EILLE

Le Corbusier

Stade Vélodrome

Avenue du Prado

Avenue du Prado

Place Castellane

Notre-Dame-
de-la-Garde

ROUCAS
BLANC

PARC DU
PRADO

LES CALANQUES →
LES GOUDES

che Kennedy

VALLON
DES AUFFES

DITERRANÉE

Miel

FRANCE

Paris

SWI

Lyon

Milan

ITALY

Barcelona

Marseille

SPAIN

Rome

N

Algier

Mediterranean Sea

ALGERIA

Tunis

Made in Marseille

Made in Marseille

FOOD AND FLAVORS FROM FRANCE'S
MEDITERRANEAN SEAPORT

DANIEL YOUNG

PHOTOGRAPHS BY SÉBASTIEN BOFFREDO

HarperCollins*Publishers*

ALSO BY Daniel Young

The Paris Café Cookbook

HarperCollins books may be purchased for educational, business,
or sales promotional use. For information, please write: Special
Markets Department, HarperCollins Publishers Inc., 10 East 53rd
Street, New York, NY 10022.

FIRST EDITION

Designed by Marysarah Quinn

Printed on acid-free paper

Library of Congress Cataloging-in-Publication Data

Young, Daniel.
   Made in Marseille / Daniel Young.
      p. cm.
   Includes index.
   ISBN 0-06-019937-7
   1. Cookery, French. 2. Marseille (France)—Social life and
customs. I. Title.
TX719.Y66 2002
641.5944'912—dc21   2002019831

02 03 04 05 06 ❖/RRD 10 9 8 7 6 5 4 3 2 1

FRONTISPIECE: *The view*
south toward the village of
Les Goudes and the islands
of Maïre and Tiboulen.

To my parents

Contents

ACKNOWLEDGMENTS ix

Discovering Marseille 1

La Cuisine Marseillaise 35

Dips, Jams, and Sauces 53

Appetizers 71

Pizzas and Tarts 95

Soups 107

Bouillabaisse 121

Fish 145

Meats 175

Vegetables 205

Desserts 219

MARSEILLE RESTAURANTS 257

INDEX 259

Monsieur André, the wine merchant in the village of L'Estaque.

Acknowledgments

Marseille is no less mysterious to me now, three years after I embarked on this culinary and cultural exploration, than it was when as a fourteen-year-old I first read of its splendor and intrigue in Alexandre Dumas's *The Count of Monte Cristo.* The city's wondrous enigmas deepen and multiply only in proportion to one's familiarity, a happy correlation that will become deliciously evident as you read this book, see the photographs, and try the recipes.

I could not make an analogous observation about another of Marseille's enduring characteristics: the notorious insularity of its inhabitants. The entrance to the great seaport appeared to widen and brighten with every visit. More doors always opened. And the extent to which I was able to develop, expand, enrich, and convey both my fascination with and appetite for France's oldest city was steadily enhanced by the generosity and candor of many initially circumspect Marseillais. I am grateful to all those who guided, encouraged, or accompanied me on my very personal quest for this town's best foods and truest flavors, including Alain Aubin, Claude Bataille, Georges Bataille, Gilbert Biton, Dominique Bluzet, Philippe Carrese, Laurent Damonte, Jean-Claude Dejuli, Didier Deroin, Laurence Gamerre, Claude Gollin, Catherine Heuzé, Jacky Israel, Jeanne Laffitte, Djamel Larbi, Jacqueline Lepetit, Michele Loubat, Brigitte Messac, Max Minniti, Maurice Mistre, Isabelle Moreni, Serge Moutarlier, Stéphan Muntaner, Fallou N'Diaye, Kassem Papa, Yvonne Perettoni, Gilles Revertegat, Sylvie Rofritsch, Thomas Saar, Marc Thépot, Martine Yana, and the members of the Cercle des Boulemanes.

I am especially indebted to my good friends and valued dining companions Catherine Chilio, Bernard Loubat, Hervé Rofritsch, and Valérie Tassara for sharing their wisdom, kindness, good taste, humor, and hospitality. I benefited too from the expertise of Jacques Bonnadier, Patrick Boulanger, Christophe Castiglione, Jean-Georges Harmelin, Frédéric Poitou, and Pierre Psaltis.

A heartfelt thank you to all the home cooks, restaurant chefs, and bakers who either offered their recipes or helped me to develop my own. In improving my understanding and appreciation of *la cuisine marseillaise,* I had not one but

Cruising under the viaduct past the Joliette Docks.

four gurus: home cook extraordinaire Renée Brunet, the estimable food writer and scholar Jacques Dupuy, the artisanal baker Enzo Fassone, and, from the Provençal cultural center La Couqueto, cooking instructor and author Marion Nazet. I also received indispensable cooking and reporting assistance from Claire Lamine and additional suggestions from New York chefs James Chew, Rick Moonen, and Marco Moreira.

Katia Zeitlin, the public relations manager at Marseille's Office du Tourisme, responded to my inquiries and indulged my curiosity with unfailing professionalism and tact. She is a treasure. At the Marseille Chambre de Commerce, I enjoyed the cooperation of Thierry Huck as well as its president, Georges Antoun.

Emotional support came from steadfast pals, most of them in New York or Paris: Steven Biondolillo, Nina Blaine, David Brower, Mitch Brower, Alan Cohen, Anne de Ravel, David Downie, Steven Forbis, Mark Giles, Alison Harris, Agnès Lozet, JoAnn Makovitzky, Anahita Mekanik, Patrick Pougeux, Arthur Schwartz, Stephanie Teuwen, Alain Weill, and Jeff Weinstein. I also enjoyed the love and backing of my parents, Mimi and David Young, my brothers, Bill and Roy Young; my sisters-in-law, Sharon Baumgold and Laurie Young; my nieces, Elizabeth, Hava, Molly, and Shoshana; and my nephew, Aaron.

My deepest appreciation to my agent, Alice Martell, whose smarts, classiness, and loyalty cannot be overestimated. I am also proud of my association with my editor, Susan Friedland, whose regard for Marseille as well as for my writing about France predate this project by several years. We, meaning this author and his subject, are both lucky to have her. I am thankful too for the insightful craft of copyeditor Ann Cahn, for Sue Llewellyn's keen eye in guiding the book through the production process, for the elegant design of Marysarah Quinn, for the dedication and enthusiasm of publicist Carrie Bachman, and for Monica Meline's tireless help in getting through the day-to-day dilemmas. And how nice to have the expressive photographs of native Sébastien Boffredo to remind us of Marseille's exceptional light and mysterious beauty.

Now, if only I could get everyone in the same room for one big, glorious bouillabaisse.

Made in Marseille

Discovering Marseille

A Tale of Two Taxis

Had the passenger known something of the Old Port's great splendor, he might have sought a grander perspective for his arrival than that from the back seat of an airport taxi. An approach by train would likely have culminated with his standing atop the landmark stairway in front of the Saint Charles station, just like the legends Yves Montand and Fernandel did in the movies. A coming into port from the sea would have revealed the ancient inlet of Lacydon from the same point of view as the Greek mariners' twenty-six centuries ago. Perhaps a beautiful maiden would have extended to him a marriage goblet brimming with romantic promise, as legend says the Princess Gyptis did to the young captain Protis.

As it happens, the arrival by taxi could not have left a stronger first impression. After whizzing past the warehouses, dockyards, hangars, cruise ships, and shipyard cranes of the Joliette basin, the passenger emerged from a sweeping left turn to be practically blinded by the luminous colors of Marseille's storied Vieux Port.

"Your city is wonderful!," he cried out. "You've got the sun, the sea, the islands, the boats, the fish markets, the cafés, the hillside villages, the exotic flavors and foreign accents, the dark-haired women."

So captivated was the passenger by the unfolding spectacle that he failed to notice the pained expression of the cabdriver as reflected in the rearview mirror.

"Take it from me," the cabby interjected during the first pause in the impromptu ode to Marseille emanating from the back seat. "This place is nothing to write home about. It's dirty. No one knows how to drive.

Entering the Panier from the Passage de Lorette.

Everyone's double-parked. There's a construction site every block. These immigrants don't work. Nothing gets done . . ."

The diatribe did not dishearten the mystified passenger, but it did persuade him to plan another approach for his return visit. No, he did not take a boat or a train. As before, he rode a taxi into town, only this time he took a different tack with its driver.

"This place is nothing to write home about," the passenger murmured as the taxi lurched from one bottleneck to the next. "It's dirty. No one knows how to drive. Everyone's double-parked. These people are lazy . . ."

"Are you kidding?" protested the cabby, gesticulating right and left between gear shifts. "This is paradise. We've got the sun, the sea, the islands, beautiful brunettes from the four corners of the Mediterranean, the best seafood in the world. You won't find a quality of life like this anywhere else."

The extent to which the tale of two taxis rings true can be seen in the knowing smiles its telling invariably elicits from native Marseillais. Dangerous as it is to draw sweeping conclusions from the windshield perspectives of two taxis, their tactless, willfully contradictory responses are illuminating. They reveal a sometimes comical, often endearing, and occasionally maddening paradox that led French novelist Blaise Cendrars to call Marseille one of the most mysterious and difficult to fathom cities in the world. How, he and countless other observers have wondered, could this great cosmopolitan harbor, this historic point of departure for world travelers, this perpetual port of arrival for refugees and immigrants, maintain such an insular outlook?

On a primitive level, the rosier view of the second cabby who, caught in dense traffic, was in an odd position to be boasting about quality of life, can be appreciated as that of a macho Marseillais coming to the defense of his *grand amour*. Although the French-Mediterranean street code grants anyone the right and, some might add, the obligation to criticize his or her beloved spouse, child, mother, foods, or hometown soccer team, you should never misconstrue his or her bellyaching as an invitation for you to do so.

Outsiders beware: There is far more behind the grumbling typified by the first cabby than the inclination to find fault with what one knows and loves best. We're talking two thousand years of emotional baggage. His unconvincing, what's-so-hot-about-Marseille argument betrays a suspicion of outsiders, most notably wide-eyed ones, ingrained in the Marseillais character since the visit to France's oldest city by an extremely impressed future dictator by the name of Julius Caesar. When Caesar battled Pompey for control of the strategic trading port in the year 49 B.C., the Marseillais backed the wrong Roman, siding with the more moderate, soon-to-be-vanquished Pompey, and suffered gravely for their miscalculation.

A Cultural Renaissance

The latest would-be conquerors to swell the hearts of the wary locals with some pride and much dread have been the turn-of-the-century—twentieth to twenty-first—Parisians. The recent invasion of Parisian artists, intellectuals, journalists, and tourists has been viewed from within as a suspicious development. The city had come to expect only one thing from the denizens of the French capital: ridicule. In their vocabulary, Marseille was synonymous with vice and vulgarity. How odd to be counting Parisians among the earliest and most enthusiastic supporters of a cultural renaissance that has established France's gateway to the south as a Mediterranean capital of food, fashion, literature, music, dance, film, and theater.

"For the famous actors, Marseille was a stopover just like any other French city," recalls Dominique Bluzet, director of the Théâtre du Gymnase. "Now it's a required destination." This statement can now be applied to a much larger group. Shortly before the new high-speed TGV Mediterranée was making its June 2001 debut, shortening the $4\frac{1}{2}$-hour train link between France's largest and second largest city to 3 hours, French national railroad president Louis Gallois confided to me that Marseille had clearly become the country's trendiest travel destination. "But please," urged Gallois, "don't tell any of your contacts in other French cities I said that."

Many local officials trace this transformation to Marseille's selection as a host city of the 1998 World Cup. The tournament was their opportunity to show a new or, more accurately, an undiscovered image of themselves to thousands of visiting soccer fans and, through the international media, millions more. But setting and achieving this lofty goal first required a metamorphosis in the city's self-image and a greater appreciation of its regional identity and southern orientation.

"We wanted to be more like a second Paris than a city of the south," explains Bernard Aubert, music director of the Fiesta des Suds, a one-of-a-kind festival of music, art, and food from, as its name—"Festival of the *Souths*"—implies, not just the South of France but many other southern regions of the world. "But people have always come to Marseille to experience what they can't find elsewhere. And that's its extraordinary mix of southern cultures."

His argument is underscored by a flashback to the night of October 28, 2000 at the tenth annual Fiesta des Suds: In the packed main concert space of the Dock des Suds, a converted, sixty-thousand-square-foot warehouse, French-Algerian rock star Rachid Taha electrifies a vivid and vibrant cross-section of the Marseille mosaic. On a second stage, Senegalese drummer Fallou N'Diaye thrills a dance floor swarming with trans-Mediterranean fusion. Elsewhere, revelers circulate between a tapas bar, three wine bars, a cyber lounge, several art galleries and installations, a North African *salon de*

The Bar de la Marine.

thé/bakery, a pizzeria (love those thin-crusted slices!), and a Provençal-Mediterranean sit-down restaurant.

Almost overnight, some of the very stereotypes that caused this city to be shunned as a pariah within the beloved region of Provence had become sources of curiosity and inspiration. Where once immigration was perceived as a root cause of social ills, now it was valued as a rich source of artistic discovery, creative cross-pollination, world music, and fusion cuisine. Where once a city suffered for its unvarnished portrayal in the movies, now it was benefiting from the same. The image of a drug-infested Marseille given to the world in 1971 by *The French Connection* and then aggravated by the Academy Award–winner's 1975 sequel was at last being replaced by a more enticing depiction in two recent French movie hits.

The best-selling soundtrack for the *Taxi*, an action comedy blockbuster written by Luc Besson and directed by Gérard Pires, promoted the local music scene, particularly its hit, multiethnic rap groups IAM and Fonky Family. Robert Guediguian's *Marius and Jeannette*, the second of three fables about working-class Marseillais living in the old fishing village of L'Estaque (from *estaco*, the Provençal word for "home port"), restored a more romantic representation of Marseille captured for the French as well as Americans in the classic 1930s *Trilogie Marseillaise* (*Marius, Fanny*, and *César*) of Marcel Pagnol. Instead of running from Pagnol's deeply affectionate but nevertheless buffoonish caricature of an earlier generation, the city's young social climbers were now descending in droves to the Bar de la Marine, a stunning retro facsimile of the Old Port haunt around which the *Trilogie* and its folkloric camaraderie were centered.

A Timeless Expectation

What was and continues to be most puzzling to many locals about this so-called renaissance is that, from their standpoint, Marseille has not changed all that much. It's difficult for them to tell what all the fuss is about. Globalization, for example, is no more a novelty than the steamship in a city of passages heralded in old travel posters as France's *Porte de l'Orient* ("Gateway to the Orient") and its *Porte de l'Afrique du Nord* ("Gateway to North Africa"). As early as 1860, the local journalist and literary ambassador

Joseph Méry wrote adoringly about restaurant feasts, where "Turkish pilaf, Indian curry, Russian caviar, and Italian pasta were as welcome as *bouille-a-baisse provençale*."

But it is precisely the direct links these and other Marseille marvels have to the near and distinct past that create a timeless expectation of discovery. It is the *perception* of the city that has been rehabilitated, not its essential character.

A modern-day visitor searching for *Massalia*, namely the Marseille of antiquity, can survey it from the great limestone cliffs of the Calanques. This sinuous series of wild fjords follows the rocky coastline to the seaside resort town and wine region of Cassis. Sormiou and Morgiou, two of the largest and most breathtakingly beautiful Calanques, miraculously fall within the borders of a large city of over eight hundred thousand inhabitants. The effect of coming upon this rugged wilderness within Marseille's 9th arrondissement is mind boggling. Their unspoiled views expose the same secluded Mediterranean seascape that first lured and then embraced the Phocaeans, the daring Greek mariners from Asia Minor who founded what is still known today as the *cité phocéenne*.

The sentimental reader searching for the Marseille of literary fame, as thousands did following the 1844–1845 serial publication of Alexandre Dumas's *The Count of Monte Cristo*, can take an excursion ferry to—or merely gaze out toward—the Château d'If, the island fortress-turned-prison from which Edmund Dantès, the classic's protagonist, escapes. Cabbies grateful for the boom in tourism during the years following the release of the Marseille-set novel refused to accept payment from Dumas for rides in their horse-driven vehicles. But money is one thing. It's doubtful the drivers succeeded at suppressing the urge to contradict anything the famous author dared to utter about their town.

More of Dumas's Marseille can be absorbed at the restaurants of the Catalans beach. Guests at the mythical engagement party of Dantès and his fiancée, Mercédès, passed around "lobsters in their dazzling red armor," "prawns of large size and brilliant color," "clovisse clams esteemed by the epicures of the South as more than rivaling the exquisite flavor of the oyster," and "all the delicacies cast up by the wash of waters on the sandy beach, which the grateful fishermen call 'the fruits of the sea.' "

Though La Reserve, the setting for that mythical feast, no longer exists, its spirit endures at two Catalans beach fish houses known for their fresh seafood and bouillabaisse, Restaurant Michel and Calypso. Elsewhere, shellfish stands are strategically stationed throughout the city. On two sides of the Cours Saint-Louis, the selection of crustaceans, raw shellfish, and other assorted sea creatures is legion at the award-winning oyster dealer and restaurant Toinou Coquillages.

The pulse of eighteenth- and nineteenth-century Marseille can still be felt amidst the diverse throng strolling La Canebière. The famous main thoroughfare follows the path of the ancient Lacydon River, ascending perpendicular from the innermost embankment of the Old Port. The Marseillais are so proud of this street, wrote Dumas, "that they say with all the gravity in the world, and with that accent which gives so much character to what is said, 'If Paris had La Canebière, Paris would be a second Marseille.' "

In the city's northwest end, painter Paul Cézanne's definitive *View of the Gulf of Marseille* is manifest in the gentle slopes of L'Estaque. Known locally for *chichi fregi* (Marseille-style funnel cakes), *panisses* (fried chickpea cakes), sardines, and other humble yet irresistible pleasures, this fishing village also nurtured two world-famous phenomena, bouillabaisse and modern art. The thirty canvases Cézanne completed while sojourning at a small house he rented near his mother's L'Estaque home signaled his liberation from impressionism and helped establish this quaint locale as the cradle of modern painting. Georges Braque's *Maisons d'Estaque*, painted in 1908, marked the invention of cubism. Views portrayed in the luminous landscapes not only of Cézanne and Braque but also of Renoir, Derain, Dufy, Marquet, and Guigou can be pinpointed today throughout the village.

The sunbathed, windswept bay of Marseille has always maintained a special appeal for colorists, painters as well as writers, aesthetes as well as amateurs. It is not at all unusual to hear local merchants and roustabouts comment on the play of the arcing sunlight and the changing hues of the sea, the sky, and the tiled rooftops, albeit somewhat less poetically than did the resident man of letters André Suarès. In *Marsiho,* a 1931 portrait of Marseille titled after the city's Provençal name in post-medieval times, Suarès wrote of the sky's dancing gold dust and of vermilion roofs blooming under a twilight inferno. The golden sunsets had a similar effect some sixty years earlier on American Mark Twain, one of the self-described "Innocents Abroad" who was thus immune to accusations of chauvinism: "[We] saw the dying sunlight gild its clustering spires and ramparts, and flood its leagues of environing verdure with a mellow radiance that touched with an added charm the white villas that flecked the landscape far and near."

The Prospect of Intrigue

Past nightfall, Marseille invites interpretations better suited to black and white. The ensembles of late-eighteenth- and early-nineteenth-century apartment houses, with their bas-relief façades, tall shutters, wrought-iron balconies and balustrades, winding stairways, and landings paved with hexagonal red *tomettes* (the classic Provençal stone tiles) evoke a romantic fascination. The unifying architectural element, the classic *trois fenêtres marseillaises,* is not so much a style as it is a measure. Sized to the standard lengths of the wood beams with which they were first built, the buildings of that era were "three windows" (just under 20 feet) in width. Larger structures of the same period were sized in multiples of three (six windows wide, nine windows wide, and so on).

Late at night, the side streets and boulevards possess an eerie beauty. The three-window façades lining both sides of the boulevard Longchamp emit a surreal glow. The atlantes, those imposing figures who carry the weight of old buildings, seem to patrol the city streets like phantoms.

The once pompous and now forlorn sameness of the rue la de République suggests a film-noir fantasy. Its seemingly endless succession of grand, nineteenth-century residences was modeled to parallel urban planner Baron Haussmann's designs for Paris. Financed by Parisian bankers, the thoroughfare was practically brand new when Twain recounted "a long walk through smooth, asphaltum-paved streets bordered by blocks of vast new mercantile houses of cream-colored stone, every house and every block precisely like all the other houses and all the other blocks for a mile, and all brilliantly lighted."

The rise of the rue de la République and other similarly grand boulevards was poorly received. The Marseillais didn't care to have their houses razed and their neighborhoods cleaned up. Critics found the architecture, however considerable its merits, doubly insulting because the overall style was Parisian rather than Mediterranean. It didn't fit in with its surroundings.

The locals expressed similar resentment toward more recent urban recon-

struction plans, even in instances where the designs were not Parisian. English architect William Alsop can expect a very long wait before the Marseillais embrace his 433-foot-long vision for the Hôtel du Département, which first suggests the high-tech headquarters for a James Bond villain rather than a French regional government. Viewed in profile, the 1994 configuration of glass boxes and curves suggests a futuristic phoenix for whose massive wings a sizable chunk of the working-class quarter of St. Just has been cleared. The *vaisseau bleu* ("blue vessel") is widely viewed as a bureaucratic island fortress, the very entity it was intended not to be.

It's taken some fifty years for the Marseillais to warm to the post–Second World War housing blocks that architect Fernand Pouillon designed for the razed tract of the Old Port. And some oldtimers still hold a grudge against Le Corbusier for constructing the revolutionary housing project they nicknamed the Maison du Fada, "house of the crackpot," amid the villas and stone houses of what was then (1947–1951) a countrified area of southern

The buildings on either side of the Cours Lieutaud are representative of the classique Marseillaise *style.*

Marseille. The *unité d'habitation* is an eighteen-story complex of 337 terraced duplex "villas" stacked over thirty-four concrete pillars. With an on-premises hotel, café, post office, gym, grocery store, nursery school, and rooftop swimming pool as part of the original plans, this landmark of modern architecture essentially discouraged interaction by its residents with their surroundings.

Time and grime do manage to cover up most of these sore spots. Now that its cream-colored house fronts are dark and dingy, the rue de la République sparks no opposition. What it does kindle is your cinematic imagination. And so, when ostensibly law-abiding tenants vanish behind the tall, darkened doorways, they can easily be mistaken for exiles eluding the authorities. A man and a woman walking a few paces apart can be imagined as imperiled lovers set to rendezvous at one of two classic cafés. Will they retreat into the warm embrace of the Café Parisien and its charismatic owner Gilbert Biton? Or will they choose to risk all and resolutely face the world from the sweeping terrace of the Samaritaine? As a longstanding fixture on picture postcards, that Marseille icon has long accompanied news from this perennial port of call to near and distant shores. With the great rounded façade of the Samaritaine suggesting a ship's bow, the rue de la République appears to point downward to the Old Port like the drifting ghost of a Parisian boulevard.

Turn off this straight, broad artery and the mystery deepens. Westbound streets invariably climb into the Panier, a labyrinthine quarter that, under cover of darkness, resembles the shadowy casbah you might expect to find in an old Humphrey Bogart movie, *Casablanca* or *Passage to Marseille*. The city's oldest surviving section is a medieval maze of narrow roads, steep stairways, crooked passages, tiny village squares, and trusted cafés known mostly by the diminutive nicknames of their owners. (Anyone who identifies these hideouts by the signs above their entrances is immediately revealed to be an outsider.) On windy nights, the mistral gusts make doors creak and shutters rattle. The tall and narrow house fronts appear to lean against each other to keep from blowing over.

Never mind that the once deserted Vielle Charité, a seventeenth-century charity hospital and baroque marvel designed according to the plans of native sculptor/painter/architect Pierre Puget, is no longer of much interest to fugitives seeking refuge in the heart of this enclave. Through a painstaking renovation, the domed chapel and the three levels of arcades that surround it now cloister nothing more sinister than two museums, a bookstore, an art house cinema, and, inevitably, a café.

In reality, the Panier, though still, as its name implies, an isolated "basket" inhabited by poor immigrant families, has become less a magnet for predators and gangsters than for bobos (bourgeois bohemians) and unstarving artists. Nowadays, much of the shady dealing is in real estate, not drugs. Having survived the perils of German occupation and demolition, organized crime, urban renewal, and political do-gooders, the resilient Panier's greatest threat may now be posed by climbing rents.

Still, the gentrification of working-class neighborhoods and the reinvention of depressed industrial sections do little to diminish the prospect of intrigue and the unusual. They merely expose the urban explorer to some dramatic plot turns in an infrastructure shifting uneasily from shipping, manufacturing, and merchandising to a service economy. There is, for example, no longer much contraband for customs agents to hunt down within the brick walls of the Docks, the monumental port warehouses that extend four football fields along the waterfront. Through a spectacular renovation, the six floors and four atriums of the 1858 structure have been transformed into an office complex.

Detectives will likewise encounter little wrongdoing other than perhaps some ill-conceived art inside an abandoned cigarette factory in the gritty Belle de Mai quarter. Its 360,000 square feet are now occupied by La Friche Belle de Mai, a thriving cultural center consisting of recording studios, artists' lofts, rehearsal rooms, performance spaces, meeting rooms, multimedia centers, and a radio station.

This sea change notwithstanding, a substantial number of locals still hold on to an image of Marseille as the French Chicago. They are invariably disappointed when American visitors fail to make the same connection. The comparison reflects a dated, narrow-minded conception of both cities. They associate the Windy City familiar to them only through old American gangster movies with a corruption-plagued Marseille overrun, according to sensational newspapers and lurid novels, by the Neapolitan Camorra, the Sicilian Mafia, and the Corsican syndicates. But I would sooner liken Marseille, with its distinctive southern accent, its taste for mixed stews and assorted mischief, and its position at the mouth of a great river, to New Orleans. Alternatively, the city of high hills, low-down pleasures, great shellfish, world travelers, and an island prison (think Alcatraz) has many parallels to the old port of San Francisco. And when you speak of Marseille's special appeal to writers of crime stories and rap lyrics, as well as its mix of exotic flavors and foreign cultures clustered within its sun-bleached communities, you could be talking about Los Angeles.

The three detective novels written in the 1990s by the late Jean-Claude Izzo, Marseille's counterpart to LA's Raymond Chandler, do exploit the terror of organized crime as well as the violence fomented in the city's *cités* (public housing projects). Lawlessness and murder are, after all, central to the genre. But Fabio Montale, Izzo's detective-protagonist, also has a dogged nose for wine, fish (both catching and eating), poetry, music, brick-oven pizza, single malt Scotch, couscous, and *cuisine provençale*.

Fanatical readers from Belgium and Italy drop into town with the express purpose of trying the real-life restaurants, bistros, canteens, cafés, and bars frequented by the fictional Montale. Many others no doubt prepare the recipes—*aïoli* and salt cod, stuffed peppers, lasagna with fennel-scented tomato sauce—that bring real pulp to Izzo's fiction. Some may even follow his advice on Provence's extra virgin olive oils (the Moulin Rossi is recommended when whipping up *aïoli;* those of Jacques Barles, Henri Bellon, and Margier-Aubert are to be used in cooked dishes and for dressing salads).

Not everything in these novels should be taken as gospel. Izzo may have had a better feel for Greek tragedy than Provençal olive oil. The extra virgin olive oil of Moulin Rossi is made with fermented olives, resulting in a disagreeable odor many wrongly associate with the true taste of oil. And speaking of a slightly bitter aftertaste, I was at first thrilled to meet and do the nighttime rounds of Old Port haunts with Claude Gollin, the retired Marseille cop, captivating Communist, and near mythical center-city figure who was a model for Montale. But I ultimately found his carousing and cynical detachment more troublesome in person than in print. Specifically, my doubts first surfaced the night he cornered me into singing *New York New York* at a packed nightclub near the Marseille opera house.

Le Melting Pot

The image of a hard-boiled detective with a parochial perspective and a worldly outlook is nevertheless worth holding onto. When it comes to the rich and varied fruits of living in a multiethnic Provençal city, of fighting crime in a cosmopolitan seaport stretched wide open to absorb continuous waves of immigration, Izzo/Montale is both connoisseur and champion.

Writing with passion and lyricism in *Total Khéops*, Izzo termed Marseille "a utopia. A utopia where anyone of any color can step off a boat or a train, his suitcase in his hand and not a cent in his pocket, and merge into the stream of other men. A city where, with his foot scarcely touching the ground, this man can say, 'here is place I can call home.' "

Had I been fortunate enough to meet Izzo, who died in January 2000, I would have immediately questioned him about his favorite restaurants, foods, home cooks, and personal recipes. That, in any event, is what I prefer to think. But when I did get to meet Philippe Carrese, a leader in Marseille's growing band of detective novelists, the first thing that came to mind had very little to do with dining or any topic directly related to my research for this book. My first question was pretty much the same one I would have asked Chandler: How did he dream up his lethal femme fatale? In a single paragraph of his fantastical third novel, *Pet de Mouche et la Princesse du Désert*, Carrese describes Nora, his female lead, as "the queen of the Berbers," "the princess of the desert," "1 meter 70 centimeters (5'7") of Mediterranean energy," and "*le melting pot*."

"Isn't she something?" responded Carrese, shaking his head as if the character were not his creation. As it happens, he had just crossed paths with Nora's living model, a Marseillaise of Kabyle (a Berber people of northeast Algeria) origin, for the first time in several years. He hadn't made her up. He couldn't have made her up. Moreover, the author's inspiration for the explosive attachment between Nora and her reluctant but ultimately obedient boyfriend José was much broader than any two individuals. Their relationship reflected that of the archetypal Mediterranean couple.

"The men make the racket," noted Carrese, "but the women make the decisions." Perhaps four or five people were sitting in the café when he offered this observation. I nevertheless imagined thousands nodding their heads. Not just Marseillais who, like the real-life Nora, came from Algeria, but also those with Armenian, Corsican, Greek, Italian, Lebanese, Moroccan, Portuguese, Spanish, Turkish, Tunisian, and, it should not be forgotten, Provençal roots. I'm never quite sure what's more striking: the differences among the city's many resident Mediterranean cultures or their commonality.

This tradition of immigration and cultural integration is as old as the city itself. Marseille's very foundation was bound by the marriage of a princess from a native Ligurian tribe and a Greek captain from abroad. But large-scale immigration did not begin until the second half of the nineteenth century and the rise of France's Second Empire. The development of the colonial empire, the digging of the Suez Canal, advances in steam navigation, and the emergence of the industrial revolution all sparked commercial development and economic prosperity. The Old Port was expanded. A new port with larger harbor basins and a rail link to St. Charles station was built. And new sources of labor were needed to man the burgeoning shipping industries, chemical plants, oil refineries, and soap works.

Le Savon de Marseille

Expanded trade with North Africa helped change the composition of the *Savon*—"soap"—de Marseille and thus the celebrated cleansing bars most of France and a sizable share of the western world used for personal washing. At the time, Marseille commanded a near monopoly on the manufacture and export of French soap.

"In Marseille they make half the fancy toilet soap we consume in America," observed Mark Twain in 1868. "But the Marseillaise only have a vague theoretical idea of its use."

From as early as 1371 until the mid-nineteenth century, the Savon de Marseille was made with olive oil (previously, soaps were made with animal fats) and a caustic soda extracted from marine plants known as barilla. Ready supplies of both commodities let Mediterranean soap makers dominate the industry. Besides Marseille, the region's great soap centers were in the Italian cities of Genoa, Savona, Venice, and Albi and the Spanish cities of Alicante and Cartegena.

In the mid-eighteenth century, less costly grain oils, chiefly palm oil and coconut oil imported from North Africa, were substituted for olive oil.

This was only the latest of many industry developments reflecting Marseille's close and evolving ties with its Mediterranean neighbors. The history of the Savon de Marseille, like that of the city's cuisine, is one of cultural fusion.

According to Patrick Boulanger, author of *Le Savon de Marseille,* the city's soap factories began poaching skilled workers from their rivals in Italy and Spain at the start of the sixteenth century. By incorporating the foreigners' secret methods of production with their own so-called "large boiler" technique, the Marseillais refined the four-step process—saponification (a chemical reaction between the oil and the soda), cooking, washing, and liquidation—for making hard soap. They also searched the Mediterranean for new sources of olive oil to diminish their dependency on nearby oils from Provence and the Italian Riviera. The formula for the renowned cubic bars of 72 percent pure Savon de Marseille soon encompassed olive oil from Crete and the Italian region of Mezzogiorno, natural sodas from Spain and Egypt, and ashes from Sicily and Sardinia.

The introduction both of cheaper grain oils and artificial sodas facilitated soap making, not only in Marseille but elsewhere in France. When, at the end of the nineteenth century, the appellation "Savon de Marseille," was recognized to identify the method but not the location or purity of its production, distant soap makers were legally entitled to engrave that important distinction on their cubic, rectangular, or round soap bars. Due to fierce competition, first from cheaper, lower-grade soaps and later from new cleansing products and fashions, the annual output of Marseille's soap industry declined from 130,000 metric tons in 1901 to 3,000 tons a century later. Although cubic bars of Savon de Marseille are back in style, most are manufactured outside its namesake city.

Twentieth-Century Passages

During Marseille's economic boom, the largest share of immigrants were Italians from Piedmont, Tuscany, and Naples. By 1914, one in four Marseillais were of Italian origin. The early twentieth century saw a steady expansion in the arrival of workers from economically depressed Corsica and, in smaller numbers, from Spain and Greece. In the 1920s, immigration took a political turn with the mass arrival of Armenian refugees fleeing Turkish persecution. Later, Italian antifascists and Spanish Nationalists were among the political émigrés.

Marseille's prosperity lasted until the Second World War. The city suffered significant material destruction under German occupation. The Pont Transporteur, a transport bridge spanning the Old Port, was demolished, leaving only the classic photographs of Germaine Krull, Laszlo Moholy-Nagy, Marcel Bovis, and others as bittersweet reminders of the twin pylons that stood over the harbor like two-legged steel monsters. Some thirty-five acres of the historic Old Port district were razed. The Hôtel de Ville, the city hall, built in 1653, was one of the few buildings deliberately spared by the Germans.

Although thousands of Jewish refugees fleeing Nazi persecution sought refuge in Marseille, the seaport was hardly a safe harbor. The Gestapo could ask the Vichy government to "surrender on demand" any foreign national, subjecting them to deportation to concentration camps. In 1940 and 1941, a New Yorker named Varian Fry managed to secure emergency visas, forged passports, and safe passage to America for more than twelve hundred refugees, among them such cultural giants as Marc Chagall, Max Ernst, Marcel Duchamp, André Breton, Franz Werfel, and Hannah Arendt. In October 2000, the city of Marseille dedicated the square in front of the American Consulate in Fry's honor.

Beginning with the reconstruction efforts of the 1950s, people from the Maghreb, from Algeria and, to a lesser extent, from Morocco and Tunisia, became the most significant group of immigrants into Marseille. Algerian independence in 1962 also brought an influx of *pieds-noirs* ("black feet"— French colonials born in Algeria) and Sephardic Jews (descendants of Jews who lived in Spain during the Middle Ages) who retained their French citizenship. Close to one million *pieds-noirs* were pressured to flee the only home they had ever known.

Most Algerian Jews followed the same path. Harassed by the Algerian government, they immigrated to France shortly after Algeria was granted independence. Those who settled in Marseille were joined by Sephardic Jews from Morocco, Tunisia, Egypt, Turkey, and Greece as well as a much smaller number of both resident and newly arrived Ashkenazim (European Jews). Marseille's Jewish population increased from an estimated ten thousand after the Second World War to its current total of eighty thousand, second only to Paris among French cities.

More recent immigrant waves have come from distant vestiges of the French colonial empire, notably Indochina, the French West Indies, and sub-Saharan Africa. The number of Marseille inhabitants from Comoros, a tiny and faraway archipelago located in the Indian Ocean between Mozambique and Madagascar, is estimated at fifty thousand, second only to the Comoran capital of Moroni.

Where All the Spice Trails Cross

The fabric and spice of this ever-changing patchwork converge, both literally and figuratively, two blocks south of the Canebière at the intersection of the rue Longue-des-Capucins, the rue d'Aubagne, and the rue Vacon. Walking north from the Old Port through the central shopping district, the storefront displays change abruptly from jeans, perfumes, cell phones, and athletic footwear to meter-wide rolls of fabrics in glittery solids, leopard prints, large polka dots, harlequin patterns, Provençal harvest motifs, and African tricolors.

Up a few steps on the left, the boxes, bins, sacks, and shelves inside the Cap Orient (aka Chez Salem) are filled with Thai rice, Tunisian olive oil, Turkish hazelnuts, French walnuts, California almonds, and hundreds of other commodities. Every grain has a different clientele: Bulgur wheat is sold mostly to Greeks, Lebanese, and Turks; coarse cornmeal to Italians and Spanish; fine-grain cornmeal to Africans from Comoros, Madagascar, the Ivory Coast, and Togo; corn flour to the Senegalese; couscous to Tunisians, Moroccans, Algerians, and French.

"Marseille is a warm, friendly place and very open to globalization," says Salem Habaieb, a Tunisian immigrant espousing a belief that, however idealistic and even illusory it might sound in other contexts, cannot be challenged inside a spice shop with no national allegiance. Here, the only apparent loyalty is to Espig, a popular brand of locally milled and packaged spices, including a notorious blend called Spigol. Over a century ago, the Algerian saffron merchant Frédéric Espig introduced that cheap saffron substitute and altered the flavor of Mediterranean food history. The red-hued powder endures to

The Saffron Connection

Marseille's participation in the saffron trade dates back to the first expeditions from the city to Alexandria, Egypt in the second century B.C. The port of Alexandria was then a great commercial center of Mediterranean and Oriental commerce, much of it in pungent and aromatic spices following the trade routes from India and Asia Minor to the markets of Greece and the Roman Empire. In ancient times, saffron was used as a golden-yellow dye for luxurious garments and fabrics, as a powdered fragrance in cosmetics and air fresheners, as an herbal remedy, as a medicinal flavoring in sweet wine, and later as a spice in sauces.

Assumed to be native to the Mediterranean region, saffron was first cultivated in Europe by the Arabs of Spain around the year A.D. 961. Its farming in Provence began during the eleventh century, and, by the time of the Middle Ages, reversed the direction of the local saffron trade. Instead of importing saffron from Egypt, Marseille merchants began exporting it to the Middle East. Still, not all the Provençal saffron was shipped overseas. It was widely used and, some might say, abused in aristocratic cuisine. Nearly every dish was ennobled with the distinctive color and flavor of the world's most expensive spice. Saffron did not seep into the cooking of the middle and working classes and, in particular, their beloved bouillabaisse until the nineteenth century.

Due to the high cost of harvesting saffron (it takes some 14,000 threads hand-picked from the blossoms of crocus flowers to yield a single ounce), the cultivation of Provençal saffron was abandoned after the First World War. The resilient Marseille merchants were obliged to switch back from exporting to importing. Major players like Espig now get most of their saffron from Spain.

this day as a pigment not only in home-cooked soups, stews, vegetables, and rice dishes but also in cheap restaurant paellas and bouillabaisses. Whereas Salem sells pure Spanish saffron threads for about four dollars per gram, Spigol, which has a saffron content of 3 percent, sells for about one dollar per gram. Sure, there are many principled home and restaurant cooks who routinely buy Spigol. But truly self-respecting ones are wont to quickly conceal it beneath other purchases on the bottom of their opaque shopping bags.

Across from Chez Salem is the Halle Delacroix, until 1980 the site of a covered fish market. It is now an open square surrounded by a live poultry market, a kosher butcher, a Southeast Asian grocery, two exotic produce markets, and a shop that sells only olives.

From here you are only steps away from the heart of the Noailles quarter and the intersection where all Marseille-bound spice trails cross. At the very bottom of the rue Longue-des-Capucins, the Coq d'Or is so specialized a butcher that lamb and mutton are sold from separate departments. The Middle Eastern supermarket Au Royaume de la Chantilly, the halal meat market Galia Viande, and the Egyptian bakery/pizzeria/rotisserie Le Soleil d'Egypt are on the same end of the same side of the same narrow block of this food bazaar.

The shopping options were not always as rich and varied. When Arax (named after Armenia's chief river) opened on the rue d'Aubagne in 1929, the grocery/delicatessen/spice emporium was the city's lone source for many Middle Eastern and southern European staples and specialties. Its first customers were mostly homesick Armenians and Greeks thrilled to get their hands on kachcaval cheese, grape leaves, phyllo dough, pastourma sausage, tarama, and cornichons à la russe. Why "Russian pickles"? Arax's owner Vartan Bandikian was among the many Armenians who immigrated to Marseille from territory controlled by the Soviets, in his case, the Caucasian city of Krasnodar.

Arax gradually expanded its selection and floor space, eventually opening a second store in 1969, to accommodate the far-flung cravings of new immigrants from the Middle East and North Africa. But although the inventory in the original and now solitary store remains comprehensive, there is a disturbing amount of open space on its shelves between the halvah and the makrouts, the loukoums and the baklava. A sad quiet pervades the shop.

"All is changing and I don't accept it," laments David Bandikian, the embittered son of the founder. "It [the Noailles quarter] was the belly of Marseille. Now there is nothing."

Nothing? You only have to walk next door to the bustling Vietnamese grocery store Tam Ky to see how mistaken Bandikian is. Opened in 1986, the family-run business has since expanded into five adjacent shops along the Halle Delacroix and extending through to the rue d'Aubagne. It stocks some two thousand canned, frozen, fresh, and prepared foods of Vietnamese, Thai, and Chinese origin on behalf of a clientele that is part Southeast Asian, part "European," as the manager and eldest brother Bertrand prefers to say. There isn't a contemporary French chef in town who doesn't comb the shelves for inspiration. Out front, Tam Ky's exotic produce market draws French West Indians and sub-Saharan Africans, especially Comorans and Madagascans. They vie with their Vietnamese counterparts for the pick of the tropical pro-

The Marché d'Afrique.

duce: plantains, cassavas, mangoes, durians, litchis, carambola (star fruit), coconuts, and so on. My Camoran friend Kassem Papa, a student in pharmacological research, will closely inspect a minimum of a dozen cassavas to find one to his liking.

In a nearby shop, Jean-Claude, the Guadeloupe-born owner of Marché d'Afrique, has not a single spare centimeter of space on his shelves for the dried fish and spicy dried shrimp adored by his customers from Senegal, the Ivory Coast, Burkina Faso, Guinea, and Mali. And neighbor Ali, the affable, Somali-born co-owner of L'Univers Alimentaire ("the food universe"), has become something of an international celebrity. Film crews invariably pass by his shop, seeking his expertise on everything from African incenses, nargileh (water pipe) tobaccos, and Maggi bouillon cubes to Marseillais mores and mannerisms.

But while the rue d'Aubagne thrives, what is painfully apparent to Bandikian and his wistful contemporaries is the irreversible evolution of the

Noailles quarter's ethnicity. The Armenians, Greeks, and Lebanese have dispersed to the outer reaches of the city, just as their Italian counterparts did years before. The only traces of the rue d'Aubagne's Italian past are a beleaguered but still excellent brick-oven pizzeria and a handful of disused Italian signs that linger over storefronts. Bandikian has steadily lost customers to outlying neighborhood grocers stocking acceptable—if sometimes inferior—alternatives to his Middle Eastern specialties. Meanwhile, Arax's Istanbul-to-Tangiers pantry cannot satisfy a marketplace that has expanded beyond the Mediterranean to encompass Moroni, Fort-de-France, and Ho Chi Minh City.

Such is the cyclical nature of immigration. Change is just about the only thing that never does. Certain Noailles customs inevitably go the way of triple-layered skirts weighted down with lead sinkers and, for added security against mistral winds, fastened at the bottom with a safety pin.

"Marseille," notes immigration expert Emile Temime, professor emeritus at the Université Aix-Marseille, "never stops remodeling and renewing itself."

Proud to Be Marseillais

Following his 1840 visit, French novelist Gustave Flaubert hailed the city as "a babel of all the nations." By adding their voices to that babel, new arrivals preserve a way of life they may just as readily be accused of threatening. Full integration and acceptance for each new wave of immigrants can be excruciatingly slow, especially when complicated by lingering issues of race and decolonization. But it is encouraging and even startling to see how quickly and how willingly recent immigrants declare themselves *fier d'être marseillais,* "proud to be Marseillais." That declaration is not merely a slogan of the OM, the Olympique de Marseille, the beloved professional soccer team. It doubles as the rallying cry of a people who have always perceived a sense of isolation from their region and, since 1481, their country.

That isn't to suggest that the Marseillais are unpatriotic. It was, after all, five hundred spirited volunteers from Marseille who, marching into Paris in 1792 during the French Revolution, sang the rousing new war song that would become the French national anthem. It didn't matter that Claude-Joseph Rouget de Lisle wrote the song in the city of Strasbourg or that he called it the "Chant de guerre de l'armée du Rhin" ("War Song of the Army of the Rhine"). "La Marseillaise" was the name that stuck.

In a similar vein, the fact that the stars of the OM come from other cities, countries, and continents is of little import. What matters most is where they live and play and what name and colors (pale blue and white) they sport on the jerseys. When I asked Kassem, who heads a Comoran community outreach group, what he thought about life in France, he wavered. His compatriots generally work at menial jobs, often to support not only themselves but also destitute family members back home. But when I asked if he was proud to be Marseillais, he did not hesitate.

"I love the OM," he responded and, though we were only two in the room, tens of thousands nodded.

The us-versus-them passions aroused by a soccer squad battling against teams representing other French cities and, in particular, Paris, resonate in the flag-waving chants that echo between the grandstands of Marseille's sixty-thousand-seat Stade Vélodrome.

Allez, l'OM. Go, Marseillais.
Hoist high the flags.
All united under the same colors.

And if, as the American food essayist and travel writer M. F. K. Fisher suggested, the Marseillais are proud of being "apart" to the point of embellishing their melodramatic quirks, this tendency appears to feed their hunger to belong. This is what it means to be "made in Marseille."

The winners, they are with Marseille, the symbol of independence.
They are born on the shores of the Mediterranean.
Immigrants, but Marseillais for life.

As a symbol of civic pride and solidarity, the OM is surpassed only by the Notre-Dame-de-la-Garde and the Old Port above which that basilica towers. Erected between 1853 and 1870, "Our Lady of the Guard" has rarely been admired for its Romanesque-Byzantine architecture. The basilica's Website comes pretty close to apologizing for its anachronistic, maladroit mix of architecture styles and alternating light and dark stone. "We must acknowledge," avow the authors of www.marseilles.com/NDdelaGarde/, "that anyone who has never seen a building of this style does get a visual shock as they arrive."

Marseille's signature building owes most of its considerable power to La Bonne Mère, the gilded statue of "The Good Mother" set atop a campanile on the basilica's west end. Cast in galvanized copper, the Madonna herself is about 37 feet tall, 81 feet if you count her pedestal. But since the basilica rests on a scenic hilltop some 500 feet above sea level, her gilded outline can be viewed from afar by sailors making their way to port. She is their beacon, their "buoy of buoys," as Suarès described, as well as an omnipresent lighthouse looked up to by Christian, Muslim, and Jewish Marseillais alike.

Reflecting the continuous class rivalry between Marseillais living on the northern bank of the Old Port and those living to the more prosperous south, the latter are inclined to boast that La Bonne Mère resides on their side.

"That's true," reply the northsiders. "But she looks upon us!"

A Great Light Joins the Conversation

The Old Port of Marseille is entered through a narrow channel flanked since the seventeenth century by two fortresses: to the southern right, the star-shaped Fort St. Nicolas; to the northern left, the Fort St. Jean. The latter's rounded watchtower guides boats from the west into the long, quadrilateral inlet. Looking back, the sailor can clearly see both forts through his binoculars but not much of the sea beyond them. Oddly, Marseille is a seaport with restricted views of the horizon. The Old Port gives the impression of closing behind arriving boats in a protective embrace. And because most of Marseille's thirty-four-mile coastline forms a gulf in the shape of an inverted C, many of its widest vistas stretch out from one end of the seashore to the other.

The innermost boundary of the Old Port is formed by the Quai des Belges. That short but magnificent axis connects the Quai du Port and the Quai de Rive Neuve, the embankments to the harbor's north and south. Stepping up to the Quai des Belges from the Vieux Port Métro Station and turning toward the water, the Quai du Port is to your right, the Quai de Rive Neuve is to your left, the Canebière is directly behind you, and the hills that insulate the Old Port are all around you. Marseille itself is surrounded by a

OVERLEAF: *The Old Port, looking east to the Quai des Belges and the Canebière.*

mountainous belt that separates the city from the region around Aix-en-Provence. When residents of the outskirts and the Provençal countryside speak of "descending" to Marseille's center, the verb should not automatically be interpreted in the moral sense. It is literally true.

Those driving or, better yet, strolling either the Quai du Port or the Quai de Rive Neuve have the impression of cutting between two endless successions: one of fishing boats and pleasure craft docked to the inside; the other, of restaurants and cafés moored to the outside. Choosing a café to rendezvous with one's friends or simply one's thoughts is a strategic calculation involving convenience, personal loyalties and habits, intermittent moods and momentary impulses, architectural preferences, situational needs, and, perhaps most decisively, solar orientation.

"Here the sun thinks out loud," wrote French poet Jules Supervielle. "It is a great light that joins in the conversation."

Ascertaining the direction of the sun and anticipating its westward progression are essential. A special sundial is built into the body clocks of the Marseillais, pointing them past the angling shadows of buildings to the warmest, brightest urban terrain. All fishermen at heart, they navigate a carefully timed circuit of choice stopovers. I know a photographer who synchronizes his late-afternoon apéritif at a corner café on the Place Jean-Jaurès to the twenty odd minutes a fleeting slice of orange sunlight shines on its tiny sidewalk terrace. He departs with the sun, decamping to nearby bohemian haunts in the vicinity of the Plaine and the Cours Julien.

Around the Old Port perimeter, the south-southeast orientation of the Quai du Port's outdoor cafés makes them the sunniest alternative for morning espressos. Those who seek out the terraces extending out from the galleries of the waterfront apartment blocks beside the Hôtel de Ville are not necessarily partial to Pouillon's scheme for postwar reconstruction. By sitting with their backs to Pouillon's concrete pillars and walls, they don't have to look at them. They face out at the harbor and the old stone houses and hotels lining the Quai de Rive Neuve and the Quai des Belges.

The western orientation of the Quai des Belges and the north-northwestern orientation of the Quai de Rive Neuve offer the most strategic settings for twilight drinks. You can't truly observe the final minutes of the sun's setting from the wide, Rive Neuve terraces of the Beau Rivage, the Transbordeur, and the Bar de la Marine. But the orange-streaked purple sky

Strolling from the Quai du Port onto the Quai des Belges.

makes a sublime backdrop for the opalescence of the city's preferred apéritif, the pastis de Marseille. Aside from considerations of sunlight and beverage/sky color coordination, those Quai de Rive Neuve cafés tend to draw a younger, slicker, more boisterous crowd than their Quai du Port counterparts.

During midday hours and barring overcast skies, the entire Old Port is awash in daylight. The Mediterranean sun casts a blinding light against all three Quais, bleaching the buildings of dirt and washing out their colors. The jade green shutters of the Hotel Mercure appear white. The taupe stone of the Hôtel de Ville turns pinkish. And the grimy façade of the Samaritaine reverts, as if from sandblasting, to the unblemished color of a sand dune.

Meanwhile, the sometimes violent mistral winds periodically blow in from the northwest to sweep clean the streets and hills of Marseille, leaving behind blue skies of exceptional clarity. Exposed to direct lighting of this brilliance, a woman sitting at an outdoor café table without the shading of an awning or an umbrella does not need a mirror to check her makeup. She can examine her reflection by looking into the dark liquid in her coffee cup.

Choosing a place to eat among the dozens of restaurants along the Quais is relatively simple. There are but three restaurants worthy of serious consideration, all of them on the Quai du Port: Chez Madie, an unassuming Provençal bistro that owes its charm to its terrace and its equally sunny hostess (her name, oddly enough, is Delphine, not Madie); Le Miramar, where the Old Port's finest and most authentic bouillabaisse is served amid 1960s kitsch; and Une Table Au Sud ("A Table Facing South"), the second-floor showcase for the inventive or, rather, "reinventive" cuisine of chef Lionel Lévy.

Lévy knew little of the Old Port's unsavory reputation for not-so-fine dining when he moved down from the Paris restaurant Spoon Food & Wine in 1999. Superstar chef Alain Ducasse warned his sous-chef and protégé he was crazy to open a restaurant in Marseille and crazier still to open it in the Old Port.

"It was pitiful," said Lévy, recalling his first visit to the abandoned restaurant space directly over the Samaritaine. "I couldn't understand how a place like this, right in the heart of the Vieux Port, could be in such disrepair."

Lévy's success may augur a new trend. In general, the best restaurants around the Old Port—Les Trois Forts, Les Echevins, Carbone, Lemon Grass, L'Oliveraie, Le Charles Livon, the 504, La Girafe, Les Arsenaulx—have opened near but not directly on the quais. The 180-degree panoramic dining room of Les Trois Forts, a hotel restaurant perched on the same rocky ridge as the Palais du Pharo, is a magnificent exception to the unwritten rule that you can't get very good food *and* a very good view of the harbor.

Price is also a factor. The front-and-center Quai restaurants, as well as those bunched in a pedestrian section between the Quai de Rive Neuve and the Cours d'Estienne d'Orves, are for the most part a collection of fast-food franchises, inexpensive chain restaurants, uninspired ethnic eateries, mediocre pizzerias, and, most maddening of all, second-rate fish houses—this in a city famous for its seafood. The problem is that few restaurateurs in this touristy area will bear the sizable expense of fresh, locally caught seafood or risk passing it on to their price-sensitive customers.

One afternoon, I noticed an American couple perusing the menu posted in the window of Le Miramar. The man punched a number into his calculator, divided it by a quotient corresponding to the applicable exchange rate, and—*voilà*—looked shocked to discover the restaurant was charging more than $40 for bouillabaisse. Wasn't that an awful lot to pay for a peasant's soup first prepared centuries ago by local fishermen seeking to salvage their ugliest, boniest, most fishy tasting, least desirable catches?

The wary travelers crossed the Quai des Belges and rushed into the Office de Tourisme to relate their encounter with the "tourist trap." They requested the addresses of fish houses serving authentically prepared and priced renditions.

"If someone is charging 200 (then about $28) francs or more," replied the official in perfectly dry English, "you at least have a chance of getting a veritable version. If they're asking less you can be sure the bouillabaisse has been made with frozen fish and that the restaurant is indeed a tourist trap."

That response, pointed as it was, rests behind all thoughtful discussions of the city's best bouillabaisse. Rascasse and chapon, the once unsellable *poisson de roche* ("rockfish") that give the soup its distinctive flavor, are now prohibitively expensive. Keeping enough of it in supply, even at times when storms strand most small fishing boats at port, requires purists like Le Miramar owners Pierre and Jean-Michel Minguella to charge as much as they do. It also depends on a line of fidelity that extends from the fishing net to the dinner table. The fishermen set aside fish for their most loyal customers, who set aside fish for their most loyal customers, and so on.

Rubbing Elbows with the Fishermen

The American travelers could have verified exactly how much the Minguella brothers fork out for some of their bouillabaisse fish by investigating the open-air fish market on the port side of the Quai des Belges. At about 9:00 A.M. on all but the most inclement mornings, local fishermen begin to pull their boats up to the Quai and unload their overnight catches. Their large blue display racks are marked with the same registration numbers painted on their boats (minus the MA prefix that identifies their Marseille origins). Their selections vary according to season, their preferred and often secret fishing locations, and the mesh sizes of the nets they employed the prior night. Fishing for rouget (red mullet), sole, and merlan (hake) require three different nets.

The market's great appeal to home cooks or, in many cases, their designated shoppers, is not only about having access to fresh, locally caught fish. There are expert fishmongers in most of Marseille's villages, including two—Martine Cappai-Silvestri in Mazargues, Neige Perez in Bompard—on whose advice this book relies. What's particularly satisfying about rubbing elbows with the fishermen, the Minguellas, and other restaurateurs and fish connoisseurs is in having a flavorsome anecdote or conversational tidbit to take back with the fish.

Aimé Bergero, the owner of Le Tiboulen de Maïre, a wonderfully simple seafood grill outside the fishing village of Les Goudes, gloats about the shoppers who follow at his heels to identify exactly where and what he buys. Hot air or not, those who do, for example, make purchases from brothers André and Eric Fromion can be sure of getting some of the same fish used not only by Bergero but also by Marseille's nationally acclaimed (two Michelin stars) Restaurant Passédat. Such a distinction can be especially important to thoughtful dinner guests who may bring a whole fish to a friend's house the way a Parisian might present a bottle of Champagne.

Essentially, the participants in this daily drama all have one thing in common: They take special delight in relaying the particulars of their fish finds, adding some local flavor with each retelling. A Marseillais may consume an outstanding piece of fish without a single herb, spice, or grain of salt. But a good fish tale never passes between his lips without savory embellishment.

Spectators too treasure the contact with these local heroes and the bluff manner in which the fishermen or their family surrogates hawk their prized catches. The exchange of vulgarities can, on occasion, make modest French-speaking visitors envy the uncomprehending foreigners standing beside them. But the fish-lover's lexicon is a resonant link between the city's past and present, connecting the Old Port to the unfolding string of charming little fishing ports and coves—Vallon des Auffes, Malmousque, Fausse-Monnaie, Les Goudes, Madrague—to its south.

Turning onto the Corniche

These rustic inlets—each one a mini-Vieux Port with its own special character—can be reached by following the Quai de Rive Neuve out of the center city and turning onto the Corniche Kennedy. This left turn out of the Old Port is nearly as dramatic as the one into it, marking as it does a sudden changeover from the congested inner harbor to the vast outer seashore. The

Native soccer star Zinedine Zidane surveys the Corniche and the coastline.

coastal view from this winding road and promenade is of rocky bluffs, soaring seagulls, cliffside villas, scattered luxurious apartment towers, beach restaurants, and, out to sea, the three islands of the Frioul archipelago: Ratonneau, If, and Pomègues.

The determined gaze of native son Zinedine Zidane, the revered French-Algerian who is possibly the world's most gifted soccer player, watches over the entire seascape from a large Adidas billboard painted on the side of a Corniche building. He is too much the married gentleman to look down at the topless sunbathers who, come noontime, recline on the flat rocks and concrete platforms of the rough-and-ready beaches below. These are not necessarily women of leisure. A good number are on lunch break.

"(In Marseille) there is a work side and a vacation side," notes Professor Temime. "Here we go for a swim for two hours in the afternoon."

Near the shore, the beauty of the sea's light green color is most apparent the moment it is snatched away. During my jaunts out on the Corniche I hated to wear sunglasses, however essential their UV protection was, because their colored tints darkened and distorted this entrancing shade of sea green. Please do not dismiss this as the nonsense of an observer emulating the Marseillais penchant for exaggeration. There is scientific evidence to prove that the gradations of this Mediterranean green are distinct from those seen in Nice, Barcelona, Alexandria, Tunis, or, for that matter, the Marseille of 1987.

According to Dr. Jean-Georges Harmelin of the Centre d'Océanologie de Marseille, the vivid, light green reflection of the seagrass meadows and whitish sand patches on the sea floor is greatly enhanced by the exceptional clarity of the sky and the sea. With dry mistral winds clearing the air of haze, as they do in the Old Port, the undiminished sunlight sharpens the contrast among the colors of the sea, land, and sky. The cleanliness of the alternately green, blue, and green-blue coastal waters is a recent development. Sewage that had been emptied from the Huveaune river into these bathing and fishing waters is now diverted to a new purification plant.

So much for Marseille's dirty image.

Around the rows of *cabanons*, those little houses and makeshift beach cabins that line both small inlets and large Calanques, the conditions are ideal for the carefree Sunday pleasures the Marseillais regard as an ancestral birthright: swimming, fishing, boating, sunbathing, playing pétanque and the card game *la contrée*, sipping pastis, lunching on aïoli, grilled fish or bouillabaisse, drinking white wine from Cassis and dry rosé from Bandol and Côtes de Provence, napping, clowning around, ribbing friends, and, when the coast is clear, bellyaching about spouses, politicians, the in-laws, neighbors, or the underachieving OM.

To demonstrate my growing empathy for the Marseillais I would occasionally utter a few carefully chosen words to voice my shared displeasure with the slumping soccer team. Neither true fan nor expert, I would invariably target my frustration at the disappointing play of Brazilian Adriano Marcelinho, one in a line of would-be saviors asked to lead the OM back to championship glory. If I was going to pick on a single player, I thought it prudent to choose someone whose origins were outside not just France and the Mediterranean but also the transcontinental triangle formed by Moroni, Fort-de-France, and Ho Chi Minh City.

I recall feeling no guilt for making Marcelinho my scapegoat (forgive me, Adriano). I was too self-satisfied, if somewhat bewildered, by my capacity to find fault with something so close to the Marseillais heart without inciting their anger. While sipping glasses of pastis and nibbling olives and anchovies at the Corniche beach café Le Petit Pavillon, I broached this confusing development with a friend intimately acquainted with two local passions. Hervé Rofritsch, in addition to being a season ticketholder, is the son of former OM player Maurice Rofritsch. Their family business, La Boule Bleue, is the sole manufacturer in Marseille of *boules*, the metal balls used to play pétanque.

How, I asked Hervé, could an outsider like me get away with criticizing the home team?

"When you involve yourself in the condition," he responded, "when you speak with compassion and sympathy and not a mocking spirit, you are accepted."

I smiled and raised my glass of pastis, first to my friend, then to the last peel of sun setting over the Mediterranean, and finally to my lips. Some three years after my first taxi ride into Marseille I had finally arrived.

La Cuisine
Marseillaise

IN THE CLASSICAL SENSE, sound arguments can be advanced to set apart the *cuisine marseillaise* from the *cuisine provençale*. Most are based on the criteria typically used to define all regional French cuisines: parochial preferences and specialties, cultural and religious practices, and, of greatest significance, the indigenous foods and agriculture from which these and other distinctions stem. In Marseille, the most obvious and defining characteristic is its historic access to the outstanding variety and quality of seafood fished off its shores. The city's "national" dish, the world-famous *bouillabaisse marseillaise,* is a magnificent manifestation of that bounty.

"There is no doubt about it," wrote M. F. K. Fisher in *A Considerable Town,* her portrait of Marseille. "Freshly caught fish, scaly or in the shell, have a different flavor and texture and *smell* there than in any other port in the world."

Besides consuming more finfish and shellfish in more ways than their counterparts in the Provençal countryside, people raised in Marseille and its vicinity are more likely to flavor their foods with such low-lying plants as rosemary, thyme, basil, garlic, olives, almonds, hazelnuts, and fennel than with lavender, sage, mint, and other highland vegetation.

Still, such distinctions, however logical and historically accurate they may be, only go so far. The universal staples in the classic cooking of Marseille and Provence are virtually the same: olives, olive oil, garlic, tomatoes, aromatic herbs, eggplant, zucchini, fennel, almonds, honey. Moreover, Marseille has no more an exclusive territorial claim on aïoli, *soupe au pistou,* daube, anchoïade, ratatouille, fougasse, and the thirteen desserts of Christmas than it does on Provence's sun-kissed fruits and vegetables. They are part of a shared heritage.

But just as Provence is a French region with its own language, culture, and Greco-Roman-Latinate origins, Marseille is a Provençal city with its own accent, customs, and multiethnic influences. In this vein, it might at first seem more helpful to think of Marseille as a city within a region within a country, and to speak of a *tradition*—as opposed to a *cuisine—marseillaise*. This tradition would take its shape from local interpretations of dishes first prepared elsewhere in Provence, and, reversing the direction, specialties that originated in Marseille and were later adopted and interpreted elsewhere. Some primary examples of this would be tapenade, *panisses* (fried chickpea cakes), *navettes* (biscuits in the symbolic shape of a small boat), and *pieds et paquets* (stuffed mutton tripe slow-cooked with tomato, white wine, and mutton trotters).

It's What the People Bring

But describing Marseille as a Provençal subdivision consisting of black olive paste, chickpea cakes, biscuits, and sheep's feet is not only unappetizing. It's insulting. Marseille's culinary influences are much larger and wider than Provence's. You can more easily fit the cuisine of Provence into a Marseille cookbook, as I've felt it not only desirable but also imperative to do here, than fit the cuisine of Marseille into a Provençal cookbook. While Provence is bordered to the west by the Rhône river and to the east by the French-Italian border, Marseille's reach extends from the French West Indies to Indochina, with heavy concentrations throughout the four corners of the Mediterranean. And nowhere on the Mediterranean is there a large seaport city with as wide and varied an aggregation of the region's cultures.

"There is not a *cuisine marseillaise* per se," notes Emile Temime, professor emeritus at the Université Aix-Marseille. "It's what the people bring."

And that is the best way to classify the cuisine of Marseille and, by extension, the collected recipes in this cookbook. It is not a pure example of what the French call a *cuisine du terroir*, meaning it is local, countrified, and closely connected to the land. (Even when, prior to the mid-nineteenth century, outstanding figs and fine wines were cultivated on Marseille soil, the city's deep-rooted attachments were largely offshore.) Neither is it a *grande cuisine* in the sense of it being built upon the creations and legacies of master chefs. Rather, the recipes and refinements of Marseille's celebrated chefs (Durand, Roubion, Meynier, Caillat, Isnard, Arnoud, Drouin, Brun) from the nineteenth and early twentieth centuries were built upon it.

"We are atypical," notes Jeanne Moreni-Garron, the chef at the Marseille-Provençal restaurant Les Echevins. "In Lyon it's very defined. Here it is diversified—Italian, Greek, Armenian—it's not homegrown."

The food of Marseille, like the culture it richly reflects, is the result of twenty-six centuries of importation, immigration, and implantation. It is a *cuisine du port*, a "seaport cuisine." It is an evolution that began with the Greek mariners who founded Marseille around the year 600 B.C. and soon after planted the region's first olive trees, fig trees, walnuts trees, and vineyards.

All Cargo Goes Through Marseille

As a large harbor city strategically situated near the mouth of the Rhône river (the French regional department to which Marseille belongs is called the Bouches du Rhône, "mouths of the Rhône"), Marseille has for centuries been the principal French port of entry for everything moving from the south to the north, not the least of all foodstuffs: spices, grains, cereals, sugar, oils, bananas, citrus fruit, teas, cocoa. A 1644 shipment of coffee beans from Alexandria to Marseille is believed to have been Europe's first. The era of commercial development and economic expansion that began in the eighteenth century and exploded during the second half of the nineteenth century brought with it a flood of goods across the Mediterranean. From its very livelihood Marseille quickly developed an extraordinary capacity to absorb foods and integrate the cuisines of southern Europe, the Middle East, and North Africa.

When you think of Provence and the natural beauty of its vineyards, olive groves, dazzling gardens, lavender fields, plane trees, and parasol pines, any suggestion of it being a barren region sounds ludicrous. But Provence is, in farming terms, a mostly dry and impoverished land with few fertile green meadows to raise livestock. Its sun-dried scrubland may be a paradise for rosemary, thyme, sage, savory, and marjoram, but only the hardiest breeds of sheep and goats dare graze there. The goats of Rove, which take their name from a village outside Marseille, are to be admired as much for their noble bearing and survival instincts as the curd cheese—*brousse de Rove*—they produce. The fact that the population of Rove has in

Olive Oil in Marseille Cookery

Prior to the nineteenth century, having your mouth washed out with soap was not quite so nasty a proposition for naughty Marseillais children. The distinctive cubes of the famous *Savon de Marseille* were until that point made with olive oil, an essential, flavorsome, and healthful ingredient not only in the cooking of Provence but also in the varied Mediterranean cuisines that together define the Marseille palate.

The historic link in French minds between Marseille soap and olive oil may, however, explain why the city's name has rarely figured prominently on the can and bottle labels of local distributors. Les Moulins de l'Estaque, a new line of herb-flavored olive oils, upholds this tradition. They were named by the Compagnie Alimentaire for the village but not the city where these specialty oils are macerated.

But though there is really no such thing as a Marseille-style olive oil, either by the origin or the variety of the olives, there is a longstanding preference among chefs and connoisseurs for Provençal oils in general and the oils of the Aix region in particular. The extra virgin olive oils of Aix tend to be very fruity, with a strong vegetal flavor (sometimes comparable to artichokes) and a peppery kick. These characteristics are well suited to the likes of pistou, aïoli, anchoïade, eggplant caviar, tapenade, fougasse, and, yes, bouillabaisse. The concern with these outstanding oils is that they are expensive: At this writing, a 500-milliliter bottle of the highly recommended and widely distributed Château Virant was selling for $32.75 at Williams-Sonoma. That works out to about $1 per tablespoon.

Home cooks might reserve a fine Provençale oil for flavoring purposes and seek out a less costly alternative for general cooking purposes. Extra virgin olive oils from the Spanish regions of Andalusia and Catalonia and the Greek regions of Peloponnesus and Crete share some characteristics with the French oils from Aix. Many Italian oils, especially those from Tuscany and Puglia, can be too overpowering for the aforementioned specialties, especially uncooked dips and sauces (aïoli, pistou) with high concentrations of olive oil.

For high-temperatured cooking like sautéing and pan frying it is not necessary to use a high-quality olive oil. You may, however, prefer to use a low-priced extra virgin olive oil (be sure to check the label for the words *extra virgin*) for its full health benefits. Only extra virgin olive oil contains the antioxidants called polyphenols. That might also be a reason to use a low-priced extra virgin olive oil in place of canola oil, peanut oil, or corn oil in deep frying.

Interestingly, despite our admiration for the Mediterranean diet and its supposedly universal reliance on olive oil, that product is today viewed in many homes as an indulgence to be used sparingly. Whether employed with restraint or in abundance, extra virgin olive oil should be appreciated as the noble ingredient it is. And its many uses in body care products notwithstanding, good olive oil ought not be wasted on the dirty mouth of a mischievous child.

the past century gone from four thousand goats and four hundred people to two hundred goats and four thousand people is due to urban sprawl and not to any weakening of the goats' resolve. Give them some thorns to chew on and they're content.

Rather than subsist on a regime of woody spines, the Provençals found other ways to adapt. They developed a simple, economical, family-style cuisine which, though limited in its selection of meats, dairy products, and, as a fortunate consequence, sources of fat and cholesterol, was enriched through an assortment of vegetables, perfumed herbs, fragrant olive oils, and exotic spices. This is especially true of the hardy people who take their name from a world spice capital, namely the Marseillais. If you think of the classic Marseille pantry as a wardrobe, it's one with just a few basic suits or dresses but enough wild and colorful accessories to fill two dressers.

Champagne or Pastis

The Marseille food wardrobe has never truly won the respect of French gastronomy. The emergence of Provençal cookery and its recent and dramatic transformation from rustic to rarefied, *grand-mère* to grande cuisine has so far eluded Marseille. This seaport's enduring but soon-to-be-endangered reputation as a desert for *haute cuisine* reflects the contempt that Parisians in particular have felt toward this working-class city of immigrants.

But the locals must share some of the blame—or, you could say, credit—for this predicament. Mediterranean by origin and independent by nature, they have rebelled against everything that smacks of pretension, be it aristocracies or groceries. Even some well-do-to Marseillais would sooner answer to accusations of being cheap than frequent the city's finer dining establishments.

"The Marseillais are not cheap," says Jacques Moréni-Garron, owner of the moderately priced Les Echevins, "but it is true they don't like to put money on the table."

In actuality, the city's aversion to *haute cuisine* is less about money than culture. Given a choice between the esoteric, intellectual, impeccably presented, and sometimes soulless pleasures of a multistarred French restaurant and the uncomplicated, unfettered, and unpolished joys of a fish house, bistro, or pizzeria, most Marseillais would opt for the latter. As someone with an insatiable appetite for both experiences, I would not take sides in this class struggle between high and low culture, linen and paper napkins, Champagne and pastis. In Marseille I was delighted to have found many wonderful tastes reflecting both notions of pleasure, as you will see just from perusing the recipes in this book. But if I were to compare audio recordings of two dinners, one at the nationally acclaimed (two Michelin stars) Restaurant Passédat; the other, at the convivial fish house L'Escale, there wouldn't be much doubt about who was having a better time.

"A Marseillais wants to have a good laugh, he wants to be near the cuisine of his childhood," explains L'Escale owner Serge Zarokian. With his gregarious charm, dark features, thick accent, and, as if by order from central casting, Armenian-Corsican-Italian-Lebanese roots, he is the right person to be making this argument. "The Marseillais is the bon vivant, the jokester, the lover of the sun, pastis, *boules,* the sea, and fish. You must keep that identity."

Non-natives, business travelers, and tourists have another motive for preferring the informal restaurant option. Accomplished, multistarred restaurants may be found throughout France and in most major cities of Europe and North America. But seaside seafood gems like L'Escale and Le Tiboulen de Maïre, both located near the fishing port of Les Goudes, and the breathtaking Le Lunch, a concrete patio wedged between the beach and the rocky cliffs of the great Calanque de Sormiou, afford an exhilarating experience particular to Marseille.

Although I successfully adapted and tested all the recipes (including three from L'Escale) for this book in my New York City kitchen, importing the sun, the sea, the colors, the breezes, the smells, and the *joie de vivre* of those restaurants proved more elusive. The best that can be done is to uncork a chilled bottle of Cassis, a dry, delicately fruity white wine possessing the bouquet of the Calanque coastline. Romantics can identify a hint of what the French call a *gout iodé*—meaning not so much iodized as tasting of the sea—in the wine's mineral-like tang. United States importers distributed several good examples of Cassis, not to be confused with the black currant liqueur of the same name.

Pastis de Marseille

The ritual begins with the scant one-ounce transfer of a clear, caramel-yellow solution from liquor bottle to juice glass. Atop that shot is poured five measures of a transparent, colorless liquid that, but for the mysterious chemical reaction it was about to effect, could not be mistaken for anything other than water. Once diluted and emulsified, the solution metamorphoses into a milky opalescence. The cloudy apéritif is complete save for an ice cube or two.

This is the method for serving a pastis, a refreshing, French-Mediterranean institution that is inseparable from the laughter, conviviality, and good times the Marseillais seem to acquire a knack for simply by drinking the local water. Well maybe it is not only the water. The regulated alcoholic content of the distilled liqueur is 45 percent. It is flavored with star anise, licorice, and, less noticeably, aromatic herbs that vary from recipe to recipe and producer to producer.

The drink that came to be known as pastis was first developed in the bars and, yes, bathtubs of the South of France as a substitute for the notoriously potent and inordinately popular liqueur absinthe. France banned the manufacture and distribution of absinthe, "the green peril," in 1914. In 1932, an enterprising twenty-two-year-old Marseillais named Paul Ricard turned a local recipe into the commercial formula for Ricard, *le vrai pastis de Marseille* ("the true pastis of Marseille"). Ricard was launched in the Sainte-Marthe quarter of Marseille, where it is distilled and bottled to this day. It is one of two brands (the other is Pernod) distributed throughout the United States, although employees estimate that more Ricard is consumed in the bar next to the Sainte-Marthe plant than in the entire *Etats-Unis*.

Most Marseille cafés, bars, and restaurants carry two brands of pastis: Ricard and Pastis 51. A third mark, Casanis, is also prevalent. (Oddly, the internationally known Pernod, which makes Pastis 51 and is now owned by Ricard, is of another style and rarely served in Marseille.) A pastis is typically ordered as a *pastaga,* a *jaune* ("yellow"), or according to either brand name or brand-name diminutive: *Casa* for Casanis, *51* or "*fly*" for Pastis 51, just *Ricard* for Ricard.

Those quick to dismiss pastis as a generic, licorice-tasting drink are probably missing both its complexity and its full significance as a definitive Marseille mélange (*pastis* is Provençal for "mixture"). Star anise and licorice, the most prominent ingredients in most pastis, are not, as Americans are inclined to believe, identical. We commonly mistake licorice for the similarly scented anise because anise oil is used as the primary flavor in so-called licorice candies. But licorice is sweeter and not as bitter as star anise. The Marseillais may instead associate star anise with the scent of the fennel that grows wildly in their scrubland.

Ricard is made with star anise imported either from southern China or northern Vietnam and thus is one of many end products of the busy spice trail between Marseille and Southeast Asia. Its licorice root comes from Syria's Euphrates valley, reflecting the Middle Eastern route to the French seaport.

The additional herbs and spices ostensibly mixed into the commercialized brands of pastis are nearly impossible to detect. They are formulated so as to be neutral and not offend. But several pleasing though mostly unfamiliar aromas are apparent in Henri Bardouin, a prestige-level, artisanal pastis produced by the Distilleries et Domaines de Provence. It is made with star anise, artemesia (a Provençal herb with a bitterness common to fine apéritifs), feverwort (another bitter herb), malaguetta (a pepper from the Ivory Coast), cardamom, white pepper, black pepper, tonka bean (a South American bean with a flavor suggestive of tobacco), cinnamon, nutmeg, and clove.

Though many Marseillais would identify the buyers of the herbaceous Henri Bardouin pastis as bourgeois dupes, its mixture is a fascinating evocation of the city's cosmopolitan nose. Besides, locals who have been drinking pastis all their lives might be surprised to learn of the herbs contained in a true and original formula. Although Ricard's recipe is a closely guarded secret, I do have the next best thing. The late Ange Scaramelli lived in the celebrated Marseille village of Eoures and claimed that his childhood friend, Paul Ricard, used his personal recipe as a source in formulating the commercial product that became Ricard. Whether the story is true, false, or somewhere in between, Scaramelli's recipe is an excellent one.

PASTIS ANGE SCARAMELLI

1 liter grain alcohol (90 percent)

1 ¼ liters water

1 tablespoon plus 1 teaspoon star anise

20 grams star anise leaves

10 grams green star anise

5 grams wild fennel stems

5 grams fresh coriander

10 grams ground licorice root

3 grams malaguetta grains

3 teaspoons sugar

1. Combine all the ingredients except the sugar in a half-gallon jar with a tight-fitting lid. Store out of the sunlight and let macerate for 1 month.

2. Pour the mixture through a fine sieve to filter out the herbs.
3. Heat the sugar and 2 teaspoons water in a saucepan, stirring continuously, until the mixture turns a dark caramel color. Pour this caramel into the pastis and mix well.

Anyone brave enough to prepare pastis at home might well find it much easier to use essential oils instead of herbs, as in the following recipe of Frédéric Poitou, a chemist at Compagnie Alimentaire in L'Estaque. The oils may be purchased directly from his company (*www.compagnie-alimentaire.com*) or from other distributors and importers in the U.S. and abroad. The preparation is the same as in the previous recipe, except that there are no herbs to filter out.

PASTIS FRÉDÉRIC POITOU

1 liter grain alcohol (90 percent)
1 ¼ liters water
3 drops star anise oil
3 drops sweet fennel oil
6 drops armoise oil
1 drop licorice extract
1 drop lavender oil
1 drop inula oil
1 drop immortelle oil
3 teaspoons sugar

In a "standard" serving of pastis, the ratio of pastis to water is 1 to 5. Many Marseillais, however, prefer less water and expect bartenders to pour accordingly to the point where the ratio is nearly reversed. Immoderate imbibers may go far as to request a *mominette* or, for short, a *momi*, a shot glass of pastis with at most a few droplets of water. At cafés, a jigger of pastis is customarily served in a four-ounce glass, with a carafe of water to accompany it so that the optimum water dosage may be gauged by each individual. A pastis may also be flavored with a variety of syrups. Each such drink is named for its appearance. One with 1 volume pastis, 5 volumes water, and 1 volume almond-flavored syrup *orgeat* is ordered as a *Mauresque* ("Moor" or "Moorish"). A pastis and grenadine is called a *tomate*, for its tomato color; with mint syrup, it is identified as a *perroquet* ("parrot"). A pastis apéritif with both grenadine and mint is known as a *feuille morte*, "a dead leaf."

Monsieur André (right) *sells wine to Monsieur Gabella.*

Authenticité and *Simplicité*

As much as the Marseillais may eschew certain pretensions, even populists like Zarokian are not without a certain arrogance. Theirs is the snobbery of *authenticité*, only they use that word in a different way than an American would. When we describe a dish as "authentic," we usually mean that its preparation was true to its origins, "just like in the old country" so to speak. But the concern here is the fidelity to the main ingredients. A tomato must taste like a tomato. A *loup* (Mediterranean bass) must taste like *loup*. You have to know what you're eating. The nightmare of the Marseillais grandparent is the grandchild who, when asked to draw a picture of a fish, draws a rectangle.

Authenticité demands "*simplicité*," itself the most overused and most misunderstood food term in the culinary world. Home cooks may interpret simplicity as meaning easy to prepare, something it rarely is. And when I interview hotshot chefs in both France and America, they often define simplicity as using no more than three ingredients. But a piece of sole covered with melted Roquefort cheese—that's two ingredients!—is not the Marseillais' idea of simplicity. Just how picky can the Marseillais be about the flavor of fish? When I asked Aimé Bergero why he served fish soup and grilled fish but not bouillabaisse at his modest but incomparable seafood grill, the owner of Le Tiboulin de Maïre answered the question with several questions:

"Do you like rib steak?" he asked. "Do you like lamb chops?"

"Yes and yes," I replied.

"Do you boil your rib steaks? Do you boil your lamb chops?"

"No and no."

"Then why would I boil my handsome *rougets* [red mullets]. I grill my fish."

I related this amusing exchange to food writer Jacques Dupuy, adding how Bergero pampers all his fish as they grill, turning them once and only with a dainty pastry spatula, and how he refuses diner requests for olive oil. The only proper way to eat *rouget*, according to purists, is naked—the fish, that is. I expected Dupuy to laugh at the absurdity of comparing the boiling of fish with the boiling of meat. But the Mediterranean fish scholar was not amused.

"The noble *rouget* merits better than grilling," noted Dupuy. "I would sauté."

Though we may revel in this purism bordering on fanaticism, it is not included here as an argument against creativity or, for that matter, a drizzle of good-quality extra virgin olive oil atop a lovely piece of fish, grilled or sautéed. I am not at all opposed to the application of seasonings, garnishes, and accompaniments that either draw out or complement the flavor of the seafood. Indeed, this cookbook features fish dishes adorned with fennel, zucchini, basil, tomato, honey, lemon, and orange—all workhorse ingredients of the Marseille kitchen.

Rather, the lesson to take home is this: A respect and appreciation for the purity of food products are most essential when their quality is as great as their selection is small. Such was the case in Marseille and the greater region of Provence before the global marketplace yielded such questionable marvels as the January tomato.

One Does the Best with What One Has

For me, one of this cookbook's breakthrough moments occurred in the kitchen of Dupuy's country home in the village of Coudoux, some fifteen miles northwest of Marseille. While sweating the onions and leeks that were to be the basis for what Dupuy wanted to call a *bouillabaisse new yorkaise*, he warned me about the necessity of using a good quality extra virgin olive oil to gently extract every last bit of flavor from the onions and leeks. This took on extra importance, he noted, because we were limiting ourselves to Atlantic ocean fish and thus couldn't count on the strong-tasting Mediterranean rockfish for cover. Scarcity necessitated selectivity.

"One does the very best with what one has," said Dupuy, sharing with me an adage I had also heard from retired fisherman Roger Silvestri at his family's fish market in the Marseille village of Mazargues. And though this was a rule of thumb they and perhaps also the fishermen who first made bouillabaisse applied to its preparation, it could be the guiding principle of all Marseille-style home cooking.

Thereafter I came to a fuller appreciation of the rigid rules handed down by Marseillais sticklers from generation to generation: the ideal combination of fish and vegetables in a bouillabaisse. The precise combination of beans and the pasta shape without which a *soupe au pistou* becomes unthinkable. The requirement that Armenian lahmajoun (pizza) be baked in a rectangular pan rather than a round pan or, according to the tradition of a competing school, vice versa. The precise cut of the vegetables in an Algerian chorma. The utter greenness of the bananas required to keep a Comoran tropical fish stew from turning mushy. I even saw the wisdom in Etienne Cassaro's insistence that his word for a pizza restaurant—"pizzaria"—is right and everyone else's spelling is wrong.

"Tell me something," Cassaro asked me, "are you eating *peetz-eh* or *peetz-ah?*"

Perhaps the "a" in *pizz-a-ria* has something to do with his baking the best pies in a truly great pizza town. Of course I don't actually believe that. But I am convinced the orthodoxy that forbids the use of a blender or mini–food processor in the preparation of pistou sauce preserves the traditions of *authenticité* and *simplicité,* even admitting that a processed pistou can be pretty darn good. One does the very best with what one has.

Marseille's Culinary Renaissance

For Marseille's best restaurant chefs, the objective should be the same: *Mettre en valeur*—"to show off to best advantage"—their food products. And this can be as basic and outrageous as Gérald Passédat's idea of chilling a fine extra virgin olive oil to the solidity of butter so that, spread on toast, it melts in the mouth, slowly unleashing its vegetal aromas, fruity flavors, and peppery notes.

For the talented young chefs who are irrigating this onetime desert of *haute cuisine* and fueling Marseille's culinary renaissance, the challenge is finding a middle ground between old and new, familiar and exotic, Bergero and Passédat. For Guillaume Sourrieu, that means keeping a traditional bouillabaisse on the menu at L'Epuisette opposite his tajine of sole with braised baby artichokes and Oriental spices. For Florent Saugeron, formerly the chef at Vong in London, that means creating a more subdued fusion cuisine at his bistro Lemon Grass that is less French-Asian than Mediterranean-Asian. Every plate must be grounded with some component or flavor to which the Marseillais palate is accustomed.

The ingenuity of Lionel Lévy, a protégé of chefs Alain Ducasse and

Gérard Garrigues, is in taking familiar foods and formats and rethinking them. At Une Table au Sud he creates desserts (stuffed tomato, olive clafoutis) inspired by appetizers and appetizers (salmon crumble) inspired by desserts. Like most of his Marseille counterparts he defines his cooking as Mediterranean as opposed to Provençal.

Tellingly, Lévy looks back at his move from Paris to Marseille in 1999 as a coming home, forgetting that he grew up in the southwest French city of Toulouse, worked only there and in the French capital, and never lived close to the sea. As the son of a Moroccan Jewish father, the perfumes and colors of the Old Port evoke an early childhood he hadn't quite remembered.

There is the magic of Marseille. Lévy can put a fork to his side dish of glazed carrots with black olives and cumin and say, "That's home. That's Marseille."

The chemist Frédéric Poitou, a native of Normandy, can dip blotters into tester bottles containing basil oil, thyme oil, and star anise oil, hold them up to his nose, sniff, and say, "That's home. That's Marseille."

And this book's author, a New Yorker, can point to any recipe in this book, home or restaurant, old or new, traditional or modern, unmodified or fusion, indigenous or global, Provençale, Italian, Armenian, Corsican, Moroccan, Spanish, Sephardic, or French, and say, "That's home. That's made in Marseille."

Pétanque

If it seems as though the Marseillais have been playing pétanque for eons, it may be because the popular bowling game runs through their Greco-Roman bloodlines. The ancient Greeks played a similar game, casting round stones as far as possible. And the ancient Romans used iron-covered wooden balls in a contest which, like pétanque, valued accuracy above brute strength.

Though comparable games were popular throughout the Middle Ages, the first official competition of pétanque, a corruption of *pèd tanco,* Provençal for "feet together," was not played until 1908 in La Ciotat, a coastal town east of Marseille.

As with lawn bowling and Italian *bocce,* the objective of the game is to toss the ball as close to the "jack" (a smaller ball that acts as the marker) as possible. In pétanque, the metal balls are called *boules,* have a diameter between 7.05 and 8 centimeters (about 3 inches), and may vary in weight from 650 to 800 grams ($1\frac{1}{2}$ to $1\frac{3}{4}$ pounds). The wood "jack" is called a *cochonnet* ("piglet").

A great attraction of pétanque is that it is a social game for which neither the player nor the playing surface require special conditioning. Pétanque can be played not only on *bouledromes,* the dirt fields made explicitly for the sport, but also on nearly any reasonably flat dirt surface (parks, playgrounds, fields, walkways) by anyone who can toss a *boule* some ten yards or so without pulling a muscle. Most healthy people between the ages of ten and eighty can manage this. Matches may be contested between teams of one, two (*doublettes*), and three (*triplettes*) players.

To start play, a competitor draws a small circle on the ground and throws the *cochonnet* between $6\frac{1}{2}$ and 11 yards from the circle. Each round begins when a player of the first team, standing with both feet together within the circle, throws a *boule* toward the *cochonnet.* The second team must then play until at least one of its *boules* is closer to the *cochonnet.* The first team must then try to best the second team's *boule* and so on. The winning team receives one point for each *boule* it has placed closer to the *cochonnet* than any *boule* of the opposing team. Most matches are played to thirteen points.

In the course of each round, skilled pétanque players generally employ one of two basic strategies: They may choose to "point" the *boule* closer to the *cochonnet,* crouching down in the starting circle and lofting the ball with a backhand motion toward the target. Or they may elect to "shoot" it at an adversary's *boule* to knock it violently away and leave one of their team's *boules* closest to the *cochonnet.* The most proficient "shooters" may hit the front of an opponent's *boule* in such a manner as to knock it far from the *cochonnet* while leaving their *boule* in its place. This adroit maneuver is known as the *carreau.*

Pointers and shooters alike must contend with the same nasty side effect. The pressure of competing in a match of pétanque under the intense Marseille sun invariably leads to a parched mouth. This intense thirst is best quenched by a glass of pastis. *Boules* can be ordered on the Web from the Marseille metalworks that has forged them since 1904, La Boule Bleue (*www.laboulebleue.com*). Sadly, pastis is not among the official accessories and supplies they ship to the United States.

Outside the Cathédrale de la Major, pétanque is a religion.

Dips, Jams, and Sauces

Tapenade

Vinaigrette Fouettée aux Olives Noires
BLACK OLIVE PUREE

Anchoïade ANCHOVY AND GARLIC PASTE

Caviar de Sardine à la Provençale
PROVENCE-STYLE SARDINE SPREAD

Pistou BASIL AND GARLIC SAUCE

Aïoli PROVENÇAL GARLIC MAYONNAISE

Rouille SPICY GARLIC SAUCE

Confiture d'Oignons ONION JAM

Confiture d'Échalotes au Vin Rouge
SHALLOT AND RED WINE JAM

Confiture de Tomates et Gingembre
TOMATO-GINGER JAM

Tomato Confit OVEN-ROASTED TOMATOES

Coulis de Tomates Provençal PROVENÇAL
TOMATO SAUCE

Huile d'Olive Glacée COLD OLIVE OIL
SPREAD

I N T H E T H E A T E R O F G A S T R O N O M Y, sauces are customarily supporting players whose role it is to either complement or heighten the natural flavor of the main act. But on the dinner table, as on stage and on screen, the character actors sometimes steal the show. Indeed, two great classics of Provençal cooking—soupe au pistou and aïoli garni (or, in its most elaborate presentations, grand aïoli)—take the name of their sauces and not the foods these sauces animate. In the former, pistou is the pesto-like basil sauce that is a last-minute addition to a hearty bean and vegetable soup. In the latter, aïoli, a garlic-powered mayonnaise sometimes referred to as the butter of Provence, is slathered over salt cod, hard-boiled eggs, and an array of cooked vegetables (carrots, potatoes, artichokes, haricots verts, cauliflower, beets).

In Marseille as elsewhere in Provence, aïoli is one of three celebrated sauces that do double duty as cold dips or spreads. The other two are tapenade (a paste of black olives, capers, anchovies, and olive oil) and anchoïade (a paste of anchovies, garlic, and olive oil). Served before the meal to accompany an apéritif, these sauces stimulate the appetite while boldly introducing some key food components—garlic, black olives, anchovies—likely to reappear during the course of dinner. With nothing to smooth these pointed flavors but extra virgin olive oil, they quickly become emblazoned in a Marseillais' taste memory.

The other sauces and condiments in this section may not all perform as solo acts. Nevertheless, the objective in their preparation is the same: concentration of flavor. The recipe for oven-roasted tomatoes is a prime example: The tomatoes are slow-cooked with garlic and olive oil to their melting point so that, when applied as a sauce or garnish, each molecule practically explodes with sweet tomato intensity. As with the jams (tomato-ginger, onion, shallot and red wine), the ultimate goal is to trap the ingredients at the moment their flavors peak.

TAPENADE

This famous Provençal paste of black olives, capers, and anchovies was invented in 1880 by Charles Meynier, chef de cuisine at the long defunct Marseille restaurant La Maison Dorée. Meynier's original recipe for "caviar *marseillais*" called for a base of capers (it took its name from *tapeno*, which is Provençal for capers), black olives, tuna, anchovies, and mustard. It was prepared to accompany eggs *mimosa* (a salad topped with chopped eggs).

As the uses of tapenade evolved, so did its composition. The proportion of black olives increased from about 30 percent to perhaps 65 percent, while the quantity of capers diminished, the anchovies became a subject of debate, and the tuna all but disappeared. Nevertheless, it is rare to find a tapenade in a Marseille restaurant without anchovies. It is most often served as a dip or spread over toast, but it does find its way into many dishes, including sautéed sea scallops with vegetables and basil panisses (page 166) and the Marseille-style BLT (page 188).

MAKES ABOUT 1 CUP

½ pound (about 1 cup) black olives, pitted

7 to 8 whole salted anchovies, rinsed, filleted, and dried (substitute 15 canned anchovy fillets, drained and dried)

3 tablespoons drained capers

1 to 2 cloves garlic, minced, optional

½ cup olive oil

1 teaspoon fresh lemon juice

Combine the olives, anchovies, capers, and minced garlic, if desired, in a blender or food processor and mix into a paste. With the machine still running, in a slow stream pour in the olive oil and lemon juice; mix until smooth. Transfer to a tightly lidded jar and refrigerate. It will keep up to 2 months.

VINAIGRETTE FOUETTÉE AUX OLIVES NOIRES

BLACK OLIVE PUREE

The consistency of Giselle Philippi's black olive puree is halfway between a paste and a vinaigrette. With no anchovies and only a little olive oil, it makes a great tapenade alternative for those who want none of the former and not too much of the latter.

MAKES 1¼ CUPS

½ pound (about 1 cup) black olives, pitted
1 tablespoon herbes de Provence (see Note)
1 teaspoon red wine vinegar
Salt
Freshly ground black pepper
3 tablespoons olive oil

1. Put the olives in a blender, and pour in just enough cold water to cover. Add the herbes de Provence and vinegar, season with salt and pepper, and blend until the mixture has the consistency of a paste, about 2 minutes.

2. Add the olive oil and blend for 1 minute. The puree should have the thick consistency of melted chocolate. If too watery, add more black olives. Transfer to a tightly lidded jar and refrigerate. This will keep for 2 months.

Herbes de Provence constitute an aromatic blend of dried herbs that can vary somewhat in content and proportion. Usually the mix includes thyme, rosemary, bay leaf, basil, and savory. To prepare your own custom blend of herbes de Provence, combine 1 tablespoon each of dried basil, thyme, rosemary, marjoram, and summer savory with 1 crushed bay leaf, and then additional quantities of these herbs or smaller quantities of other aromatics (lavender, fennel seeds, sage) according to taste.

ANCHOÏADE

ANCHOVY AND GARLIC PASTE

A staple of the Provençal table, anchoïade is a pungent paste of anchovies, garlic, and olive oil that is most often served cold as a dip for crudités (raw carrots, celery, carrots, red pepper, cauliflower, radishes) or as a spread on toasted slices of country bread or baguettes. It can also be used as a sauce, topping, or condiment to enliven a hard-boiled egg, tomato sauce, slab of meat, or any recipe that calls for—or could benefit from—a hit of anchovy paste. To this basic formula you may add chopped parsley, chopped black olives, or capers, but certainly not more than two of those and only in small quantities. Your result should be recognizable as an anchoïade and not halfway between it and a tapenade or pistou.

MAKES 1¼ CUPS

4 cloves garlic

15 salted anchovies, rinsed, filleted, and dried (substitute 30 canned anchovy fillets, drained and dried)

½ cup olive oil

2 teaspoons red wine vinegar

¼ teaspoon freshly ground black pepper

1. Crush the garlic cloves in a garlic press or grate against the prongs of a fork held down on a cutting surface. Combine in a mortar or mini–food processor with the anchovies and pound with a pestle or process into a paste.

2. Gradually add the olive oil and vinegar, season with pepper, and mix, using a whisk if you'd like your anchoïade to be a little fluffy, until smooth.

The "King of Olives,"
a stall within the food
bazaar at the Marché des
Arnavaux, Marseille's
flea market.

Monia, a waitress at a café on the Place Jean-Jaurès.

CAVIAR DE SARDINE
À LA PROVENÇALE
PROVENCE-STYLE SARDINE SPREAD

In writing *Le Roman de la Sardine* ("The Story of the Sardine"), Marseille native Jacques Bonnadier set out to rescue the reputation of the sardine, a fish unjustly maligned—or merely ignored—for being too ordinary, too abundant, and too darn puny. His admirable effort of culinary scholarship is epitomized by the noble name he gave his recipe for a sardine spread, Caviar de Sardine à la Provençale.

MAKES ABOUT 1½ CUPS

20 to 25 fresh basil leaves
2 tablespoons olive oil
2 cans (3¾ ounces each) oil-packed sardines
3 slices white bread
1 cup milk
1 tablespoon lemon juice
Salt
Freshly ground black pepper

1. Place the basil leaves in a mortar and mash with a pestle. Add the olive oil and mash into the basil.

2. Drain the oil from the sardines, add the sardines to the mortar, and mash with the basil and olive oil.

3. Place the bread slices in a bowl, cover with the milk, and let soak for 1 minute. Squeeze out as much milk as possible from the bread with your hands, add the bread to the mortar, and mash into the sardines until you have a smooth paste. Add the lemon juice, season with salt and pepper, mix well, transfer to a jar or plastic container, cover, and refrigerate. This will keep for 3 days. Serve with toast, raw tomatoes, or steamed potatoes.

PISTOU

BASIL AND GARLIC SAUCE

The Provençal counterpart to Genoese pesto, *pistou* is a sauce of crushed basil, garlic, and olive oil. The word *pistou* comes from the Provençal verb *pista,* meaning to crush or pound. A *pistou* refers to a pestle, the instrument used to reduce the ingredients to a homogeneous paste. Is it permissible to instead mix together a *pistou* in a blender or mini–food processor? Yes, of course. But only if you're willing to defy common wisdom, accept an inferior result, and change its name to *sauce au mixer* (blender) or *sauce au robot* (food processor). An essential part of *soupe au pistou* (page 109), it may also be used as an uncooked sauce for pasta.

MAKES 1 TO 1½ CUPS

8 garlic cloves
Salt
Freshly ground black pepper
4 cups loosely packed fresh basil leaves
3 plum tomatoes
1 cup (about ¼ pound) shredded Gruyère or
    Emmental cheese
½ cup (about 3 ounces) grated Parmesan
6 to 8 tablespoons olive oil

1. Put the garlic cloves in a marble mortar and crush with a pestle. Add the salt, pepper, and basil leaves, and pound into the garlic.

2. To peel the tomatoes, cut a small X in their smooth ends and plunge into boiling salted water for 30 seconds. Peel the tomatoes, cut each into 5 or 6 sections, and remove their seeds.

3. Chop the tomato sections and add to the mortar along with the shredded Gruyère and grated Parmesan. Pound the tomato and cheese into the mixture, very gradually adding the olive oil, until the mixture turns into a uniform paste (there should be few remaining patches of dark deep green). Transfer to a jar or plastic container, cover, and refrigerate. This will keep for one week.

AÏOLI

PROVENÇAL GARLIC MAYONNAISE

The initial challenge when first preparing aïoli, as with any mayonnaise, is getting the egg yolks and olive oil to thicken into a rich and creamy emulsion. Having the egg yolks, garlic, olive oil at room temperature, and slowly, patiently, adding the olive oil drop by drop will greatly reduce the chance of a failed aïoli. Moreover, the addition of the mustard, though an affront to purists, will provide further insurance against such a collapse.

Still, if despite all precautions your mixture turns muddy do not despair: Your aïoli may rise to live again. Empty the aïoli into a bowl. Place a single egg yolk in the mortar and mash it in a circular motion with the pestle. Add the aïoli little by little, continuing to mash the mixture in a circular motion. Slowly the mixture should thicken to the texture in which the pestle can stand on its own. Mash in any unused oil by slowly adding it drop by drop. Serve with assorted crudités.

MAKES ABOUT 2 CUPS

2 egg yolks
6 cloves garlic, crushed
½ teaspoon salt
1 small pinch freshly ground white pepper
¼ to ½ teaspoon Dijon mustard, optional
2 cups olive oil

1. Take out the eggs from the refrigerator 1 hour in advance. If you must use cold eggs you will probably need an additional ¼ cup or so olive oil.

2. Place the garlic, salt, and white pepper in a mortar and mash with a pestle into a paste.

Add the egg yolks and mustard, if desired, and mash with the pestle in a circular motion until fully incorporated and thickened, about 2 minutes. Let stand for 5 minutes.

3. Very gradually add the olive oil, drop by drop, never ceasing to mash the mixture in a circular motion until the aïoli has thickened to a consistency in which the pestle can stand up on its own. Add 2 teaspoons of lukewarm water, continuing to mash in a circular motion for 1 minute. Taste, and correct the seasonings. Refrigerate for up to 24 hours. Bring to room temperature before serving.

ROUILLE

SPICY GARLIC SAUCE

The bouillon of a bouillabaisse is traditionally poured into shallow soup bowls and directly over small toasted bread slices topped with the thick, spicy garlic sauce known as rouille. Since Jacques Dupuy's recipe, like most authentic versions, calls for cooked potato slices and hot fish soup lifted from a bouillabaisse-in-progress, its preparation must be coordinated with that of the fish stew itself. This requires good planning and organization.

Step 1 can be done in advance. Step 2 can be accomplished once the fish soup is very hot. But steps 3 and 4 cannot be undertaken until the potatoes are tender and the bouillabaisse nearly done.

When a bouillabaisse is prepared with rouget, the liver of that fish is mashed into the rouille to enrich its texture and flavor. Though the resulting grayish color may alarm diners expecting a rust-colored sauce—*rouille* is, after all, French for "rusty"—connoisseurs recognize the taupe tint as an indicator of a great delicacy that is part sauce and part fish liver mousse.

MAKES ABOUT 1 CUP

2 to 3 cloves garlic, crushed
1 small pinch cayenne
1 small hunk country bread, crust removed
2 to 3 tablespoons hot fish soup
2 to 3 potato slices cooked in the bouillabaisse, mashed
¼ cup olive oil
Salt
Freshly ground black pepper

1. Combine the garlic and cayenne in a mortar and mash with a pestle.
2. Dunk the country bread into the hot fish soup, squeeze out the soup, add the soaked bread to the mortar, and mash with a pestle.
3. Add the mashed potato slices and mash with the pestle into a thick paste.
4. Gradually add the olive oil, drop by drop, never ceasing to mash the mixture with the pestle in a circular motion until the rouille is thick (if the mixture breaks up, mash in a teaspoon or two of the hot fish soup or a little more of the soup-soaked bread). Season with salt and pepper.

CONFITURE D'OIGNONS

ONION JAM

A caramelized onion jam such as Giselle Philippi's becomes a workhorse condiment that can be served as a spread or garnish for steak, fish, sausages, toast, pâté, foie gras, and Giselle's "poor man's" version of the last, *terrine de foie de volaille,* chicken liver terrine (page 93).

MAKES ABOUT 1 1/2 CUPS

3 onions, chopped

2 tablespoons olive oil

1 tablespoon sugar

1 teaspoon lemon juice

1/4 teaspoon cayenne

1 tablespoon honey

1/2 cup red wine

Salt

Freshly ground black pepper

1. Combine the onions, olive oil, sugar, and 1/2 teaspoon lemon juice in a saucepan, cover, and cook over low heat for 15 minutes.

2. Add a cup of water, cover, raise the heat to medium, and cook for 5 minutes.

3. Add the cayenne, honey, and the remaining 1/2 teaspoon lemon juice, raise the flame to high, and cook uncovered until the onions are nearly dark and caramelized, about 5 minutes.

4. Pour in the red wine and cook until the wine has evaporated, about 5 minutes. Lower the heat, add 1/2 cup water, cover and cook until the water has evaporated, 7 to 10 minutes. Season with salt and pepper. Pour the mixture into jars and seal and refrigerate.

CONFITURE D'ÉCHALOTES AU VIN ROUGE

SHALLOT AND RED WINE JAM

This is a classic bordelaise sauce reduced to a handy jam. It serves as an accompaniment for *steak au poivre* (page 200).

MAKES 1 CUP

3 tablespoons olive oil

6 shallots, peeled and cut into thin slices

Salt

Freshly ground black pepper

½ cup veal stock or beef stock

2 cups dry red wine

1 teaspoon grenadine syrup

¾ cup sugar

1. Heat the olive oil in a saucepan over medium heat. Add the shallots and cook, stirring occasionally, until they begin to turn golden, 4 to 5 minutes. Season with salt and pepper.

2. Pour in the veal stock, then the red wine and grenadine, stir in the sugar until dissolved, and cook until the liquid thickens and becomes syrupy, 30 to 35 minutes. Let cool. Pour the mixture into a tightly lidded jar and refrigerate for up to 4 weeks.

CONFITURE DE TOMATES ET GINGEMBRE

TOMATO-GINGER JAM

Olivier Vettorel adds ginger to his tomato confiture to give it some piquancy. He serves it as an accompaniment to zucchini fritters (page 210).

MAKES 1¼ CUPS

2 pounds ripe tomatoes
2 cups sugar
1 tablespoon finely chopped fresh ginger

1. To peel the tomatoes, cut a small X in their smooth ends and plunge into boiling salted water for 30 seconds. Peel the tomatoes, cut each tomato into 5 or 6 sections, and remove the seeds.

2. Combine the tomatoes, sugar, and chopped ginger in a heavy-bottomed saucepan over medium heat and cook just to a boil. Lower the heat to very low and cook gently, stirring occasionally, for 2 hours. Remove from the heat and let cool. Pour the mixture into a jar, seal, and refrigerate up to 3 weeks.

TOMATO CONFIT

OVEN-ROASTED TOMATOES

2 pounds ripe plum tomatoes
5 cloves garlic
1 sprig fresh thyme
1 pinch of sugar
Salt
2 tablespoons olive oil
Freshly ground black pepper

1. Preheat the oven to 175 degrees or the lowest possible temperature setting. To peel the tomatoes, cut a small X in their smooth ends and plunge into boiling salted water for 30 seconds. Peel the tomatoes, cut each tomato into 5 or 6 sections, and remove the seeds.

2. Slice the garlic cloves in half and place on the bottom of a nonstick baking pan. Place the tomato sections over the garlic, sprinkle with fresh thyme and sugar, season with salt and pepper, drizzle with olive oil, and cook slowly in the oven for 3 hours.

3. Transfer the tomatoes, along with the garlic, tomato juices, and olive oil, to a jar, seal, and refrigerate for up to one week.

COULIS DE TOMATES PROVENÇAL

PROVENÇAL TOMATO SAUCE

An indispensable sauce in any Marseille kitchen, the tomato sauce may be prepared well in advance and stored in the freezer.

MAKES 2 CUPS

2 pounds ripe plum tomatoes (substitute 2 cups canned plum tomatoes)
2 tablespoons olive oil
2 to 3 cloves garlic, chopped
2 onions, chopped
2 teaspoons chopped fresh thyme
2 teaspoons chopped fresh rosemary
1 bay leaf
Salt
Freshly ground black pepper
1/2 to 1 teaspoon sugar, optional

1. To peel the tomatoes, cut a small X in their smooth ends and plunge in boiling salted water for 30 seconds. Peel and quarter the tomatoes and squeeze out the seeds and much of the water.

2. Heat the olive oil in a large saucepan over medium heat. Add the garlic and sauté for 1 minute. Add the onions, tomatoes, thyme, rosemary, and bay leaf and season with salt and pepper. Lower the flame to very low and cook uncovered, stirring occasionally, for 1 hour. Add some sugar, if desired, to neutralize the acidity of the tomatoes.

3. For a smooth tomato sauce, pass through a food mill. For a chunky version, leave as is.

HUILE D'OLIVE GLACÉE

COLD OLIVE OIL SPREAD

If extra virgin olive oil is the result of cold pressing, then this spread could be described as cold cold-pressed olive oil. Through freezing and partial thawing, Gérard Passédat of the Restaurant Passédat transforms extra virgin olive oil from a liquid to a solid before serving it as a bread spread or condiment. It can be used as you would table butter—spread over toast, cut into cubes to scatter atop vegetables and potatoes, sliced and placed over a piece of fish, and so on. It also opens up the possibility of "compound" cold olive oils, meaning herb-flavored olive oil chilled in a like manner. However, a benefit of Passédat's chilling is being able to discover the character of a good-quality extra virgin olive oil as it melts in your mouth, so it may be counterproductive to hide that character by introducing herbs or other flavors.

MAKES 4 TO 6 SERVINGS

2 tablespoons extra virgin olive oil

1. The day before: Pour the oil into a small ramekin or relish dish and freeze for at least 24 hours.
2. About 6 hours before serving the oil, transfer to the refrigerator. Remove from the refrigerator immediately before serving.

Appetizers

Panisses CHICKPEA CAKES

Biscuits au Parmesan et Olives Noires PARMESAN AND
BLACK OLIVE BISCUITS

Oeufs en Cocotte Provençale PROVENÇAL-STYLE EGGS
IN COCOTTE

Boreg au Fromage ARMENIAN-STYLE CHEESE TURNOVERS

Fromage de Chèvre Rôti aux Herbes en Croute de Baklava
WARM BAKLAVA OF HERBED GOAT CHEESE

Rouleaux de Fromage au Sésame RICOTTA SESAME ROLLS

"Crêpes" Marocaines MOROCCAN SAVORY TURNOVERS

Blinis de Poissons FISH BLINIS

Crumble de Saumon SALMON CRUMBLE

Tartare de Thon Mariné aux Herbes Fraîches et Panisso
TUNA TARTARE WITH FRESH HERBS AND PANISSES

Supions Frits en Persillade "Chez Etienne" CHEZ ETIENNE'S
PAN-FRIED CALAMARI WITH PARSLEY AND GARLIC

Terrine de Poisson FISH TERRINE

Terrine de Poulpe OCTOPUS TERRINE

Terrine de Foie de Volaille CHICKEN LIVER TERRINE

The Café Parisien.

THE DISHES COLLECTED FOR THIS SECTION reflect the diversity and natural affinity of Marseille's many resident cuisines. Although selecting an appetizer may be akin to spinning a culinary compass, most of the recipes are brought home by their reliance on fresh and dried herbs. From the fresh basil in the Parmesan biscuits, the fish terrine, the panisses, and various fillings for the Moroccan crêpes to the fresh parsley in the Armenian cheese turnovers, pan-fried calamari, and eggs in cocotte to the assorted herbes de Provence—thyme, rosemary, marjoram, savory, bay leaf—in the fish blini, cheese baklava, and chicken liver terrine, the essence of these aromatic herbs vouch for a made-in-Marseille identity. When guests sit down at the dinner table, their noses will get the first and clearest notification of the meal's whereabouts.

PANISSES

CHICKPEA CAKES

Proper etiquette dictates that when a proud local recites the adage about it always being sunny in Marseille, you pay little notice to the droplets of water that happen to be raining down from the gray sky. And so when any typically chauvinistic Marseillais tells Aldo-Christian and Renée Ronzonelli that the round little chickpea cakes known as panisses are a specialty unique to Marseille, the owners of the fried snack stand Chez Magali in L'Estaque do not dare speak of the *panizze* they ate in Tunisia and Sicily. Besides, the existence of these similarly named street treats as well as *socca*, the flat chickpea cakes of Nice, does not make panisses any less a Marseille classic. It is logical that both Nice and Marseille would have their own chickpea cakes, situated as those two cities are at the southeast and southwest corners of a region where wheat farming is scarce. Chickpeas, popular throughout the Mediterranean and, in particular, North Africa, provided Provence's best homegrown substitute for wheat flour.

Panisses were particularly trendy in the 1930s around Marseille's Old Port as a snack, or paired with a salad as a meal. Today they are back in vogue in an entirely different format. Accomplished French chefs like Alain Ducasse and Daniel Boulud use them within main courses as they would polenta to accompany or cushion meats, fish, and stews. They are also great with daube or daube sauce (see page 190). Prepared with a porridge-like batter of chickpea flour, the interior of a fried panisse is almost comparable to fried cheese in its creaminess.

As a snack, the panisse may be served in a paper cone, even one made from a folded newspaper page. Under ideal circumstances, this would be a sports clipping from *La Provence* or *La Marseillaise* heralding the latest exploits of OM, the beloved hometown soccer team that never loses.

MAKES 4 TO 6 SERVINGS (30 TO 35 PANISSES)

2 cups chickpea flour
1 tablespoon olive oil
Frying oil
Salt
Freshly ground black pepper

1. Sift the chickpea flour and combine in a large saucepan with 1 quart hot—but not boiling—water and the olive oil. Heat over moderately high heat, mixing continuously with a whisk, until the mixture thickens and starts to bubble, 2 to 3 minutes. Exchange the whisk for a wooden spoon and cook, stirring continuously, for 10 minutes more. The mixture should be thick and heavy.

2. Spread out a clean dish towel on a work surface. Place the panisse mixture along the bottom of the dish towel. Wrap the towel over the mixture and roll it into a log 2 to 3 inches in diameter. Refrigerate for 2 hours. As an alternative to this towel method, which can be tricky, spread out the mixture on an oiled baking sheet to a depth of $1/3$ inch, cover with a dish towel and refrigerate for 2 hours. Later you can cut out the panisse rounds using a cookie cutter, biscuit cutter, or small jar.

3. Heat some frying oil in a skillet (the oil should be about $1/4$ inch deep) over moderately high heat. Cut the panisse log into slices roughly $1/3$ inch thick and fry in small batches until golden, about $1\frac{1}{2}$ minutes on each side. Drain on paper towels. Sprinkle with salt and pepper and serve immediately on a dish or, better yet, in a paper cone.

PANISSE FRIES: Immediately following step 1, pour the mixture into a square cake pan or baking pan to a depth of roughly $3/4$ inch. Refrigerate for 2 hours. Heat the frying oil in a deep fryer or heavy-bottomed saucepan to 350 degrees. Cut the panisse mixture into sticks of any length but no wider than $3/4$ inch and fry until crisp and golden brown, 5 to 6 minutes. Drain on paper towels, season with salt and pepper, and serve immediately.

BASIL PANISSES: At the beginning of step 1, add 2 tablespoons of finely chopped fresh basil to the mixture of chickpea flour, water, and olive oil.

BISCUITS AU PARMESAN ET OLIVES NOIRES

PARMESAN AND BLACK OLIVE BISCUITS

Neither hard nor chewy, not dry or soggy, these savory biscuits can be served as hors d'oeuvres, snacks, or a little something extra to put out with salads, cold dips, and appetizers. Try to grate the Parmesan with the large holes of the grater, which will give the biscuits an appealing, crumbly texture. The recipe comes from Yvon Cadiou, a resourceful chef who built a cult following at a number of short-lived Marseille restaurants.

MAKES 12 TO 14 BISCUITS

2 cups flour

2 cups ($\frac{1}{2}$ pound) coarsely grated Parmesan cheese

2 egg yolks

10 ounces (2$\frac{1}{2}$ sticks) unsalted butter, melted and cooled (1$\frac{1}{4}$ cups)

3 tablespoons water

$\frac{1}{4}$ cup whole black olives, pitted and chopped

1. Preheat the oven to 375 degrees. Combine the flour and Parmesan cheese and mix well.

2. Beat the egg yolks into the butter. Pour into the flour-and-cheese mixture and mix well. Add the water and olives and mix until the texture is even and the bits of olives are well distributed.

3. Roll small clumps of the batter between the palms of your hands into smooth balls about 1$\frac{1}{2}$ inches in diameter. Place these balls on a nonstick baking sheet at least $\frac{1}{2}$ inch apart and press down lightly on each with a spatula or the back of a spoon so they're slightly flattened into a biscuit shape. (They will eventually take the shape of chubby oatmeal cookies.) Bake in the oven until lightly golden on top and golden brown on the bottom, 25 to 30 minutes. Serve warm or store in tightly lidded cookie jars for up to one week.

OEUFS EN COCOTTE PROVENÇALE

PROVENÇAL-STYLE EGGS IN COCOTTE

Oeufs en cocotte is a standard French dish in which eggs are placed in little *cocottes* or ramekins and poached in a bain-marie. There are many classic garnishes, including *à la tartare* (raw ground beef), *à la Lorraine* (bacon, cheese, and cream), *à la Maraichére* (spinach and sorrel). Jeanne Moréni-Garron of the restaurant Les Echevins makes hers *à la Provençale,* with the addition of tomatoes, parsley, garlic, and olives. It is all of Provence in a single *cocotte.*

Chopping the garlic together with the parsley creates what's known as a *persillade.* The garlic softens the parsley's pronounced perfume. Cooking time ultimately depends on personal taste: 3½ minutes of poaching will produce barely set egg whites and runny egg yolks, 5 minutes of poaching leads to creamy whites and yolks just on the point of hardening.

MAKES 4 SERVINGS

4 to 5 ripe plum tomatoes

1 clove garlic

1 tablespoon coarsely chopped parsley

2 tablespoons olive oil

Salt

Freshly ground black pepper

4 eggs

2 teaspoons chopped fresh basil, optional

1 small baguette, cut into diagonal slices and toasted

1. To peel the tomatoes, cut a small X in their smooth ends and plunge into boiling salted water for 30 seconds. Peel the tomatoes, cut each tomato into quarters, remove the seeds, and chop.

2. Combine the garlic and parsley and finely chop the mixture.

3. Place the tomatoes, the garlic-parsley mixture, and the olive oil in a saucepan over low to medium heat, season with salt and pepper, and simmer, stirring occasionally, for 15 minutes.

4. Spoon a heaping tablespoon of the tomato mixture into the bottom of 4 ovenproof ramekins. Flatten with the back of a spoon.

5. Delicately break 1 egg inside each ramekin. Set the 4 ramekins in a saucepan and pour in just enough boiling water to reach halfway up the sides of the ramekins. Cover tightly, place the saucepan over medium heat, and steam for 4 minutes.

6. Place one napkin on the center of 4 plates, place the ramekins over the napkins, season with salt and pepper, sprinkle with basil, if desired, and serve with a baguette.

BOREG AU FROMAGE

ARMENIAN-STYLE CHEESE TURNOVERS

It would take a connoisseur of linguistics rather than ethnic cuisine to identify the respective nationality of the savory turnover known throughout the Middle East, North Africa, and therefore Marseille as either *berag, boerag, boreg, borek, bourek,* or, in French, *chausson oriental.* Though often prepared with phyllo, Armenian immigrant Berthe Baghtchejian makes her turnovers with bread dough. The addition of Gruyère to the feta cheese betrays some French influence.

MAKES 6 SERVINGS (18 TO 24 TURNOVERS)

1 tablespoon active dry yeast

$3\frac{1}{2}$ cups all-purpose flour

Salt

$\frac{1}{2}$ cup vegetable oil

$\frac{1}{2}$ pound feta cheese, crumbled

1 cup (about 4 ounces) shredded Gruyère cheese

$\frac{1}{4}$ cup chopped parsley

1 tablespoon chopped fresh mint

Freshly ground black pepper

Frying oil

1. Pour $\frac{1}{2}$ cup warm water in a measuring cup, stir in the yeast, and let stand for 5 minutes, until the yeast dissolves and turns creamy.

2. In the bowl of a heavy-duty standing mixer combine the flour and a pinch of salt. Add 1 cup cold water, vegetable oil, and the dissolved yeast. Attach the dough hook and mix on low speed for about 4 minutes. If the dough appears dry, add a teaspoon of water. Gather the dough into a smooth ball, place in a bowl, cover with a dishcloth, and let rise for 15 minutes.

3. Combine the cheeses, parsley, and mint in a bowl, and season with salt and pepper.

4. Pull off a small piece of dough, place it on a powdered work surface, and flatten it out with a rolling pin to a thickness of about $\frac{1}{8}$ inch. Using a large jar or a bowl, cut out rounds 3 to 4 inches in diameter. Repeat until all the remaining dough is used, including unused portions of the rolled-out dough.

5. Place up to a tablespoon of the cheese filling in the center of the dough rounds. Fold each round over the stuffing to form a crescent shape and seal the edges by pressing down with the end of a fork.

6. Heat $\frac{1}{4}$ inch of the frying oil in a skillet over moderately high heat. Working in batches, fry the turnovers until golden and crisp, 2 to 3 minutes on each side. Drain on paper towels.

FROMAGE DE CHÈVRE RÔTI AUX HERBES EN CROUTE DE BAKLAVA

WARM BAKLAVA OF HERBED GOAT CHEESE

Giselle Philippi of the restaurant Le Sud en Haut ordinarily fills her "baklava," so-called since it's a pastry made with thin sheets of phyllo, with Saint Marcellin cheese. If you can get your hands on that soft, nutty, cow's milk (originally goat's milk) cheese from the Rhône-Alpes region, you'll see that the standard 80-gram wheel is a perfect fit for each baklava. Nevertheless, you'll achieve excellent results with a good quality goat cheese to which you apply the herbes de Provence. In either case, your pastry will not look anything like a baklava. These resemble large phyllo pouches that may be served as a dinner appetizer or lunch entrée.

MAKES 4 SERVINGS

2 tomatoes
Herbes de Provence
Salt
Freshly ground black pepper
Olive oil
12 ounces goat cheese, cut into 4 rounds
6 tablespoons butter
6 sheets phyllo dough
1 to 2 teaspoons confectioners' sugar
Black Olive puree (page 56)
Mixed greens

1. Preheat the oven to 275 degrees.
2. Cut a small X on the smooth end of the tomatoes. Drop them into boiling water for 1 minute. Plunge the tomatoes into cold water and use a sharp knife to peel off their skins. Cut the tomatoes in half, scoop out the seeds, and place in an oiled baking dish. Sprinkle the tomato halves with herbes de Provence, salt, and pepper, drizzle with olive oil, and cook in the oven for 20 minutes.
3. Remove the goat cheese from the refrigerator and let soften at room temperature.
4. To clarify the butter, place in a small saucepan and melt over low heat. Remove from the heat, skim off the foam, and set aside until the solids have settled to the bottom. Carefully pour off and reserve the clear fat, discarding the residue.

5. Unravel the thawed sheets of phyllo dough and cover with a damp kitchen towel so they don't dry out. Lay out two sheets of phyllo on a dry work surface, brush with clarified butter, and fold in half. Each folded sheet constitutes 2 of the 3 phyllo layers needed for each baklava. For the third layer, take out a second sheet of phyllo, brush with clarified butter, cut in two, and place a half on each folded sheet of phyllo. Repeat with the remaining 3 sheets of phyllo to assemble the pastry for 4 baklava.

6. Raise the oven temperature to 350 degrees. Butter a large baking pan. Place half a tomato at the center of each baklava, top each with a goat cheese round (3 to 4 ounces), sprinkle liberally with herbes de Provence, season with salt and pepper, and drizzle with olive oil. Lift up the four sides of the phyllo to form a pouch over the goat cheese, pinching the phyllo together above the bundle to fully enclose it. Transfer this bundle to the buttered baking pan. Repeat to form 4 bundles.

7. Dust the baklavas lightly with confectioners' sugar and bake in the oven until the cheese is fully melted, testing with a knife, about 15 minutes. Drizzle with black olive puree and serve with mixed greens.

ROULEAUX DE FROMAGE AU SÉSAME

RICOTTA SESAME ROLLS

Think savory cannoli with a molten cheese filling and you have some idea of the ricotta sesame rolls Florent Saugeron of the bistro Lemon Grass serves alongside gingerbread-crusted chicken breasts (page 179). These sesame rolls are great too as finger foods, appetizers, or snacks.

MAKES 4 SERVINGS (4 ROLLS)

4 spring roll wrappers

1 cup ricotta cheese

Salt

Freshly ground black pepper

2 egg yolks, beaten

3 tablespoons sesame seeds

½ cup frying oil

1. Place a square spring roll wrapper on a work surface so that one of its corners is pointing toward you. Place 2 tablespoons of ricotta cheese diagonally across the bottom third of the wrapper. Season the cheese with salt and pepper. Fold the bottom corner of the wrapper over the cheese and tuck it under the cheese. Roll once to enfold the cheese, fold in the sides of the wrapper, and continue rolling almost to the end.

2. Brush the top corner with egg and press to seal the roll. Brush the spring roll with egg yolk on all sides and roll in the sesame seeds. Repeat with the remaining wrappers.

3. Heat the frying oil in a skillet over high heat and fry the spring rolls until golden on all sides, about 3 minutes. Drain on paper towels.

"CRÊPES" MAROCAINES

MOROCCAN SAVORY TURNOVERS

The designation "crêpes" is somewhat of a misnomer applied by Fatima Rhazi to make her savory turnovers accessible to her French clientele at the music, arts, and food festival known as La Fiesta Des Suds. But a clearer reference, especially for her Marseille audience, might have been Armenian *bouregs*, French *chaussons*, or Italian *calzoni* since the pastries served at the kiosk run by the organization Femmes D'Ici et D'Ailleurs ("women from here and there") are made with a bread dough rather than a crêpe- or pancake-like liquid batter. Rhazi starts with the same circle of dough she uses for the Moroccan pastries called *m'essémen*, but then replaces the traditional honey filling with the chickpea puree, ratatouille, or any stewed vegetables, shredded or ground meats, spreads or leftovers at her disposal. The four sides of the circle are then folded over the filling to make a square turnover that may be fried in a skillet or baked in the oven.

In this recipe I've proposed La Bohemienne, the Gypsy-style vegetable stew, as the turnover stuffing. But I suggest you make and freeze the dough well in advance and use it whenever you have leftovers (preferably mushy ones) on hand to make hors d'oeuvres, appetizers, or sandwich substitutes. Some suggested stuffings from this book: ratatouille (page 214), daube (page 190), dafina (page 193), onion jam (page 64), tomato-ginger jam (page 66), lemon potatoes (page 208), and any leftover cheeses.

MAKES 8 TO 10 TURNOVERS

1 tablespoon active dry yeast
3½ cups flour
1 teaspoon salt
1 quart Gypsy-style vegetable stew (page 213)
Vegetable oil for frying, optional

1. Pour 1½ cups warm water in a measuring cup, stir in the yeast, and let stand for 5 minutes, until the yeast dissolves and turns creamy.

2. In the bowl of a heavy-duty standing mixer, combine the flour and salt. Add the dissolved yeast and a scant cup warm water. Attach the dough hook and mix on low speed until the dough detaches from the sides of the bowl and comes together, about

2 minutes. Increase the speed to medium and mix for 2 minutes more. Turn off the mixer, pull down the dough from the hook, and gather it into one mass. If the dough appears dry and hard, add a little water. If it is wet and extremely sticky, add a little flour. Restart the mixer at medium speed and mix the dough for 5 minutes more until it has a smooth, elastic consistency and is no longer sticky.

3. Transfer the dough to a lightly floured work surface and shape into a smooth ball. Dust the ball with flour, place in a bowl, cover with a dishcloth, and let rise for 15 minutes.

4. If baking the turnovers, preheat the oven to 450 degrees and butter a large baking dish or baking sheet.

5. Tear off a small hunk (about $\frac{1}{8}$) of dough, leaving the rest of the dough covered, and form it into a smooth ball. Place the ball on a lightly floured surface and flatten the dough, rotating it as you press down with your fingertips, into a thin disk 6 to 7 inches in diameter. Place about 2 tablespoons of the filling over the center of the circle of dough. Fold in the dough from the top, bottom, and two sides of the circle so that they meet at the center and fully enclose the filling inside a square pouch. Repeat with the remainder of the dough.

6. If baking the turnovers, place on a greased baking dish or sheet and bake until lightly browned, about 15 minutes.

7. If frying the turnovers, pour vegetable oil into a skillet to a depth of about $\frac{1}{4}$ inch and heat over moderately high heat. Place the turnovers in the skillet and fry, turning once, until golden and lightly crisp on both sides, about 3 minutes. Drain on paper towels.

BLINIS DE POISSONS

FISH BLINIS

The silver dollar–sized blinis of Dominique Frérard, chef at Les Trois Forts, are all-inclusive, meaning the fish and the crème fraîche are mixed into the batter and cooked together. The most amusing way to serve them is to divide the batter in four and to mix a different Marseille-styled sauce or seasoning into each. Frérard proposes fresh herbs, tapenade, *pistou*, and chopped fresh herbs, which served together as an assortment turn the fish blinis into a Provençal tasting platter. You may serve any of the blinis with a garnish of tapenade, but you should never mix the herbs and the tapenade into the same blini. The blini can be prepared up to an hour in advance and then reheated in a warm (but not hot) oven.

MAKES 4 SERVINGS (ABOUT 16 BLINI)

¼ pound fish fillets (salmon, trout, cod, or red snapper)
½ cup crème fraîche (substitute sour cream)
2 eggs, beaten
1 pinch cayenne
Salt
Freshly ground black pepper
2 tablespoons all-purpose flour
1 egg yolk, beaten

For seasoned fish blinis, add one of the following:
2 tablespoons chopped fresh herbs (basil, thyme, rosemary)
3 tablespoons Tapenade (page 55)
2 tablespoons Pistou (page 61)
2 tablespoons chopped dill

Olive oil, for garnish

1. Place the fish fillets (use only one kind) in a food processor and pulse several times until the fish is finely chopped. Add the crème fraîche, beaten eggs, cayenne, salt, and freshly ground pepper and process into a mousse-like texture, about 2 minutes.

2. Transfer the fish mousse to a large bowl, add the flour, the beaten egg yolk, and any desired optional flavoring, and mix well.

3. Preheat the oven to 200 degrees.

4. Heat a large nonstick skillet (coated, if desired, with a little butter or no-stick cooking spray) over medium heat. For each blini, drop a heaping tablespoon of the batter onto the skillet and, if necessary, flatten it a bit with the back of a spoon. Fit as many blinis as possible in the skillet without touching, and cook until lightly browned on the bottom, about 1½ minutes.

Turn and cook until the second side is done. Place the finished blini on a warm plate or baking sheet in the oven until all are done.

5. Divide between 4 plates and drizzle lightly with olive oil, or serve with a teaspoon of tapenade.

*The morning fish market
at the Quai des Belges.*

CRUMBLE DE SAUMON

SALMON CRUMBLE

The fish crumbles (the salmon is only one of several) Lionel Lévy introduced at Une Table au Sud were plainly inspired by fruit crumbles, English cousins to American cobblers and crisps that became all the rage at French bistros and even multistarred restaurants during the late 1990s. But this ingenious, dessert-inspired appetizer may also be appreciated as an adaptation of two additional, fin de siècle food trends: nut-encrusted fish and French-Asian fish tartares. The chopped almonds, ginger, and garlic in the brittle-like topping constitute a nutty-textured topping for the silky raw fish. And the ginger in that topping and the acidity in the tomato sauce impart strong Asian accents.

MAKES 6 APPETIZER SERVINGS OR 4 MAIN-COURSE SERVINGS

1⅓ pounds salmon fillets

4 tablespoons chopped garlic

2 tablespoons chopped fresh ginger

2 limes

1 lemon

2 tablespoons olive oil

Salt

Freshly ground black pepper

½ cup heavy cream

4 tablespoons (½ stick) unsalted butter, softened

¼ cup brown sugar

½ cup blanched almonds, chopped

¼ cup red wine vinegar

¼ cup sugar

1 tablespoon tomato paste

1. Cut the salmon into ¼-inch cubes and place in a bowl.

2. Add 1 tablespoon chopped garlic and 1 tablespoon chopped fresh ginger to the salmon. Grate the zest of 1 lime and add to the salmon along with the juice of both limes and the lemon. Add the olive oil, mix well without mashing the salmon, season with salt and pepper to taste, and refrigerate. This is the salmon tartare.

3. In a bowl combine the cream, butter, brown sugar, chopped almonds, the remaining tablespoon chopped fresh ginger, and the remaining 3 tablespoons garlic, and mix well. Refrigerate this mixture for the crumble topping for 30 minutes.

4. To prepare the ketchup-like condiment: Combine the red wine vinegar, sugar, tomato paste, and ½ teaspoon pepper in a saucepan and bring to a boil. Let cool.

Transfer to a bowl and refrigerate.

5. Preheat the oven to 325 degrees.

6. On a nonstick baking sheet, spread the crumble into a thin layer no more than $\frac{1}{8}$ inch thick. Bake until caramel in color, about 20 minutes. Remove from the oven and refrigerate immediately.

7. TO SERVE, spoon the salmon tartare into 6 small soufflé dishes or ramekins or in a small mound on the center of 6 plates. (For a flatter, smoother, rounder tartare, pack a sixth of the salmon tartare into a ramekin or round mold, turn over the center of the dish, and tap the bottom to unmold. Repeat to form 6 servings.) Flatten the salmon tartare with the back of a spoon. Crush the crumble and place the pieces atop each serving of salmon tartare to fully cover. Garnish each plate with either a circle or some squiggles of the tomato condiment.

TARTARE DE THON MARINÉ AUX HERBES FRAÎCHES ET PANISSO

TUNA TARTARE WITH FRESH HERBS AND PANISSES

This is a pairing of the exotic and the familiar. At the restaurant Les Trois Forts, the fresh ginger and curry powder in chef Dominique Frérard's boldly spiced tuna tartare are a reflection of Marseille's increasingly Asian palate. The panisse (chickpea) fries are a traditional local snack.

MAKES 6 APPETIZER SERVINGS OR 4 MAIN-COURSE SERVINGS

1 pound fresh tuna

1/2 cup olive oil

Grated zest of 1 lime

2 teaspoons chopped ginger

1 tablespoon plus 1 teaspoon chopped fresh dill

1 tablespoon chopped chives

Salt

Freshly ground black pepper

2 tablespoons chopped shallots

1/4 teaspoon curry powder

1/2 teaspoon cayenne

2 to 3 drops Tabasco sauce

1/2 cup crème fraîche

2 teaspoons lemon juice

1 teaspoon chopped fresh chervil (substitute chopped parsley)

Panisse Fries (page 73)

1. Cut the tuna into 1/4-inch cubes. Combine the tuna, olive oil, grated lime zest, chopped ginger, 1 tablespoon chopped dill and chopped chives in a bowl, season with salt and pepper, and let marinate in the refrigerator for at least 1 hour.

2. Combine the tuna with the chopped shallots, curry powder, cayenne, and Tabsco. Mix well without mashing. Correct the seasoning (the tartare should be moderately spicy). Spoon the tuna mixture into 6 small soufflé dishes or ramekins (or in small mounds in the middle of 6 plates). (For a smoother, flatter, rounder tartare, pack a sixth of the tuna tartare into a ramekin or round mold, turn over the center of the dish, and tap the bottom to unmold. Repeat to form 6 servings.)

3. Whisk the crème fraîche with the lemon juice and chervil, season with salt and pepper, and drizzle around each tartare mold. Serve with 4 to 6 panisse fries per person.

SUPIONS FRITS EN PERSILLADE "CHEZ ETIENNE"
CHEZ ETIENNE'S PAN-FRIED CALAMARI
WITH PARSLEY AND GARLIC

Devotees of the Chez Etienne's *supions,* as the small cuttlefish are known in the South of France, generally assume that this great Marseille passion is either Italian or, owing to the *persillade* (chopped parsley and garlic), Provençal in origin. But if Etienne Cassaro is to be taken at his word (and those who appreciate a good story or a good table invariably do), the prevailing wisdom is misguided. In a rare moment of calm and candor that, judging from the direction of his gaze, had far less to do with my curiosity than that of my ravishing lunch companion, Cassaro revealed the source of his superior *supions.* They were introduced at Chez Etienne in 1965 by Van Lhu, which, you're right to conclude, is not an Italo-Provençal name.

"Bring me some calamari," the Vietnamese cook demanded of his Sicilian boss over thirty-five years ago, "I'm going to make a fish fry."

Let me tell you why I choose to believe what many Marseillais will dismiss as just another fish story. In the first place, if the proud Cassaro had any motivation to misrepresent the source of his *supions,* it would be to steer credit *away from* a long departed Vietnamese cook few remember. In the second place, I've spent time in the Chez Etienne kitchen and have seen how the otherwise dictatorial boss defers to his current, moody *supion* cook. Those cephalopods are his lifeblood. Finally, the Indochinese role in this French-Mediterranean classic begins a wonderful, only-in-Marseille tale that only gets better. Lhu passed on the recipe to Asman, his Egyptian-born successor, who passed it on to Ali Omori, the current Comoran cook, who passed it on to this New Yorker. I watched Ali prepare batch after batch of the *supions* and took careful notes in a tiny memo pad. The oil-splattered recipe is a priceless keepsake from an enlightening experience. Immigrants don't just introduce new and exotic flavors to a melting pot like Marseille. Sometimes, through their underappreciated work in the restaurant trade, they help sustain and, in Van Lhu's case, reinvent what is cherished as traditional and folkloric.

The *supions* are neither battered nor deep-fried, as fried calamari typically are in the United States, but instead lightly floured and pan-fried in shallow oil. It therefore becomes necessary to sweat out the water from the squid before those liquids can dilute the hot oil. This process adds to the cooking time and thus the risk of tough squid. Although extremely tender pan-fried calamari may prove an elusive goal, I discovered that cutting the squid into small pieces rather than rings produces a far less chewy outcome.

When pan frying the squid, try to resist the temptation to continually scrape up and liberate pieces that stick to the bottom of the skillet. This sticking makes possible the delectably crisp, browned edges to which the parsley and lightly browned garlic so lovingly cling. It's the sticky business that turns Van Lhu's *supions frits* into candy.

MAKES 6 APPETIZER SERVINGS OR 4 MAIN-COURSE SERVINGS

2 pounds clean squid
$\frac{1}{4}$ cup all-purpose flour
$\frac{1}{2}$ teaspoon salt
$\frac{1}{4}$ teaspoon freshly ground black pepper
Vegetable oil for frying
3 cloves garlic, chopped
3 tablespoons chopped parsley

1. Wash the squid well in cold water and rinse. Cut their bodies into small pieces 1 to $1\frac{1}{2}$ inches in length and $\frac{1}{4}$ inch wide. (This is best done by cutting the squid bodies in half lengthwise and then cutting diagonal, $\frac{1}{4}$-inch-wide slices from each half.) Cut the tentacles in half if they are too large.

2. Heat a large skillet, preferably cast iron, over low heat. Spread the squid pieces in the pan and cook, tossing once or twice, to release the liquid from the squid, $1\frac{1}{2}$ to 2 minutes. Drain the squid, place between paper towels, and dry the squid as thoroughly as possible. Clean and wipe dry the skillet.

3. Combine the flour, salt, and pepper in a mixing bowl. Add the squid and toss with the dry ingredients until lightly covered with flour.

4. Pour vegetable oil into the skillet to a depth of about $\frac{1}{3}$ inch and heat over high heat until very hot. Place the squid evenly in the skillet and fry, tossing the squid only two or three times, until they begin to brown, 2 to $2\frac{1}{2}$ minutes. Scatter the chopped garlic over the squid and fry, stirring and tossing more often, for 1 minute. Add the chopped parsley and toss with the squid until evenly distributed. Remove the squid with a slotted spoon, drain on paper towels, and serve.

TERRINE DE POISSON

FISH TERRINE

You may wish to think of Giselle Philippi's *terrine de poisson* as a salmon mousse loaf. As with the other terrines she serves at Le Sud en Haut, the fat content is reduced with the use of evaporated milk in place of heavy cream. Wonderful as an hors d'oeuvre or appetizer, served whole or presliced, it may be seasoned by adding fresh herbs, dry spices, lemon juice, or olive oil to the mixture just before it is pureed in the blender. Covered in plastic and refrigerated, it will keep for 3 or 4 days.

MAKES 6 SERVINGS

1 slice lemon
$1/2$ pound salmon fillets
$1^3/4$ cups evaporated milk
4 egg yolks, beaten
1 teaspoon salt
1 teaspoon white pepper
Seasonings
Tomato Confit (page 67)
1 baguette or country bread, sliced and toasted

1. Bring a large pot of water to a boil, add the lemon slice and fish fillets and cook for 5 minutes. Drain, peel off any skin from the fillets, and cut into chunks.
2. Preheat the oven to 250 degrees. Butter a 1-quart terrine or loaf pan.
3. Combine all the ingredients except the tomato confit and the baguette in a blender and puree until smooth, 3 to 5 minutes. Pour the mixture into the buttered terrine or loaf pan and cook in a bain-marie for 90 minutes. To verify the terrine is cooked through, insert a knife into the center. If it comes out dry and hot, it's done. Remove the terrine from the bain-marie and the oven and let cool. Pass a knife around the perimeter to unmold the terrine. Let cool, cover in plastic wrap, and refrigerate for up to 1 week.
4. You can serve the terrine whole and let guests cut slices as they would from a layer cake. Or you can cut the terrine into $1/2$-inch slices (2 per serving). The terrine should be served with tomato confit and slices of toasted bread.

CURRY FISH TERRINE: Add $1/4$ teaspoon curry powder and $1/4$ teaspoon turmeric powder.

ANISE FISH TERRINE: First marinate $1/4$ to $1/2$ teaspoon anise seeds in 2 teaspoons lemon juice and 2 teaspoons olive oil for 30 minutes. Then drain and add the anise seeds to the terrine mix.

BASIL FISH TERRINE: Add 10 chopped basil leaves.

TERRINE DE POULPE

OCTOPUS TERRINE

I've never succeeded at getting my terrine to resemble Gérald Passédat's beautiful terrazzo of octopus, with its white rounds clustered together like Carrara pebbles. It's hard enough to hold the octopus down in the pan and to keep its tentacles from curling up. But the advantage of a terrine like this is that no matter how unevenly its solid ingredients are distributed in the pan, any inch-thick cross section sliced from the terrine will still have the impressive appearance of a mosaic.

The cork is added to the braising liquid, according to Passédat, to tenderize the octopus. It's just one of dozens of tough-octopus folk remedies practiced around the Mediterranean. I tried cooking octopus with and without a wine cork and could swear the cork had an effect. I don't think it mattered, however, that the wine cork was taken from a bottle of Bandol cultivated on a vineyard beside the Provençal seacoast some thirty miles east of Restaurant Passédat.

Keep in mind that the broth needs to be aggressively seasoned. The salt and spices become less evident once the terrine is chilled. The simple sauce is mine, not Passédat's, who uses squid ink in his.

MAKES 10 TO 12 SERVINGS
(1 ONE-QUART TERRINE)

3 tablespoons olive oil
1 onion, diced
1 clove
1 large carrot, diced
1 leek (white part only), diced
1 celery branch, diced
Salt

1 large octopus (about 2½ pounds), defrosted
1 small dried chile pepper (substitute tiny pinch of red pepper flakes)
1 cork from wine bottle
2 packets powdered unflavored gelatin
1 tablespoon balsamic vinegar
Juice of 1 lime

1. Heat the olive oil in a large saucepan over moderately high heat. Pierce a piece of the diced onion with the clove and add it to the saucepan, along with the remaining onion, diced carrot, leek, and celery. Season with salt and cook, stirring occasionally, until the vegetables begin to soften and deepen in color, 6 to 7 minutes.

2. Pour $1\frac{1}{2}$ cups water into the saucepan and bring to a boil. Remove the head of the octopus and add the rest of the octopus to the boiling liquid with the chile pepper and cork. Cover, lower the heat to medium, and cook for 1 hour.

3. Remove the octopus from the saucepan and set aside. Pour the liquid from the saucepan through a fine sieve and remove the vegetables. Reserve 3 cups of the broth for the terrine and then refrigerate the remainder to be used for the sauce.

4. Sprinkle the gelatin over $\frac{1}{4}$ cup cold water and let soak until the mixture is translucent, about 3 minutes. Pour the gelatin into the broth and heat over low heat, stirring continuously, until fully dissolved, 2 to 3 minutes.

5. Line an oiled 1-quart terrine or loaf pan with plastic wrap (the plastic wrap should hang at least an inch over the sides of the terrine or loaf pan).

6. Peel the red outer layer off the octopus with the help of a clean dishcloth. (You might find it a lot simpler to leave the reddish skin on. This will mostly affect the appearance of the terrine.) Cut the tentacles and place them lengthwise as neatly as possible along the bottom of the terrine. Do your best to straighten out the curly ends, but do not be overly concerned if they do not stay even and parallel.

7. Pour enough of the gelatin-broth mixture (about 2 cups) over the octopus to cover. Set aside the remainder of the gelatin-broth mixture. If the octopus won't stay submerged, you will need to weigh it down by topping it with a second pan half filled with water or a few heavy jars. Refrigerate, making sure the terrine pan is as even as possible, for 1 hour.

8. Remove the terrine from the refrigerator and carefully lift whatever was holding down the octopus. Reheat the remaining gelatin-broth mixture, stirring until fully dissolved (making sure there are no hardened pieces), and pour it in the terrine to cover the octopus by at least $\frac{1}{4}$ inch liquid. Refrigerate, again making sure the terrine is as even as possible, for at least 2 hours.

9. Turn the terrine over a serving dish and unmold by delicately lifting up the pan while holding down the exposed plastic wrap. Peel off the plastic and, using a sharp knife dipped in hot water, delicately cut the terrine into $\frac{3}{4}$-inch slices.

10. Immediately before serving, combine the balsamic vinegar, the lime juice, and octopus broth in a saucepan over moderately high heat and stir until heated but not boiling, about 2 minutes. Place a slice of the terrine on the center of each of 4 dishes and spoon a small amount of the octopus sauce around each.

TERRINE DE FOIE DE VOLAILLE

CHICKEN LIVER TERRINE

This mousse-like terrine of chicken (not duck) livers is Giselle Philippi's take on what you, like her Marseillais diners, may come to recognize and appreciate as poor man's foie gras.

MAKES 6 SERVINGS

½ pound chicken livers
1 tablespoon olive oil
1 teaspoon herbes de Provence
2⅓ cups evaporated milk
3 egg yolks, beaten
2 teaspoons salt
1 teaspoon freshly ground white pepper
Onion Jam (page 64)
1 baguette or country bread, sliced and toasted

1. Trim off the white fat from the chicken livers, place in a bowl, and toss with the olive oil and herbes de Provence.
2. Heat a saucepan over moderately high heat (no butter or oil) and sauté the livers until golden on all sides, 5 to 6 minutes.
3. Preheat the oven to 250 degrees.
4. Combine the livers with the remaining ingredients, except the onion jam and the baguette, in a blender and puree until smooth, 3 to 5 minutes. Pour the mixture into a buttered 1-quart terrine or loaf pan and cook in a bain-marie for 90 minutes. To verify the terrine is cooked through, insert a knife into the terrine. If it comes out dry and hot, it's done. Remove the terrine from the bain-marie and the oven and let cool. Pass a knife around the perimeter to unmold, cover with plastic wrap, and refrigerate for up to one week.
5. You can serve the terrine whole and let guests cut slices as they would from a layer cake. Or you can cut the terrine into ½-inch slices (2 per serving). The terrine should be served with onion jam and toast.

Pizzas and Tarts

Pâte à Pain BREAD DOUGH

Pizza "Chez Etienne"

Lahmajoun ARMENIAN PIZZA

Fougasse au Romarin ROSEMARY FOUGASSE

Tarte à la Scarole ESCAROLE TART

Etienne Cassaro in his
"pizzaria," Chez Etienne.

A MONG THE PEOPLE who would be most surprised to hear Marseille described as a great pizza town are the Marseillais. They would prefer the city maintain its close association with bouillabaisse, even if pizza long ago surpassed the native fish stew as Marseille's most prevalent Sunday food habit. It would be easy for me to bemoan this development as another tragic example of cultural degradation if the pizza in Marseille were not so darn good and I myself had not made it my lunch and dinner choice so many times.

Not all the pizza is terrific. Indeed, some of it is very bad. But there are a number of pizzerias who turn out beautiful, thin-crusted, Neapolitan-style pies from their wood-fired brick ovens. Moreover, pizza trucks the size of postal delivery trucks are equipped with brick ovens and parked all over town. (They don't deliver. They don't even move. They set up for the night and stay put.) The rolling pizzerias even have their own alliance: La Federation des Artisans Pizza en Camion Magasin, "The Federation of Truck-Store Pizza Artisans." Though not all its members qualify as artisans, some of the pies are surprisingly good. I used to buy a crisp, cheesy, lightly charred slice or two from Massilia Pizza, which was parked outside the Notre-Dame du Mont church on Monday nights, and consume the order with a glass of rosé at a nearby sidewalk café.

Marseille pizza departs from its Italian origins in its frequent use of Gruyère or Emmental cheese in place of mozzarella, the addition of herbes de Provence to the tomato sauce, and the widespread availability of a kind—the *armenienne*—topped with ground beef, bell peppers, and onions.

This section includes recipes for *lahmajoun*, the true Armenian pizza, and two regional specialties, rosemary fougasse and escarole tart, that can be described as genuine Provençal counterparts to pizza.

PÂTE À PAIN

BREAD DOUGH

From this rudimentary formula for bread baking may rise two of Marseille's great classics: the thin-crusted master pizza of Chez Etienne (page 99) and chichi-fregi (page 240) as those spirals of fried dough are prepared in the fishing village of L'Estaque. It may also be used for Armenian-style cheese turnovers (page 77), Armenian pizza (page 101), and Moroccan savory turnovers (page 81). You can also bake this workhorse dough to make croutons for soups and bouillabaisses, the bread filling for both fish balls (page 159), the *cannelloni de daube* (page 192), and the semolina meat patties (page 196), and the toast for the Marseille-style BLT (page 188). To store unused portions of the dough in the freezer, first form the dough into either two or four small smooth balls, pack each ball in a plastic bag, press out as much air from the bag as possible, and seal it tightly with a twist tie. Keep the dough in its bag when thawing out.

MAKES 2 ROUND LOAVES, FOUR 10-INCH PIZZA CRUSTS,
OR 8 TO 10 SERVINGS OF CHICHI-FREGI

1½ cups warm water
1 tablespoon active dry yeast
3½ cups flour
1 teaspoon salt
2 teaspoons grated orange zest (for chichi-fregi only)

1. Pour ½ cup warm water in a measuring cup, stir in the yeast, and let stand for 5 minutes, until the yeast dissolves and turns creamy.

2. In the bowl of a heavy-duty standing mixer, combine the flour and salt. Add the dissolved yeast and a scant cup warm water. Attach the dough hook and mix on low speed until the dough detaches from the sides of the bowl and comes together, about 2 minutes. Increase the speed to medium and mix for 2 minutes more. Turn off the mixer, pull down the dough from the hook, and gather it into one mass. If the dough appears very dry and hard, add a little water. If it is wet and extremely sticky, add a little flour. Then restart the mixer at medium speed and mix the dough for 5 minutes more (add the orange zest if preparing chichi-fregi) until it has a smooth, even, elastic consistency and is no longer sticky.

3. Transfer the dough to a lightly floured work surface and shape into a smooth ball. Dust the ball with flour, place in a large bowl, and cover with plastic (plastic conserves the humidity and prevents it from developing an

outer crust). Let rise until doubled in bulk, 45 minutes to 1 hour (the former in very warm conditions, the latter in cooler ones).

4. Punch down the dough and divide into 2 equal parts to bake bread loaves or 4 parts both for pizza and chichi-fregi. For the pizza and chichi-fregi, proceed to the directions in their respective recipes. For bread, continue as follows.

5. Working with one part of the dough at a time (leaving the other one covered in plastic), form it into a ball, place it on a floured work surface, crush it with the palm of your hand in a twisting motion, and then re-form into a ball. Repeat this several times, the last time placing the dough on the powdered surface and turning it between your cupped hands to form a smooth round loaf. Place on a greased baking sheet, cover with plastic, and let rise for at least 1 hour. Repeat with the second part of the dough.

6. Preheat the oven to 450 degrees. Put a small ovenproof bowl, pot, or skillet of water on the bottom shelf of the oven to unleash some steam in the oven.

7. Using a single-edge razor or sharp knife make a cross-shaped slash on the top of each loaf. Lower the oven temperature to 400 degrees and bake the loaves until brown, about 45 minutes.

PIZZA "CHEZ ETIENNE"

The notion of duplicating the best pizza in a truly great pizza town is admittedly hopeless. First, it's impossible to reproduce the conditions in Chez Etienne's wood-fired brick oven. An accomplished baker furnished with flour from the same mill, tomatoes from the same cannery, cheeses from the same dairy, and water from the same reservoir could not possibly bake the same thin, slightly charred but never brittle or hard crust. Second, it's foolish to imagine anyone would love this pizza as much without the hospitality of Etienne Cassaro, the loquacious, lovably grumpy owner and his cousin Annie, the sweet-tempered redhead who has worked at his side since 1955.

Nevertheless, there is something special you can do about the cheese. Initially, I believed that Marseille pizzerias offered Gruyère or Emmental cheese in place of—or in addition to—mozzarella to save money, both theirs and yours. (In many instances, this is probably true. A Swiss cheese pizza is often priced five or ten francs below a mozzarella pie.) But Etienne explained that placing the sliced mozzarella directly over a layer of shredded Gruyère helps the mozzarella spread out over the entire surface of the pie as it bakes.

He's right. I baked half a pie with Gruyère and the other without and discovered that the mozzarella on the Gruyère was oozy and less stringy. When the Gruyère melts, it gets slippery and seems to loosen up the mozzarella. And I longed for the Gruyère's nutty flavor when sampling the half without it.

The remaining details of this Italo-Provençal pizza come from Azedine, Etienne's French-Algerian pizza chef. I urge inexperienced *pizzaiollos* not to assemble the entire pizza outside the oven before sliding it in, as most recipes suggest. The chances of their flinging the toppings right off the dough is perhaps one in three. Better to pull the oven rack that is holding the pizza stone halfway out, lay the pizza dough directly over the stone, spoon the tomato sauce over the dough, and let the pie bake for 2 minutes without the remaining toppings. (Better to cope with an oven that's lost some of its heat than one splattered with tomato and cheese.) Cooking the pie for 2 minutes without the cheese lets some of the tomato sauce's water evaporate, which in turn humidifies the oven and improves the crust. And the shorter heat exposure for the cheese ensures that it stays milky white, melted but not burned.

MAKES ONE 10-INCH PIZZA

1 ball Bread Dough (the recipe on page 97 yields 4 such balls)

4 Italian canned plum tomatoes, drained, seeded, and crushed (or passed through a food mill)

1 teaspoon herbes de Provence

$\frac{1}{2}$ teaspoon minced garlic

$\frac{1}{4}$ teaspoon salt

8 to 10 black olives

$\frac{1}{4}$ cup (about 1 ounce) shredded Gruyère or Emmental cheese

4 ounces mozzarella cheese, thinly sliced

1 tablespoon olive oil, optional

1. Place a baking stone or pizza stone atop an oven rack positioned on the lowest level. If possible remove all other racks from the oven. Preheat the oven to 500 degrees and let the stone heat for at least 30 minutes.

2. Place the dough ball on a well-floured work surface and pound flat with the palm of your hand into a thick disk. Continue to flatten the dough, rotating it as you press down on it with your fingertips. With your hands close together, lift up the dough by its rim, letting it hang down so that the dough stretches itself. Turn the dough between your fingers, each time spreading apart your hands, until the dough is roughly 10 inches in diameter and between $\frac{1}{8}$ and $\frac{1}{4}$ inch in thickness.

3. Transfer the dough onto a well-floured wooden pizza peel or flat baking sheet. Spoon the shredded tomatoes over the dough into a thin even layer, leaving a $\frac{1}{2}$-inch border untouched. Sprinkle the crushed tomatoes with the herbes de Provence, minced garlic, and salt.

4. Open the oven door and put the end of the pizza peel in contact with the surface of the baking stone. Tilt the pizza peel up, jiggle it and, as the pizza slides onto the stone, slowly pull back to completely dislodge the pizza. Close the door and bake for 2 minutes.

5. Open the oven door, slide out the oven rack if necessary, and quickly top the pizza with the black olives, the shredded Gruyère and, directly over it, the sliced mozzarella. Drizzle with olive oil, if desired. Bake until the outer crust begins to brown, 6 to 8 minutes. Use a pizza cutter or sharp knife to cut into quarters and serve immediately.

LAHMAJOUN

ARMENIAN PIZZA

Pizza Armenienne appears on the menus of Marseille's pizza shops and trucks the way you might see a Margherita or a Quattro Stagioni at pizzerias in Italy. An influence of the city's large Armenian community, it has become a standard variety loosely based on the ground meat pie lahmajoun. Marseillais of Armenian ancestry like Serge Zarokian love to tell friends that the meat-topped Armenian pizzas sold at pizzerias is nothing like what their grandmothers made. Of course they are right. Below is Serge's family recipe, with an assist from another Armenian grandmother, Berthe Baghtchejian. The lahmajoun is typically served with a simple salad.

MAKES 8 TO 10 APPETIZER SERVINGS
OR 6 TO 8 MAIN-COURSE SERVINGS

1 pound ripe plum tomatoes
1 pound ground lean beef or ground lean lamb
   (or ½ pound of each)
2 small onions, chopped
1 clove garlic, chopped
1 small green bell pepper, chopped
¼ cup chopped fresh parsley
1 teaspoon salt
1 pinch cayenne
1 pinch freshly ground black pepper
1 recipe Bread Dough (page 97)
1 lemon
Olive oil (for greasing pan and for salad)
Salad greens

1. Cut the tomatoes in quarters, remove and discard most of the seeds, and then chop the tomatoes. Transfer to a large mixing bowl, add the ground meat, onions, garlic, green pepper, parsley, salt, cayenne, and black pepper and mix well. Cover with plastic wrap and refrigerate until ready to use.

2. Preheat the oven to 450 degrees. Oil a 15 by 10 by 1-inch jelly-roll pan.

3. Place the dough on a floured work surface and alternately stretch and flatten to roughly the size of the jelly-roll pan. Transfer the dough to the pan and flatten it to completely cover the bottom. Pinch the dough up along the perimeter so it comes up the sides of the pan by ½ inch or so.

4. Spread the meat filling evenly over the top of the dough. Place on the bottom rack of the oven and bake until the rim of the crust is golden brown, about 15 minutes.

5. Remove from the oven and drizzle the top of the pizza with lemon juice. To cut into squares and rectangles, make one long lengthwise cut down the middle (assuring that every slice includes a portion of the crusty rim) and then several lateral cuts according to your needs. Serve with salad greens dressed only with olive oil, lemon juice, salt, and pepper.

FOR INDIVIDUALLY SIZED PIZZETTES: Divide the dough into 8 or 10 balls, roll out each ball into $\frac{1}{2}$-inch-thick rounds, place the rounds on a greased cookie sheet, top each with about $1\frac{1}{2}$ tablespoons of the meat mixture, leaving a $\frac{1}{2}$-inch rim uncovered, and then bake.

Though Serge suggests baking the pizza on one rectangular pan and then cutting it into squares, you can get the same results by spreading the dough on the bottom of greased round pie pans and then cutting the finished pies into wedges.

FOUGASSE AU ROMARIN

ROSEMARY FOUGASSE

As the Provençale counterpart to Italian focaccia, the fougasse plays naturally into the skillful hands of Enzo Fassone, a great Marseille baker with Piedmontese bloodlines. Flavored with fresh herbs (in Fassone's recipe it is rosemary), black olives, anchovies, or onions, the olive oil–enriched fougasse has evolved from a decorative holiday specialty into an "ordinary" yet dependably impressive bread served throughout the year. (The sweetened version of fougasse, *la pompe à l'huile*, page 231, is the centerpiece of Provence's celebrated thirteen Christmas desserts.) Smaller fougasse made with no more than 2 ounces of dough, though less imposing than the large, leaf-patterned classic, are far easier to shape and to stretch open its interior incisions before it is baked. Those incisions give the bread its decorative, latticelike form. Such mini-fougasse may be served as part of a bread basket or as hors d'oeuvres at the apéritif hour. Unused portions of the dough separated into similarly small pieces may also be used to bake rolls, pizza crusts (bakers like Fassone tend to prefer thick pizza crusts over the thinner counterparts championed at pizzerias like Chez Etienne), savory tarts, and *gressins* (French for the breadsticks—*grissini*—of Turin).

Whatever the size, shape, design pattern, filling, or usage, Fassone's expert advice for home bakers is ultimately the same. "It mustn't be too uniform," he says, making an argument for imperfection characteristic of a Marseillais's reverse snobbism. "You want to preserve the rustic, artisanal spirit."

MAKES 2 LARGE FOUGASSE

2 tablespoons active dry yeast
3 cups unbleached all-purpose flour
1½ teaspoons salt
¼ cup olive oil
2 teaspoons chopped fresh rosemary

1. Pour ½ cup of warm water into a measuring cup, stir in the yeast, and let stand for 5 minutes, until the yeast dissolves and turns creamy.

2. In the bowl of a heavy-duty standing mixer, combine the flour and salt. Add 1 cup cold water, olive oil, and dissolved yeast. Attach the dough hook and mix on low speed until the dough detaches from the sides of the

bowl and comes together, about 2 minutes. Increase the speed to medium and mix for 4 minutes more. Turn off the mixer, pull down the dough from the hook, and gather it into one mass. If the dough appears very dry, add a teaspoon of water. Then restart the mixer at medium speed and mix the dough for 4 to 6 minutes more, until it has a smooth, even, elastic consistency, 8 to 10 minutes. With the mixer still running, slowly add the chopped rosemary and mix for 1 minute.

3. Transfer the dough to a lightly floured work surface and shape into a smooth ball. Dust the ball with flour, place in a bowl, and cover with plastic (plastic conserves the humidity and prevents it from developing an outer crust). Let rise until doubled in bulk, 45 minutes to 1 hour.

4. Return the dough to the lightly floured surface and cut into two equal parts. Shape each into a smooth ball, parting the dough by making a depression beneath it with your fingers and, as you turn it inward, folding the dough over itself. Dust each ball with flour, cover with plastic, and let relax for 15 minutes.

5. Place each ball of dough on the lightly floured surface and gently pull and stretch it into an oval roughly 12 inches in length, 6 inches in width, and $\frac{3}{8}$ inch thick. To make the leaf pattern, pretend there is a line dividing the fougasse lengthwise and, using a sharp knife, make four diagonal incisions on each side of the imaginary line. Gently lift the fougasse, being careful not to pinch the dough, and stretch to widen the openings made by the incisions. If

necessary, gently push your fingers through the gaps. Lay the fougasse on an oiled baking sheet, scatter pieces of the rosemary stem over the top, cover with plastic, and let it puff up a bit for 30 minutes.

6. Preheat the oven to 425 degrees.

7. Remove the plastic from the fougasses and bake on the middle shelf of the oven until lightly golden on top and bottom, about 15 minutes. Transfer to a cooling rack for 2 minutes and serve.

OLIVE FOUGASSE: Substitute $\frac{1}{2}$ cup chopped pitted black olives for the rosemary. After the olives are added to the dough at the conclusion of step 2 and while the mixer is still running, slowly add 2 additional teaspoons flour to absorb the liquid contained in the olives.

GRESSINS: Complete steps 1 through 5 of the fougasse recipe. For each gressin, place a small ball (roughly the size of a billiard ball) of the dough on a lightly floured surface and stretch it out into a flattened sausage about 6 inches in length and 2 inches in width. Fold the dough in two lengthwise by pinching along the middle of the sausage with your thumb, folding the dough over itself, and then pressing down on the open seam with the heel of your hand. Roll out the dough using the palms of both hands and then pull at each end to stretch it into a long cord about $\frac{1}{2}$ inch in diameter. Sprinkle gressins with fresh chopped rosemary, coarse salt, or grated Gruyère cheese, if desired, place on an oiled baking sheet, and bake at 425 degrees until golden, 15 to 17 minutes.

TARTE À LA SCAROLE

ESCAROLE TART

A variation of the pissaladière, a deep-dish onion tart from Nice most often accessorized with anchovies and onions, home cook Renée Brunet's *tarte à la scarole* adds the taste and just enough of the bitterness of wilted escarole to that mix. The escarole-onion-anchovy topping is so yummy that you might find yourself eating it right off the tart.

MAKES ONE 12-INCH TART

1 small-to-medium head escarole
3 tablespoons olive oil
1 medium onion, finely chopped
1 tablespoon Anchoïade (page 57)
½ Fougasse recipe (page 103), omitting the
    chopped rosemary and stopping after step 4
6 anchovies packed in oil, drained and dried
¼ cup black olives, pitted

1. Wash the escarole, place it in a saucepan over high heat, and cook covered to release its bitter liquids, 2 to 3 minutes. Drain, rinse in cold water, and then chop. (You should have about 2 cups.)

2. Heat the olive oil in a saucepan over low heat. Combine the escarole and onion in the saucepan and cook gently, stirring occasionally, for 15 minutes. Add the anchoïade and mix well.

3. Preheat the oven to 400 degrees. Oil a 12-inch tart pan with a removable rim or a 12-inch quiche baking dish.

4. Roll out the dough on a lightly floured surface to a 12-inch circle and place in the oiled tart pan. Press the dough with your fingertips to spread it out and push the dough up the sides of the pan. Top the dough with an even layer of the escarole-onion mixture. Place the anchovies over the tart in a starburst pattern, with each anchovy extending out from the center toward the outer rim. Scatter the black olives over the top and bake until the tart crust is golden brown, about 40 minutes. Remove the rim of the pan if necessary and serve immediately.

Soups

Soupe au Pistou
VEGETABLE SOUP WITH BASIL AND GARLIC

Soupe de Pois Cassés SPLIT PEA SOUP

Soupe de Haricots Vert Comme au Roucas Blanc
HARICOT VERT SOUP "ROUCAS BLANC"

Soupe Courte PROVENÇAL "SHORT" SOUP

Chorba ALGERIAN RAMADAN SOUP

Bourride PROVENÇAL FISH SOUP WITH AÏOLI

Looking west from the Monument aux Morts d'Òrient to the three islands of the Frioul Archipelago: If (front center), *Ratonneau* (right), *Pomègues* (left).

FOLLOWING THE EXAMPLE of virtually all French-English dictionaries instead of the physical evidence, I've translated the French word *soupe,* as it applies to the recipes to follow, as "soup." But although there was really no other viable alternative, the term *soup* is, if not a misnomer, a bit misleading. These hearty Marseille soups all push, penetrate, or pass across the murky boundary between a hot liquid food and something more solid, a ragoût perhaps.

The haricot vert soup, though thickened with mashed potato and containing more vegetables than broth, would be recognized by most observers as a soup, that is, if you told them it was intended to be a soup. But the only sure indications that the classic *soupe au pistou* (Provence's version of minestrone) and the split pea soup are soups may be the bowls you choose to serve them in and the spoons you position conspicuously at their sides. Both are thick and rich to the point of being solid foods.

The *bourride,* like bouillabaisse, could be described as a Provençal fish stew. The Algerian chorba is also a meat, vegetable, and pasta stew. And calling the short soup short is a ridiculous understatement. It isn't done cooking until all the liquid has vanished. Don't even think of serving it with a spoon.

SOUPE AU PISTOU

VEGETABLE SOUP WITH BASIL AND GARLIC

What impressed me most about the *soupe au pistou* competition held in the late summer of 2000 at Marseille's Cours Julien was less the accomplishment of the first-prize winner than the disbelief expressed by the runner-ups. There is certainly nothing odd about any Marseillais thinking his or her mother's or grandmother's *soupe au pistou,* the Provençal counterpart to Italian mine-strone, was the best in the world. In many families it would be traitorous to believe otherwise. But so certain were the participants of their respective soup's superiority that the contrary opinion of the judges left them shell-shocked. That the winner, Lolita Doullay, was the listings editor of the weekly alternative newspaper *Taktik* only intensified their skepticism. In an irresistible bit of wordplay, a rumor spread through Marseille quicker than garlic flavor in hot olive oil that the champion *soupe au pistou* had been *piston-née* (or, in a corruption of that verb to fit the alleged misdeed, *pistounée*), meaning that strings were pulled on behalf of the well-connected winner.

Soupe au pistou is comparable to bouillabaisse in the passions it arouses over the most minor details, not only between various regions of Provence but also within them. Some Marseillais are against the very idea of details. When listing quantities in his *soupe au pistou* recipe, food writer Jacques Bonnadier refuses to be any more specific than "some" or "a little."

"There's no need to say anything more," says Bonnadier, who views the indication of precise measurements, as I've done below, as a heresy. "It's up to the individual to determine the dosage that suits him and is based on the number of his guests."

To avoid controversy, I've created a composite recipe incorporating various interpretations. The addition of tomatoes and the use of elbow macaroni rather than cut spaghetti reflect preferences prevalent in Marseille. As it happens, the unavailability in the U.S. of certain Provençal beans (freshly hulled white beans known as *cocos;* flat haricots verts known as *écheleurs* or *barra-quets*) prevents an American cook from insisting on purity. Still, I fully expect my descendants to one day champion my *soupe au pistou* as indisputably the best one west of Marseille.

Note that *soupe au pistou* means a soup "with"—and not "of"—*pistou* (basil and garlic) sauce. Its chunky base consists of beans and vegetables. The *pistou* paste should not be added until the soup has been taken off the fire either immediately before it is served or, as my friend Jacqueline Lepetit, one of the incredulous losers in the *pistou* competition urges, 10 minutes before (this allows the sauce's basil to permeate the beans to their core without getting cooked out). If you want to set aside some of the soup for later in the day, do so before adding the *pistou*. Leftover *soupe au pistou* does not, however, take well to reheating, with or without the *pistou*. It is best served cool or, even better, at room temperature.

MAKES 6 MAIN-COURSE SERVINGS

1 cup (about ½ pound) dry cannellini beans
1 cup (about ½ pound) dry red kidney beans
Salt
Freshly ground black pepper
½ pound haricots verts, ends clipped and cut into 1-inch lengths
4 tomatoes, quartered and some of the seeds removed
4 whole zucchini
1 onion, finely chopped
4 whole Idaho potatoes, peeled
⅓ pound elbow macaroni
Pistou (page 61)

1. The day before: Soak the cannellini beans and the red kidney beans overnight in separate pots of water to cover them. Drain well.
2. Place 3½ cups of water in a large soup pot, add salt and pepper, and bring to a boil.
3. Add the haricots verts, cannellini beans, kidney beans, tomatoes, zucchini, onion, and potatoes. Cover the pot tightly, lower the heat to medium, and boil for 2½ hours.
4. Add the macaroni to the soup and cook covered until soft, about 15 minutes (you probably don't want the macaroni to be al dente).
5. Meanwhile, prepare the *pistou* sauce. Add a tablespoon or two of the soup broth to the *pistou*, and mash it into the *pistou* with the pestle.
6. Remove the soup from the fire, correct the seasoning, stir in the *pistou* sauce, cover, and let stand for 10 minutes. Serve.

SOUPE DE POIS CASSÉS

SPLIT PEA SOUP

When Yvon Cadiou was cooking at a small Sunday-only restaurant at Marseille's flea market, the use of the pressure cooker was not only about saving time. It produced a thick, rich, velvety puree in which the peas were not quite fully dissolved and you could just make out the last red strands of tomato within the beautiful yellow-orange. The split pea soup's amalgam of garlic, thyme, cumin, and coriander is akin to the scent that drifts from kitchen windows in the old Panier quarter of Marseille.

If you are not using a pressure cooker, you will have to soak the split peas overnight. Then follow the directions, cooking the soup at a simmer until the peas turn mushy, about 1 hour.

MAKES 6 APPETIZER SERVINGS OR 4 MAIN-COURSE SERVINGS

1 cup dried split peas (preferably yellow)
4 tablespoons olive oil
2 onions, peeled and sliced
4 cloves garlic, chopped
2 large carrots, peeled and thinly sliced
2 tomatoes, quartered
1 teaspoon chopped fresh thyme leaves
1/4 teaspoon cumin
1/4 teaspoon coriander powder
2 bay leaves
2 teaspoons tomato paste
Salt
Freshly ground black pepper
Extra virgin olive oil, optional

1. Soak the dried split peas in cold water for 30 minutes.

2. Heat the olive oil in a pressure cooker over moderately high heat. Add the onions, garlic, carrots, tomatoes, and cook, stirring occasionally, until the onions are translucent and the carrots somewhat softened, about 5 minutes.

3. Add the peas, thyme, cumin, coriander, bay leaves, tomato paste, and 2 quarts cold water, and season with salt and pepper. Cover, set control of the pressure cooker at 15 pounds and cook until the control jiggles. Reduce heat and cook for 45 minutes more. Reduce pressure instantly. Pour into soup bowls and drizzle with extra virgin olive oil, if desired.

SOUPE DE HARICOTS VERT COMME AU ROUCAS BLANC

HARICOT VERT SOUP "ROUCAS BLANC"

Like many a Marseillaise, the late Germaine Langevin attached her identity—and, in this instance, that of her most trusted soup—less to the entire city than to one of the 111 villages within it. Just a couple of miles south of the Vieux Port, Le Roucas Blanc (literally: "white rock") is named for the rocky slope that, with steep roads and stairways descending to the Corniche and the beach, affords its hilltop villas a panoramic view of the Mediterranean coastline. With squinting eyes, a little imagination, and a hearty appetite you can begin to imagine the spindly pine trees as slender haricots verts taking root in a rocky terrain of white potatoes starting below and then emerging above sea—that is to say, soup—level. From that perspective it is not so much a landmark Marseille dish at it is a landscape one.

The neighborhood's affluence and climbing real estate values notwithstanding, Langevin's version of this rustic classic of green beans and potatoes meets the three essentials of a dish championed by any *bonne mère de famille:* it's economical, it's nourishing, and it's good. An instructor in Provençal cuisine at the cultural center La Couqueto, Langevin added pork to her soup to make it a meal and then poured the enriched broth over fork-mashed potatoes to thicken it. Any further doctoring of this simple soup is discouraged. The particular flavor of the haricots verts is fragile and would likely be overwhelmed by the addition of most herbs, spices, and vegetables, as it is by garlic and basil in *soupe au pistou.*

MAKES 6 MAIN-COURSE SERVINGS

2 pounds haricots verts, ends trimmed and cut
into 1-inch lengths (substitute green beans)
3 pounds Idaho potatoes, peeled
2 large onions, minced
1/2 to 3/4 pound bacon lardon, cut into chunks
1/2 to 3/4 pound sweet country sausages, cut in
chunks
Salt
Freshly ground black pepper

1. Put the vegetables and meats in a large
   stockpot, cover with cold water, season with
   salt and pepper, and cook covered over a low
   flame for 2 hours. Correct the seasonings.
2. TO SERVE, place one of the potatoes that
   have cooked in the stockpot on the bottom
   of 4 soup bowls and mash with a fork. Ladle
   some of the potatoes, haricots verts, and
   meat chunks in the bowls and cover with hot
   broth.

SOUPE COURTE

PROVENÇAL "SHORT" SOUP

The word *short* in this dish's name is thought to refer to the height of the broth in the soup pot. During its cooking, the liquid level gradually sinks down in the pot until virtually all the soup has either evaporated or been absorbed by the pasta. All that's left of the broth is a thickened, stewlike sauce that clings to the shells. Essentially it is a pasta and meat dish as well as a robust example of Provençal's cuisine of economy. Since the *soupe courte* is featured irregularly at the Marseillais-Provençal restaurant Les Echevins according to the whims of its chef, Jeanne Moréni-Garron, I am proud to be passing along that grandmother's hearty recipe. Now we can have it whenever we want!

MAKES 4 MAIN-COURSE SERVINGS

2 tablespoons vegetable oil

4 lamb chops (as lean as possible)

2 tablespoons olive oil

1 onion, chopped

4 cloves garlic

1 tablespoon chopped parsley

1 tablespoon tomato paste

1 teaspoon chopped thyme leaves

1 bay leaf

1 tablespoon chopped parsley

Salt

Freshly ground black pepper

½ pound pasta shells

¼ pound grated Parmesan or Gruyère

1. Heat the vegetable oil in a casserole over high heat. Add the lamb chops and brown on both sides, about 1 minute on each side. Remove the chops from the heat and set aside.

2. Clean the bottom of the casserole. Heat the olive oil in the casserole over medium heat. Add the onion and 2 cloves garlic and cook until the onion is translucent but not colored, about 10 minutes.

3. Chop the remaining garlic and combine with the chopped parsley. Add to the casserole, along with the tomato paste, thyme, and bay leaf. Cover with 1 quart water, season with salt and pepper, raise the heat, and cook to a rapid boil.

4. Place the lamb chops into the boiling liquid, add the pasta shells, lower the heat to medium, and cook at a boil until all the liquid has been absorbed. There is virtually no broth. What liquid there is left clings like a sauce to the pasta. Serve the chops and the pasta together with the grated cheese.

CHORBA

ALGERIAN RAMADAN SOUP

During Ramadan, the evening meal at Zohra Sahnoune's house in the neighborhood of Belle de Mai is not much different than it would be in Tlemcen, the Algerian province she left with her parents in 1953. It consists of chorba, the traditional main-course soup that, with its lamb, tomato, saffron, and chickpeas, is very much at home in Marseille. The Algerian counterpart to Moroccan harira is lavishly stocked with enough lamb, grains, and vegetables to sustain Muslims through the sunrise-to-sunset fasts carried out throughout their holy month. So concerned was Zohra about her family's nourishment that she, like many Algerian mothers, long ago adopted the practice of crushing the vegetables in a food mill to thwart the efforts of her eight children to sort out the veggies they didn't like. But those who don't need to trick their kids, their spouses, or themselves into eating turnips should prepare the chorba with vegetables cut in a fine dice.

MAKES 8 TO 10 MAIN-COURSE SERVINGS

1 cup dried chickpeas

1 teaspoon baking soda

1 pound ripe tomatoes (or 28-ounce can crushed tomatoes)

3 tablespoons vegetable oil

½ pound boneless lamb shoulder or neck, cut into 1-inch cubes

1 onion, chopped

1 celery stalk, chopped

½ cup finely chopped fresh cilantro

1 teaspoon allspice

1 pinch saffron threads, crumbled

1 tablespoon tomato paste

1 teaspoon salt

½ teaspoon freshly ground black pepper

1 carrot, diced

1 medium Idaho potato, peeled and diced

1 zucchini, diced

1 turnip, diced

4 ounces vermicelli

1 lemon, cut into wedges

1. The day before: Combine the chickpeas and baking soda in a pan or large bowl, cover to a level at least 2 inches over the chickpeas with cold water, and let soak overnight. Drain the chickpeas and rinse well in cold water.

2. If using fresh tomatoes, first peel them: Cut a small X in their smooth ends and plunge in boiling salted water for 30 seconds. Peel the tomatoes and crush with the back of a wooden spatula.

3. Heat the vegetable oil in a casserole or stew pot over medium heat. Add the lamb cubes, onion, celery, half the chopped cilantro, allspice, and saffron. Cook, turning the lamb once or twice, until golden on all sides, 6 to 8 minutes. Add the crushed fresh or canned tomatoes, tomato paste, salt, and pepper.

4. Pour in 1 cup of water, lower the heat to low, and cook, stirring continuously, until the liquid and tomatoes are well blended, about 5 minutes.

5. Add the carrot, potato, zucchini, and turnip. Pour in enough water ($1\frac{1}{2}$ to 2 quarts) to completely cover the meat and vegetables. Raise the heat to high and bring to a boil.

6. Add the drained chickpeas, cover, lower the heat to low, and let simmer until the meat is tender, at least 2 hours. Add some water, if necessary, to maintain a souplike consistency. Put aside any soup you might be saving for another meal. Add the vermicelli and the remaining cilantro and cook for 2 minutes. Season with salt and pepper. Serve with lemon wedges.

BOURRIDE

PROVENÇAL FISH SOUP WITH AÏOLI

Although it shares some of a bouillabaisse's essential flavors, a bourride differs from its more famous cousin in two important ways: First, it is prepared with firm, mild-tasting, white-fleshed fish such as cod, red snapper, sea bass, halibut, and turbot instead of the stronger-flavored, bottom-feeding rockfish that give bouillabaisse its unique character. Because those rockfish or acceptable alternatives are difficult to find off U.S. shores or in American fish markets, an authentic bourride can be a more practical and achievable goal for home cooks without access to imported fish. Second, in a bourride the garlicky aïoli is mixed directly into the soup to both thicken and enrich it. This is considered not only acceptable but downright desirable since the white-fleshed fish in question are, at least by comparison, bland. The high note of garlic that resounds atop the resulting, sensationally silky soup is the unmistakable call of a bourride.

This recipe is largely adapted from the bourrides of two passionate Marseillais, professional opera singer Alain Aubin and restaurateur Serge Zarokian. Each offers one bit of indispensable advice in his own distinctive voice:

Zakorian, in his raspy baritone, exhorts you not to pour the broth over the fish, as you would with a bouillabaisse. This can crush their delicacy. He suggests you first pour the broth into the bowl and then delicately lay the fish into the broth.

Aubin, in his honey-voiced countertenor, insists you not answer the telephone during the phase in which the aïoli is stirred into the bourride to thicken it. You might even want to turn down the volume of the answering machine so you won't be tempted to pick up. Leaving the bourride unattended for even a few seconds can allow the mixture to bubble and quickly coagulate the egg yolks in the aïoli. A scrambled bourride, Aubin knows from sad experience, is a tragedy of operatic proportions.

MAKES 4 MAIN-COURSE SERVINGS

¼ cup olive oil

2 onions, chopped

2 leeks (white parts only), halved and chopped

¼ cup chopped parsley

1 teaspoon fennel seeds

1 bay leaf

3 ripe tomatoes, quartered

2 cloves garlic, crushed

3 pounds fish trimmings, heads (gills removed), carcasses, and bones (substitute 3 cups fish stock or clam juice)

Salt

Freshly ground black pepper

1 pinch cayenne

1½ cups dry white wine

2 pinches saffron threads, crumbled

2 pounds firm, white-fleshed fish fillets (monkfish, red snapper, sea bass, halibut, turbot), about 1 inch thick and cut into pieces no longer than 4 inches

½ pound large or jumbo shrimp, optional, peeled and deveined

2 cups Aïoli (page 62)

1 baguette or country bread, cut into ½-inch slices and lightly toasted

1. Heat the olive oil in a large stockpot over medium heat. Add the onions, leeks, parsley, fennel seeds, bay leaf, tomatoes, and crushed garlic. Cook, stirring occasionally, until the vegetables are soft but not brown, 8 to 10 minutes.

2. Rinse the fish trimmings, heads, carcasses, and bones in cold water and pat dry. Add to the stockpot. (If the carcasses are very large, break into smaller pieces.) Season with salt, black pepper, and cayenne, turn the heat to low, and cook, stirring occasionally with a wooden spatula or spoon, for 15 minutes.

3. Bring 3 quarts of water to a boil and pour it into the stockpot. Add the white wine, raise the heat to high, and bring the mixture to a boil. Turn the heat to low and cook gently for 10 minutes. Remove from the heat and pass the mixture through a food mill, mixing the fish scraps with ample amounts of broth, to help press and squeeze out as much juice from the fish scraps as possible. Add the saffron to the strained broth.

4. Heat the strained fish broth over moderately high heat to a boil, add the fish fillets and the shrimp, if desired, lower heat to medium-low, and cook uncovered until the fish fillets are opaque in the center, about 6 to 10 minutes, and the shrimp are firm and pink, about 3 to 4 minutes. Once the fillets and shrimp are done, remove them from the broth with a slotted spoon, place on a platter, spoon some broth over the fish, and cover to keep warm.

5. Place the aïoli in a large mixing bowl and, while whipping the aïoli with a whisk, very

gradually drizzle in several ladlefuls of fish broth until 1 quart of the fish broth has gone into the aïoli. Pour the aïoli-broth mixture back into the stockpot and heat over medium heat, stirring continuously with a wooden spoon, until it thickens enough to coat the spoon, about 5 minutes, making sure the liquid does not bubble. The thickened broth will have a smooth, silky texture and rich, creamy yellow color.

6. Place 3 slices of the bread (save the rest for second helpings) on the bottom of each of 4 soup bowls and ladle enough aïoli–fish broth into each bowl to cover the bread. Delicately arrange the chunks of fish in the bowls and serve immediately.

Bouillabaisse

Fond de Poisson pour Bouillabaisse Marseillaise
FISH STOCK FOR MARSEILLE-STYLE BOUILLABAISSE

Bouillabaisse Marseillaise
MARSEILLE-STYLE BOUILLABAISSE

Bouillabaisse du Pêcheur
FISHERMAN'S BOUILLABAISSE

Compressé de Bouillabaisse Porte de L'Orient
BOUILLABAISSE TERRINE

Fond de Légumes pour Bouillabaisse
VEGETABLE STOCK FOR BOUILLABAISSE

Bouillabaisse Borgne
ONE-EYED BOUILLABAISSE

Bouillabaisse d'Epinards
SPINACH BOUILLABAISSE

Bouillabaisse de Poulet
CHICKEN BOUILLABAISSE

Bouillabaisse de Morue
SALT COD BOUILLABAISSE

The Tassara family enjoys a fisherman's bouillabaisse.

I am hard at it, painting with the enthusiasm
of a Marseillais eating bouillabaisse.
—VINCENT VAN GOGH, in a letter to his brother Theo, 1888

T HE STORY OF BOUILLABAISSE ordinarily begins with Greek sailors, local fishermen, some ill-favored fish, and a cauldron filled with seawater. It's a beautiful legend and I'll get to it shortly. But to truly appreciate the greatness of the celebrated *bouillabaisse marseillaise,* as opposed to other fish stews and assorted pretenders, it is necessary to know something about the Gulf of Marseille's unique geography, geology, oceanography, and meteorology.

The historic Mediterranean seaport is situated between two distinctly different marine environments. The sandy plains of the delta to the west of Marseille are generously fed by France's Rhône River, which runs some five hundred miles south from Switzerland. To the east, following the Côte Bleue from the town of Martigues to Marseille and then the Calanques from Marseille to the town of La Ciotat, the coastline is rocky and craggy. The islands, cliffs, and underwater canyons provide a wide selection of cozy habitats, both shallow and deep, for discriminating fish. (It is against this rocky backdrop that rascasse, the fish most closely associated with bouillabaisse, prefer to hide out.) Taken together, these environments attract an unusually wide variety of fish species. The Bay of Marseille turns out to be a model of diversity for seafood as well as people.

Futhermore, as the Mediterranean northern and Liguro-Provençal currents pass near Marseille, they frequently run into the mistral and other provocative winds, as anyone who has ever navigated these rough shores can attest. The ensuing upswelling and downswelling may strand boats at port, but they ultimately help fishermen in other ways, attracting marine nourishment and cleaning the sea floor. The Bay of Marseille turns out to be prime seafood dining destination for carnivorous fish as well as people. And the better the trolling is for the former, the better it is for the latter.

Now, back to the Greeks. Since fish soup has always been a primal source of sustenance for seafaring peoples, it's likely the sailors who colonized Massalia around the year 600 B.C. had a primitive version. The Greek fish soup *kakavia* may or may not be a forerunner of bouillabaisse, as some food historians believe. Regardless, the Marseillais have no claim and make no claim to the invention of fish soup. Their proprietary interest is in one particular variation of fish soup.

The lack of any historical record establishing the origins of bouillabaisse prevents few locals from repeating the most credible hypothesis as fact. Centuries ago, hungry fishermen coming in from the sea had two immediate objectives: feed themselves and make use of the unsellable fish and fish scraps caught in their nets. They presumably accomplished both by building a wood fire on the beach, setting a cauldron over it, and boiling their disfigured or just plain ugly fish in seawater. They must have also thrown their stale hunks of bread into the soup to render them chewable and stretch the meal.

The term *bouillabaisse* is widely thought to be a conjunction of *bouillir* ("to boil") and *abaisser* ("to turn down" or, in its culinary usage, "to reduce"), thereby summarizing the manner in which this hodgepodge was cooked. In 1785, the *Dictionaire de la Provence et du Comté-Venaissin* defined *bouilhe-baisso* as the fisherman's term for a "sort of ragout of fish boiled in seawater," so-named because once the pot boils the heat is turned down. But food scholar Jacques Dupuy points out that it is the liquid that was reduced, not the flame. He believes the dish's name might just as likely have been a corruption of *bouillir* and *peis*—the latter a Provençal term for "fish"—and thus translates as "boiling fish" or "fish boil." His theory should be considered if for no other reason than you not be tempted to reduce the flame when preparing your own *bouilhe-baisso*. The soup should be cooked at a violent boil.

We must again rely on logic to advance the story. It stands to reason that this crude fisherman's soup was not very appetizing. For one thing, Marseille seawater is extremely salty. And so, if the fishermen themselves did not add any sources of vegetable flavor to the soup, it's probable that their wives did once the cauldron was conveyed indoors from the beach to the hearth. The first additions to render the soup more palatable and nourishing were, judging from the earliest recipes, garlic and olive oil. With rascasse and bread, they constitute the four essential elements of a *bouillabaisse marseillaise.*

The subsequent evolution of the bouillabaisse recipe may be followed through the recorded recipes of the Marseille chefs who transformed the humble, home-cooked ragoût into a glorious *soupe d'or,* "a golden soup." This culinary ennobling coincided with the commercial expansion of the city during the nineteenth century. Deluxe hotel-restaurants rose along the Canebière and near the Saint Charles train station. Their chefs prepared increasingly refined bouillabaisses for eminent travelers passing through Marseille, among them Alexandre Dumas, Gustave Flaubert, and Emile Zola. They in turn carried their fond memories of the exotic specialty to Italy, North Africa, the Middle East, or back home. The city and the soup were henceforth inseparable.

The list of possible ingredients gradually expanded to include onions, leeks, parsley, orange peel, basil, thyme, bay leaf, fennel, and tomatoes. Potatoes were a comparatively late addition, not finding their way into restaurant bouillabaisses until the twentieth century. The addition of saffron, the world's most expensive spice, was recorded as early as 1830 in the published recipe of Charles Durand. He may have added the touch of saffron powder to his bouillabaisse for the same reason he did so in his rice casserole and his timbale of macaroni *à l'indienne:* color. If you're accustomed only to the clean, shellfish-stocked bouillabaisse interpretations you come across in North America, the sight of a soup made with some of the same Mediterranean fish used by Durand is a dirty surprise. In particular, the juices extracted from the small rockfish make the soup grayish and granular. Although I now esteem that dull color and granular (but not gritty) texture as indicators of purity, it's easy to understand why Durand wanted to touch it up with some orange-yellow powder for his guests at the Hotel Beauvau.

Other notable bouillabaisse recipes from this golden age are credited to Clément Marius Morard, an assistant to chef Roubion at La Réserve (Alexandre Dumas published Roubion's version in his *Grande Dictionaire de Cuisine*). The great Appolon Caillat of the Grand Hôtel du Louvre et de la Paix created the definitive version transcribed by Auguste Escoffier in his authoritative *Le Grande culinaire.* This *soupe d'or* recipe, like many of its precedents, is that it cannot truly be described as merely "garlicky," "saffron-scented," "fennel-flavored," "peppery," or "rascasse-infused." The wonder of a bouillabaisse is that it constitutes a jazzy ensemble in which all these aggressive flavors are heard to best advantage.

The subtle differences among the restaurant versions (assortment of fish, crustaceans or no crustaceans, thickness of the bread slices, parsley chopped or in branches, lemon or no lemon) are less compelling than the variance between a chef's bouillabaisse and its rustic, fisherman's counterpart.

When you hear about the two stages of a bouillabaisse, you usually think of the manner in which it is properly served. First the soup makes a solo appearance, accompanied only by toasted slices of baguette or country bread and the rouille (the spicy garlicky mayo) you spread atop them. But since the days of Durand and Caillat, almost all restaurant renditions have been cooked in two separate stages. Together they are almost akin to making two bouillabaisses:

STAGE 1: A fish stock is prepared by first sautéing tiny rockfish (or, as a substitute, fish heads) with garlic, onions, and leeks in olive oil and then cooking this mixture with tomatoes, orange peel, celery, thyme, wild fennel, and a Scotch bonnet pepper in several quarts of boiling water. All is passed through a food mill or chinoise to press out the seasoned fish juices. The fish scraps and bones are then discarded.

STAGE 2: Brought back to a boil and scented with saffron, the fish stock becomes the poaching liquid for the potatoes and fish that go into the bouillabaisse.

The result of this two-step process is a richer, more fragrant soup—the famous *soupe d'or*. And no one can claim it is not far superior to the thinner, pallid bouillon you get in a one-step version in which all the ingredients are brought to a boil in a large pot of water. Nevertheless, my first experience with a so-called *bouillabaisse du pêcheur* ("fisherman's bouillabaisse") was a revelation. Certainly, the locale—Adrienne Tassara's home overlooking the Marseille fishing port of Vallon des Auffes—and the company—four generations of Tassaras—had a major influence. Nevertheless, the rough, homespun quality of the thin, practically clear bouillon convinced me I was sampling the real thing for the first time. Here was the primitive soup improvised on the beaches of Marseille. And it was a delicious dream.

Fishermen from Marseille and other ports along the French-Mediterranean coast rarely if ever eat a bouillabaisse in a restaurant. It's a self-imposed prohibition that has less to do with the relative merits of one-step and two-step versions than the very notion of the dish. For them, a bouillabaisse is a festive, convivial, Sunday-kind-of-experience best enjoyed with the entire family and dear friends either in their dining rooms or, ideally, in one of the tiny coastline *cabanons*.

During the nineteenth century, affluent families typically escaped Marseille's summer heat waves by moving into their *bastides*, as Provence's country houses are known. Respite for their working-class counterparts was largely limited to outings in public gardens and outdoor dance halls, until these resourceful Marseillais devised their own alternative to the *bastide*. Without title or sanction they put up makeshift beach, harbor, and hillside cabins, which sprouted wildly like rosemary along the rocky coastline. These so-called *cabanons* played a central role in the development of the bouillabaisse recipe and, more importantly, experience. Even the great chef Apollon Caillat would agree. "Anyone who has not tasted the authentique bouillabaisse," he noted, "and not joined in a cabanon party knows nothing and has seen nothing."

The bouillabaisse is not just a fish soup. It is a way of life. Perhaps the best recipe of all is the one in the popular 1950 song *La Bouillabaisse* immortalized by Fernandel:

To make a good bouillabaisse
It's necessary to rise early in the morning
To prepare pastis and cold water
To tell jokes with the hands

FOND DE POISSON POUR BOUILLABAISSE MARSEILLAISE

FISH STOCK FOR MARSEILLE-STYLE BOUILLABAISSE

This is the fish stock in which a *bouillabaisse marseillaise*—the classic *soupe d'or*—is prepared. In Marseille, the stock is made with tiny, cagey, flavorsome Mediterranean rockfish and eels: *congre* or *fiela* (conger eel), *girelle* (rainbow wrasse), *sar rouge* (from the sea bream family). I was not able to identify anything similar being widely available in North American fish markets, with the notable exception of purveyors in New York's and San Francisco's Chinatowns. As a result, it is necessary to use fish heads, frames, bones (perhaps from the very fish you will be using in your bouillabaisse) to extract as much flavor as possible. Ask your fishmonger which of his small and medium fish heads would be most suitable for a fish stock. Relatively bland fish (whiting) and oily fish (mackerel, bluefish, sardines) are out. The greater the variety the better the soup will be. Make sure that the fish are scaled and that the gills are removed.

MAKES 4 QUARTS

¼ cup olive oil

2 large onions, minced

2 leeks (whites only), minced

4 cloves garlic, crushed

3 pounds small to medium-sized fish heads, frames, and bones

6 to 8 ripe plum tomatoes, quartered

Peel of 1 orange, cut in strips

1 celery stalk, cut in pieces

2 sprigs thyme

3 bay leaves

¼ to ½ teaspoon cayenne

2 teaspoons pastis (Ricard or Pernod)

Salt

Freshly ground black pepper

4 quarts boiling water

1. Heat the olive oil in a large, heavy-bottomed stockpot over medium heat. Add the onions and leeks and cook gently, stirring often and making sure the onions and leeks do not turn color, for 10 minutes. Add the garlic and continue to cook, stirring often and lowering the heat if necessary so that the mixture does not brown, until the onions and leeks have softened and "melted" into the olive oil.

2. Add the fish heads, bones, and scraps, raise the heat to high, and cook, stirring often and

vigorously without concern about crushing, mashing, or otherwise bruising the fish parts, until the fish heads begin to fall apart, 7 to 10 minutes.

3. Add the tomatoes, orange peel, celery, thyme, bay leaves, cayenne, and pastis; season with salt and pepper. Cook, stirring continuously, and lowering the heat slightly if necessary to prevent burning, for 10 minutes.

4. Pour the boiling water over all, lower the heat, and cook at a simmer for 25 minutes.

5. Pass the mixture through a food mill or chinoise, working with small quantities of fish scraps and vegetables, wetting down with the bouillon to ease the flow. Be sure to press down on the fish scraps with a pestle or wooden spoon so their juices seep out. When crushing and squeezing the fish through the food mill or chinoise, do not give up early. Some of the tastiest and richest juices will be the last to be extracted. Use the hot bouillon judiciously, periodically wetting each batch of fish heads, bones, and scraps at the bottom of the food mill or chinoise to help you press out the juices. When you are sure there is no more juice to be had, discard the fish scraps and begin anew with the remaining batches. Let cool. Store in the refrigerator or freezer until ready to use.

VARIATION: Marseille chefs generally advise against preparing a bouillabaisse stock with mussels because their strong flavor changes the essential nature of the dish. Adding the juices of steamed mussels may, however, be encouraged whenever the supply of rockfish and their characteristic flavor is either limited or nonexistent. To prepare the mussels: Place 24 to 30 scrubbed and debearded mussels and 1 cup of water in a pot over medium heat, cover, and steam the mussels, shaking the pot frequently, until the mussels open, about 7 to 9 minutes. Remove the mussels with a slotted spoon, set aside, and, if not preparing the bouillabaisse until hours or days later, refrigerate. (The cooked mussels should be served alongside the fish and potatoes from the finished bouillabaisse.) Pour the mussel broth into the fish stock.

BOUILLABAISSE MARSEILLAISE

MARSEILLE-STYLE BOUILLABAISSE

One of the great challenges in putting together this cookbook was identifying suitable North American replacements for the distinctive Mediterranean fish used in an authentic *bouillabaisse*. Jacques Dupuy helped me undertake this courageous task. Together we sampled and analyzed the flavors and character of a rendition at a Marseille restaurant famous for bouillabaisse. Later we attempted to concoct a genuine-tasting interpretation and thus create a fine recipe using only fish from the Atlantic.

According to the Charte de la Bouillabaisse Marseillaise, a 1979 charter drawn up and signed by eleven restaurants, the classic *soupe d'or* must be prepared with at least four of the following fish types to be genuine: *rascasse* (scorpion fish), *chapon* (similar to rascasse), *galinette* (a gurnard), *Saint Pierre* (John Dory), monkfish, and *fielas* (conger eel). For an American without access to—or spare cash for—expensive imports, getting a hold of two of these fish, much less four, is a tricky business. But let's start with the easy part: There is no excuse for making a bouillabaisse without the one definitive fish that is readily available: monkfish.

American counterparts to *rascasse, chapon,* and *fielas* can be fished from the Pacific Ocean kelp forests and rocky sea bottoms off the California coast. But due to a number of environmental factors, the California eels, rockfish, and moray eels are increasingly rare. Most of us will have to make do without them.

John Dory is, however, found in quality fish markets. And red mullets, a great Mediterranean passion, may also be available (if they are, snatch them up). Otherwise, the best, widely distributed replacement fish are (in order of preference): red snapper (to replace rascasse), halibut, porgy, pompano, turbot, striped bass, Chilean sea bass, grouper, tilapia, hake. Whichever you do choose, variety produces the best possible bouillabaisse. Fillets are easier to work with, but, by eliminating the bones, their flavor goes with them. I am, however, generally against the addition of shellfish. A fish soup made with heaps of lobster, shrimp, mussels, and clams may be delicious. But it is not a Marseille-style bouillabaisse. It is fine to enrich your soup with some mussels, prawns, and shrimp or shrimp shells. But do not overdo it.

A bouillabaisse is generally served in two stages: first the soup, then the fish. But dissenter André Rieusset, owner of the Restaurant Camors in L'Estaque, makes a good case for reversing the order. Because the fish are the stars of this great dish, why risk filling up your dinner guests on soup and croutons long before the fish has made its entrance? The best solution is to serve the bouillabaisse in three stages: first croutons and soup (but not too much), then fish and potatoes, then more soup!

This recipe, like much of this book's bouillabaisse lore, was put together with the invaluable assistance of food scholar Jacques Dupuy. Part of his current research involves tracing the origins of bouillabaisse and proving his theory that they are Gaul, which is to say, French, rather than Greek. Regardless, this bouillabaisse here is unmistakably Marseillaise.

MAKES 8 TO 10 SERVINGS

6 to 8 pounds fish (less if using fillets), choosing among John Dory, red mullets, red snapper (the smaller the better), porgy, pompano, turbot, striped bass, Chilean sea bass, grouper, tilapia, hake

1 tablespoon pastis (Ricard or Pernod)

1 to 1½ teaspoons saffron threads, crumbled

½ cup olive oil

Salt

Freshly ground black pepper

1 recipe Fish Stock for Marseille-Style Bouillabaisse (page 127)

2 pounds potatoes, peeled and cut into ⅓-inch slices

Cayenne, optional

1 cup Rouille (page 63)

1 baguette or country bread, cut into slices and dried in oven

2 cloves garlic, optional

1. Cut the firm-fleshed fish, notably the monkfish, into uniform pieces, removing any heads, bones, skin, and scraps as necessary. Cut the cleaned and gutted whole fish crosswise into sections about 3 inches in width.

2. Place all the fish pieces, sections, and fillets in a very large mixing bowl. Add the pastis, 2 pinches of crumbled saffron, and the olive oil. Season lightly with salt and pepper, and mix well without breaking up the fish. Cover the bowl with plastic wrap and let marinate in the refrigerator for at least 3 hours.

3. Pour the fish stock into a large, heavy-bottomed stockpot and set it over high heat. Add the remaining crumbled saffron, and bring the stock to a rapid boil.

4. Add the potatoes to the pot, bring the stock back to a boil, and cook the potatoes for 5 minutes. Add the monkfish and any other firm fish, bring the stock back to a boil, and

cook for 5 minutes. Add the remaining fish, firmer pieces on the bottom and flakier pieces and fillets on top, and boil for 10 to 15 minutes more. Correct the seasoning, adding some cayenne, if desired. You'll know the bouillabaisse is done when the potatoes are tender. Once they are, use some of the stock and the potatoes to complete the rouille.

5. TO SERVE, Delicately remove all the fish and potatoes from the soup with a slotted spoon and set aside. Rub the croutons with the garlic cloves, arrange on a serving dish, and place on the table alongside the rouille. (The diners will dab the croutons with rouille.) Have the diners place the croutons on the bottom of their shallow bowls and ladle the soup over them.

6. Next, remove whatever bones, skin, and inedible scraps you can from the fish. Arrange all the fish and potatoes on a large serving platter. Ladle some hot soup over the fish and potatoes and serve.

A bouillabaisse set to cook at the restaurant Le Miramar.

BOUILLABAISSE DU PÊCHEUR

FISHERMAN'S BOUILLABAISSE

This is a one-step bouillabaisse. Its thin bouillon evokes the rustic soup first prepared by fishermen on the beaches of Marseille and the French-Mediterranean coast. It is based on the recipe of Adrienne Tassara, who lives in a house in Vallon des Auffes beside the famous restaurant Chez Fonfon.

MAKES 8 TO 10 SERVINGS

6 to 8 pounds fish (less if using fillets), choosing among monkfish, John Dory, red mullets, red snapper, porgy, pompano, turbot, striped bass, Chilean sea bass, grouper, tilapia, hake
1 tablespoon pastis (Ricard or Pernod)
1 to 1½ teaspoons saffron threads, crumbled
¾ cup olive oil
3 large onions, sliced
4 cloves garlic, crushed
1 bulb fennel, chopped
6 to 8 ripe plum tomatoes, quartered
1 bay leaf
Salt
Freshly ground black pepper
2 pounds potatoes, peeled and cut into ¼-inch slices
Cayenne, optional
1 recipe Rouille (page 63)
1 baguette or country bread, cut into slices and dried in oven

1. Cut the firm-fleshed fish, notably the monkfish, into uniform pieces, removing any heads, bones, skin, and scraps as necessary. Cut the cleaned, gutted, and very carefully dried whole fish crosswise into sections about 3 inches in width.

2. Place all the fish pieces, sections, and fillets in a very large mixing bowl. Add the pastis, 2 pinches crumbled saffron, and ½ cup olive oil and mix well without injuring the fish. Cover the bowl with plastic wrap and let marinate in the refrigerator for at least 3 hours.

3. Heat the remaining ¼ cup olive oil in a large, heavy-bottomed stockpot over medium heat. Add the onions and cook gently, stirring often and making sure the onions do not turn color, for 10 minutes. Add 3 garlic cloves and fennel and continue to cook, stirring often and lowering the heat if necessary so that the mixture does not brown, until the onions and fennel have softened and "melted" into the olive oil. Add the tomatoes and the bay leaf, season with salt and pepper, and cook, stirring

continuously, and lowering the heat slightly if necessary to prevent burning, for 5 minutes.

4. Place the potatoes in an even layer on the bottom of the pot over the vegetables. Top with the fish in even compact layers, first the monkfish, the flakier fish, and the fillets. Top all with just enough water to cover. Raise the heat to high and bring to a rapid boil. Continue to cook until the potatoes are tender. This should occur soon after the mixture reaches a rapid boil. After adding the water, the total cooking time should be between 25 and 30 minutes. Correct the seasoning, adding some cayenne, if desired. Use some of the stock and the potatoes to complete the rouille.

5. TO SERVE, Delicately remove all the fish and potatoes from the soup with a slotted spoon and set aside. Pour the soup through a strainer to remove the vegetable pieces. Rub the toasted baguette slices with the remaining garlic clove, arrange on a serving dish, and place on the table alongside the rouille. (The diners will dab the croutons with rouille before putting them into their soup bowls.) Have the diners place the croutons on the bottom of their shallow bowls and ladle the soup over them.

6. For the next course, remove whatever bones, skin, and inedible scraps you can from the fish. Arrange all the fish and potatoes on a large serving platter. Ladle some hot soup over the fish and potatoes and serve.

COMPRESSÉ DE BOUILLABAISSE PORTE DE L'ORIENT

BOUILLABAISSE TERRINE

Admittedly, Gérald Passédat's bouillabaisse terrine lacks the gusto of a great fisherman's stew. Upon first view, I noted that the intricate fish loaf resembled not so much a terrine as some ingenious or dehydrated food developed for explorers from Planet Mars, as Marseille was tagged by the rap group IAM. But my condescension was soon replaced by admiration when I came to appreciate Passédat's accomplishment: In compressing the essential elements of a bouillabaisse, this great fish chef showed me just how well these strong and unwieldy flavors play together and solo. (In a terrine served cool, the broth needs to be much more densely seasoned than it would be in a hot bouillabaisse.) The garlicky, peppery rouille was clearly the rhythm section, beating loudly and drawing out but not drowning the fish, the saffron, and the familiar medley of olive oil, leeks, potatoes, pastis, and tomato.

One of the two fish Gérald uses in his terrine, the galinette, is impossible to find in U.S. markets; the other, rouget, is scarce. As substitutions I've proposed monkfish, an authentic bouillabaisse ingredient whose firmness holds up well in the terrine, and porgy, whose conspicuous flavor is roughly comparable to rouget's. (Remember to check for bones down the middle of the porgy fillet, pulling them out with tweezers.) Naturally, if you can get your hands on rouget (or red mullet), that would be even better.

MAKES 10 TO 12 SERVINGS

2 large potatoes, peeled and thinly sliced

1 pinch saffron threads, crumbled

Salt

1 onion, minced

1½ teaspoons coarse salt

1 pound monkfish fillets, cut into slices about ¾ inch thick

1 pound porgy fillets

2 cups Fish Stock for Marseille-Style

Bouillabaisse (page 127)

2 packets powdered unflavored gelatin

½ pound ripe plum tomatoes, diced

1 tablespoon chopped fresh thyme

2 tablespoons Rouille (page 63) or 2 tablespoons Aïoli (page 62) combined with a pinch of cayenne

1 baguette or country bread, thinly sliced and toasted

1. Place the potatoes and saffron threads in 3 cups boiling salted water and cook until the potatoes are tender, 20 to 25 minutes. Remove the potatoes with a slotted spoon, place in a bowl, cover with cold water, and set aside. Add the minced onion to the same liquid and cook at a simmer to flavor the broth, about 10 minutes. Pass the saffron broth through a fine sieve to strain out the onion. Discard the onion. Set aside the broth.

2. Scatter the coarse salt over the bottom of the saucepan and heat over high heat. Add the monkfish and porgy fillets and cover with the fish stock. When the liquid begins to bubble, lower the heat, and poach the fish at a simmer, not letting the liquid boil again, until the fish is cooked through, about 10 minutes for the porgy, a little longer for the monkfish. Remove the fish with a slotted spatula. Set aside the monkfish and refrigerate the porgy. Leave the fish broth in the saucepan.

3. Sprinkle one packet of the gelatin into ¼ cup cold water and let soak until the mixture is translucent, about 3 minutes.

4. Reheat the fish broth over low heat, stir in the gelatin, and cook until fully dissolved, 2 to 3 minutes. Remove from the heat.

5. Line an oiled 1-quart terrine or loaf pan with plastic wrap (the plastic should hang at least an inch over the sides of the terrine or loaf pan).

6. Drain the potatoes and place in an even layer on the bottom of the terrine or loaf pan.

7. Combine the tomatoes with the thyme and rouille, season with salt, and mix well. Spread the tomato mixture in an even layer over the potatoes.

8. Cut the monkfish fillets into large fingers and distribute them in an even layer over the tomatoes (if you have 12 monkfish fingers, make 4 evenly spaced columns of 3 fingers each).

9. Stir the fish stock to make sure the gelatin is still fully dissolved (if it is not, it must be reheated). Pour it into the pan, pressing down the monkfish so that the fish pieces are covered by the liquid. Refrigerate, making sure the terrine pan is on an even level, for 1 hour.

10. A few minutes before taking out the terrine, sprinkle the second gelatin packet into ¼ cup cold water and let soak until the mixture is translucent, about 3 minutes. Heat 1½ cups of the saffron broth in a saucepan over low heat, stir in the gelatin, and cook until fully dissolved, 2 to 3 minutes.

11. Remove the terrine from the refrigerator and make sure the gelatinized fish stock has solidified (if it has not, refrigerate for 30 minutes more). Remove the porgy fillets from the refrigerator, cut into fingers or small pieces, and distribute evenly inside the terrine over the solidified fish stock. Pour the gelatin-saffron broth over porgy fillets and refrigerate, again making sure the terrine is as level as possible, for at least 2 hours.

12. Turn the terrine over a serving dish and unmold by delicately lifting up the pan while holding down the exposed plastic wrap. Peel off the plastic and, with a serrated knife, delicately cut the terrine into ¾-inch slices. Serve with toast. The terrine will keep for two days.

FOND DE LÉGUMES POUR BOUILLABAISSE

VEGETABLE STOCK FOR BOUILLABAISSE

You will be hard-pressed to find a recipe, published or otherwise, for a vegetable bouillabaisse in which you are required to make a *fond*—"stock"—before assembling and preparing the actual bouillabaisse. Although a classic fish bouillabaisse is doubly enriched by cooking its potatoes and assorted fish in a previously made fish stock (a serious Marseille restaurant would not contemplate doing otherwise), going through the trouble of that initial phase is almost always eliminated for vegetable bouillabaisse. Its vegetables and seasonings are instead cooked in water that little by little absorbs its flavors and eventually turns into a fragrant soup.

This to me makes little sense. Since the soup in a vegetable bouillabaisse does not absorb the rich seafood juices that fortify the standard fish version, it becomes necessary to employ an abundance of onions, garlic, herbs, and tomatoes and to extract every last drop of taste from them. And the best way to accomplish that is by first preparing a vegetable stock whose ingredients are pressed and squeezed through a food mill.

Renée Brunet's recipe accomplishes exactly that. Her vegetable stock is the base for three fishless bouillabaisses, spinach (page 139), pea (page 140), and "one-eyed" (page 138), as well as a salt cod bouillabaisse. It is very much worth the trouble.

MAKES 3 QUARTS

¼ cup olive oil

2 onions, finely chopped

1 leek, white parts only, chopped

2 pounds ripe plum tomatoes, cut into chunks and some of the seeds removed

1 head of garlic, crushed

2 teaspoons pastis (Ricard or Pernod)

1 bouquet garni (thyme, rosemary, bay leaf)

½ teaspoon ground coriander seeds

Salt

Freshly ground black pepper
Cayenne

1. Heat the olive oil in a large saucepan or stockpot over medium heat. Add the onions and leek and cook until translucent but not yet golden, about 5 minutes.

2. Add the tomatoes, garlic, pastis, bouquet garni, and ground coriander. Season with salt, pepper, and cayenne. Raise the heat to

moderately high and cook, stirring occasionally, until the tomato chunks have softened and the onions and leek have turned a deep golden color, 5 to 7 minutes.

3. Add 3 quarts cold water and bring to a boil. Lower the heat to very low, cover tightly, and cook for 1 hour.

4. Pass the stock and vegetables through a food mill, extracting as much liquid and flavor from the vegetables as possible. Let cool and store in the refrigerator.

Chef Jean-Michel Minguella prepares his bouillabaise with vive, a Mediterranean rockfish.

BOUILLABAISSE BORGNE

ONE-EYED BOUILLABAISSE

Known alternatively as the poor man's bouillabaisse, this fishless Provençal classic known as *borgne*—"one-eyed"—for the single poached egg that floats atop each serving. Serving the bouillabaisse with a side salad stretches a soothing soup into a satisfying meal.

MAKES 6 SERVINGS

¼ cup olive oil

4 pounds medium potatoes (about 12), peeled and cut into ½-inch slices

1 recipe Vegetable Stock for Bouillabaisse (page 136)

2 pinches saffron threads, crumbled

6 eggs

1 country bread or baguette, cut into ½-inch slices, dried in the oven

½ cup Rouille (page 63) or 1 clove garlic

½ cup (2 ounces) freshly grated Parmesan cheese or shredded Gruyère

¼ cup chopped fresh parsley

1. Pour the olive oil into a large stockpot. Place the potato slices over the olive oil in even layers on the bottom of the pot. Heat over high heat for 2 minutes. Pour in the vegetable stock, add the saffron, and cook until the potatoes are soft, 25 to 30 minutes. Taste the broth and correct the seasoning.

2. Working in batches of 2 or 3 eggs at a time, crack each egg, and, holding it over the broth, lightly drop it in. Cook at a simmer for 4 minutes. Remove the poached eggs with a slotted spoon and place in cold water to stop the cooking. You may find it much easier to handle the poached eggs, as this recipe's author, Renée Brunet, suggests, by poaching them separately one or two at a time in a smaller saucepan with some bubbling broth from the bouillabaisse.

3. TO SERVE, place 3 slices of bread on the bottom of each of 6 soup bowls. Top each slice of bread with a teaspoon or so of rouille, if desired, (if not using rouille, rub a clove of garlic over the bread slices) and then a generous amount of grated cheese.

4. Place some potato slices and then a single poached egg in each bowl. Ladle the broth over the bread, the potato slices, and the poached egg. Sprinkle all with parsley.

BOUILLABAISSE D'EPINARDS

SPINACH BOUILLABAISSE

I first accepted spinach bouillabaisse as a substitute for the fish bouillabaisse after sampling Jeanne Moreni's wonderfully hearty and homespun version at her fine Marseille restaurant, Les Echevins. I stopped thinking of spinach bouillabaisse as a substitute for the fish bouillabaisse after preparing Renée Brunet's recipe for family and friends at my apartment in New York. When my cousin Philoméne noted with glee that she could not identify a single dominant flavor, say garlic or saffron, I knew the soup possessed the balanced medley of flavors that distinguish an outstanding bouillabaisse. The spinach variety stands on its own.

MAKES 6 SERVINGS

2 pounds spinach

¼ cup olive oil

1 onion, chopped

2 pounds medium potatoes (about 6), peeled and cut into ½-inch slices

2 pinches saffron threads, crumbled

1 recipe Vegetable Stock for Bouillabaisse (page 136)

Salt

6 eggs, optional

1 country bread or baguette, cut into ½-inch slices, dried in the oven

½ cup Rouille (page 63) or Aïoli (page 62)

1. Thoroughly wash the spinach leaves in water and remove the tougher stems. Plunge the spinach into a large pot of rapidly boiling water and blanch for 2 minutes. Remove, drain, and coarsely chop the spinach.

2. Heat the olive oil in a large stockpot over medium heat. Add the chopped onion and cook until translucent, about 5 minutes. Place the potato slices over the onion, add the saffron, spinach, and top all with the vegetable stock. Raise the heat and cook until the potatoes are tender, about 25 minutes. Taste the broth and correct the seasoning.

3. If serving with poached eggs: Working in batches of 2 to 3 eggs at a time, break each egg, and, holding it over the broth, lightly drop it in (you may wish to poach the eggs separately in a small saucepan half-filled with bubbling broth). Cook at a simmer for

4 minutes. Remove the poached eggs with a slotted spoon and place in cold water to stop the cooking.

4. TO SERVE, place 3 slices of bread on the bottom of each of 6 soup bowls. Top each slice of bread with a teaspoon or so of rouille or aïoli, if desired. Place the potatoes, spinach, and a poached egg in each bowl, if desired, and top all with the broth.

A PEA BOUILLABAISSE, which is every bit as traditional as the spinach and salt cod versions, can be made by substituting 1 quart shelled fresh peas (about $1\frac{1}{3}$ pounds) for the spinach (there is no need to blanch the peas). You may also combine the two, using 1 pound spinach and 2 cups peas. The peas do not have to be blanched.

BOUILLABAISSE DE POULET

CHICKEN BOUILLABAISSE

If bouillabaisse can be made with vegetables, why not chicken? The traditional flavors—garlic, saffron, pastis—make for an excellent chicken soup. This recipe comes from home cook Janine Palazzolo.

MAKES 4 SERVINGS

¼ cup olive oil

1 medium onion, sliced

3 cloves garlic

5 canned plum tomatoes, sliced

1 whole chicken (4 pounds), cut into 8 pieces

1 bouquet garni (thyme, bay leaf, parsley)

2 cups chicken broth

1 cup water

1 cup dry white wine

2 pinches saffron threads, crumbled

1 teaspoon pastis (Ricard or Pernod)

1 small pinch cayenne

Salt

Freshly ground black pepper

½ cup Rouille (page 63) or Aïoli (page 62)

1 baguette or country bread, sliced and lightly toasted

3 cups cooked rice

1. Heat the olive oil in a casserole over medium heat. Add the onion and garlic and cook, stirring occasionally, for 5 minutes.

2. Add the tomatoes, chicken pieces, and bouquet garni and cook, occasionally stirring the chicken with the vegetables, for 4 minutes.

3. Add the chicken broth, water, white wine, saffron, pastis, and cayenne, season with salt and pepper, raise the heat to high, and heat to a boil. Lower the heat to medium and cook at a boil for 25 minutes.

4. TO SERVE, Arrange the toasted baguette slices on a serving dish, and place on the table alongside the rouille or the aïoli. Have the diners dab the slices with rouille or aïoli and place them on the bottom of their shallow soup bowls. Ladle soup over the slices.

5. For the next course, spoon some rice into each bowl and top with one or two chicken pieces. Ladle soup over the chicken and rice and serve.

BOUILLABAISSE DE MORUE

SALT COD BOUILLABAISSE

The salt cod bouillabaisse is a rustic and not terribly noble version traditionally prepared by inland Provençals for whom fresh fish was either geographi-
cally or financially out of reach.

Nevertheless, there are those who use salt cod in their soup out of personal preference. It holds its firm texture under poaching, its flavor is a natural match for the soup's garlic and saffron, and there are few bones to contend with. Other Marseillais may regard the preserved salt cod as fish
insurance should mistral winds strand the local fishermen at port.

The salt cod bouillabaisse can be served, like the more famous Marseille
version, in two stages: first the soup alone over the croutons; later the potatoes and salt cod, kept warm periodically with some hot broth.

MAKES 6 SERVINGS

2 pounds salt cod fillets

$\frac{1}{4}$ cup olive oil

1 onion, chopped

2 pounds medium potatoes (about 6), peeled and
   cut into $\frac{1}{2}$-inch slices

3 pinches saffron threads, crumbled

1 recipe Vegetable Stock for Bouillabaisse
   (page 136)

6 eggs, optional

1 country bread or baguette, cut into $\frac{1}{2}$-inch
   slices, dried in the oven

$\frac{1}{2}$ cup Rouille (page 63) or Aïoli (page 62)

1. The day before you plan to serve: Soak the
   salt cod fillets in cold water, changing the
   water 3 or 4 times, for 24 hours. Drain.

2. Heat the olive oil in a large stockpot over
   medium heat. Add the chopped onion and
   cook until translucent, about 5 minutes.
   Place the potato slices over the onion, add
   the crumbled saffron, and top all with the
   vegetable stock. Raise the heat and cook for
   15 minutes.

3. Lower the temperature to take the broth
   down from a boil to a simmer. Cut the salt
   cod fillets into 3-inch pieces, add to the pot,
   and cook at a simmer for 15 minutes. (If the
   potatoes are not yet tender, remove the salt
   cod with a slotted spoon, top with a little
   broth to keep warm, and continue to cook
   the potatoes 5 minutes more.) Taste the
   broth and correct the seasoning.

4. If serving with poached eggs: Working in batches of 2 to 3 eggs at a time, break each egg, and, holding it over the broth, lightly drop it in. (You may wish to poach the eggs separately in a small saucepan half-filled with bubbling broth taken from the bouillabaisse pot.) Cook at a simmer for 4 minutes. Remove the poached eggs with a slotted spoon and place in cold water to stop the cooking.

5. TO SERVE, place 3 slices of bread on the bottom of each of 6 soup bowls. Top each slice of bread with a teaspoon or so of rouille or aïoli, if desired. Place the potatoes and salt cod fillets over the bread slices, place a poached egg over each serving, and top all with the broth.

Fish

Filet de Sole Farci aux Epinards, Beurre Blanc Safranée
FILLET OF SOLE STUFFED WITH SPINACH IN A SAFFRON BEURRE BLANC

Saumon en Peau de Courgette et Chèvre Frais, et Coulis de Tomates
ZUCCHINI-WRAPPED SALMON FILLETS WITH GOAT CHEESE AND TOMATO SAUCE

Filet de Saumon Farci de Fenouil, Gratiné à la Confiture D'Oignon
FENNEL-STUFFED SALMON FILLET WITH ONION JAM

Truite à la Tomate
FILLET OF TROUT WITH TOMATO

Filet de Poisson au Beurre de Colombo
FISH FILLETS WITH CARIBBEAN CURRY BUTTER SAUCE

Millefeuille de Loup en Croustillant de Tapenade, Tomates Confit et Poêlee de Différents Pois
NAPOLEON OF SEA BASS AND TAPENADE WITH TOMATO CONFIT AND PEAS

Filet de Poisson aux Aromates dans Son Fumet de Champignon
NUT-ENCRUSTED STRIPED BASS FILLET WITH ASIAN SPICES AND SOY MUSHROOM CONSOMMÉ

Boulettes de Poisson à la Sauce Tomate
FISH BALLS IN TOMATO SAUCE

Poisson Grillé à L'Escale
WHOLE FISH GRILLED IN THE STYLE OF L'ESCALE

Ragoût de Lotte et Gambas au Jus de Bandol
MONKFISH AND PRAWN STEW WITH BANDOL WINE JUS

Marmite du Pêcheur
FISHERMAN'S STEW

Noix de Saint Jacques Poêlées aux Légumes, Panisses au Basilic, et Tapenade avec Tomates Confites
SEA SCALLOPS WITH SAUTÉED VEGETABLES, BASIL PANISSES, TAPENADE, AND TOMATO CONFIT

Coquilles Saint-Jacques au Sel d'Orange, Endive Caramelisée
SAUTÉED SEA SCALLOPS WITH CARAMELIZED ENDIVE AND ORANGE SALT

Gambas Rotis au Miel et Gingembre
GINGER HONEY SHRIMP

Brochette de Langoustines aux Saint Jacques, Bisque de Crustacés
PRAWN AND SCALLOP BROCHETTE WITH SEAFOOD BISQUE

MY MAIN REGRET in adapting my favorite Marseille fish dishes for North American cooks is in not having suitable saltwater substitutions to suggest for some of the prized Mediterranean fish largely unavailable in our markets. Yes, it would be nice to go to my local fishmonger and behold the brilliant gray-silver sheen of the legendary loup; the pink skin, blue-dotted line, and beautiful eye—*bel oeil*—of the pageot; the distinctive black mark under the gills of the daurade royale; and the fine pink skin of the smallest rouget (red mullet). But though we do not have anything that quite matches the delicate flavor of the Marseillais daurade, pageot, and sar (a third member of the sea bream family), we can count on striped bass or Chilean sea bass to cover for loup and medium-sized red mullets to stand in for the tiniest rougets. Moreover, we have our own sources for tuna, monkfish, and sole.

What I miss most is not having access to fish that has just been pulled up from the sea and has not spent the previous several hours, much less days, over ice. A freshly caught loup grilled that same day has considerably more flavor and finesse than a striped bass packed in ice long before it reaches the grill; there is no doubt of this. But if I can't physically transport you to the open-air fish market of Marseille's Quai de Belges, where fishermen unload their prized catches nearly every morning at 9:00 A.M., the following recipes will bestow upon Atlantic and Pacific fish the look and, more important, the taste of France's great Mediterranean seaport. Besides, as this book makes very clear, you don't have to be born in Marseille to be Marseillais.

The Thumbprints of Saint Pierre

In the Book of Matthew, chapter 17, Jesus instructs Peter to "go thou to the sea, and cast a hook, and take up the fish that first cometh up; and when thou

PAGE 144: Fishermen Bernard Grondona (left), his son Pierre (center), and Eric André leave the Old Port.

hast opened his mouth, thou shalt find a piece of money there." According to popular legend, the two dark round spots found on the backs of the fish known in English as John Dory are the thumbprints forever left by Saint Peter when he extracted the coin. Hence the alternative name for the fish— Saint Peter or, in French, Saint Pierre.

The legend overlooks one significant detail. The John Dory is a saltwater fish unlikely to be found in the freshwaters where Saint Peter would have cast his hook, namely Lake Geneserah or the Sea of Galilee. Yet if the fish were somehow swimming in so unnatural a habitat, that might explain how he came to swallow a gold coin.

What is not easily disputed is the quality of the Saint Pierre. Its flesh, at once firm and delicate, and delectable flavor make it one of the most refined and sought-after fish of the Mediterranean. The young Saint Pierre, caught off the shores of Marseille in late spring, are the most prized by chefs if not always by fishermen. The smaller size of the young Saint Pierre compounds the problem of there not being much to eat on them in the first place. The head and bones of a Saint Pierre account for over half their total weight. That, rather than the gold coin that might be found in its mouth, accounts for the Saint Pierre's high price.

The Sardine That Blocked the Port of Marseille

In a city that would like to dispel its reputation for exaggeration, no fish tale is taller, better known, or, to many Marseillais, more irritating than the legend of the sardine who blocked the port of Marseille. "The Marseillais are justly irritated by this story," says writer Philippe Carrese. "Like all clichés that tread over this city it passes us off as likable cretins. Likable, yes, but cretins none the less." Their aggravation might be alleviated if everyone could get together and agree upon the story's factual origins. The continuing presence of several hypotheses, coupled with the lack of irrefutable historical documents, only enhances the storytelling stereotype.

In most accounts, the explanation for this preposterous event—the tiniest of fish blocking the greatest of France's seaports—is simple: Sardine is either the name or something close to the name of a boat, presumably a very large boat. According to one version, a five-hundred-fifty-ton frigate carrying the name of *M. de Sartine*, the Count of Alby, ran aground at the entrance to the Old Port in May 1780. This event is confirmed in the memoirs of the Viscount Paul-Nicolas-François Barras, who was aboard the *Sartine* at the time, and blamed the event on the poor steering and, perhaps also, if the story is to be believed, the bad diction of the inexperienced captain.

Another telling dates back to 1793 and the heroic intervention of Captain Georges-Jean Danjard, commander of the brig *La Sardine*, then based in the French Port of Toulon. When the Port of Marseille was threatened by the English fleet, Danjard navigated the *Sardine* in a position to protect merchant ships from the English menace. In a deposition dated March 30, 1793, Captain Danjard confirmed the entrance of his boat, *La Sardine*, in the Port of Marseille.

I give less credence to the first account, as it requires two leaps of faith. I can accept the fact that a sardine blocked the Port of Marseille. Pound for pound it's one powerful beast. But I cannot fathom anyone mistaking a sartine for a sardine.

Loule Fromion watches his sons André and Eric unload their prized catch.

FILET DE SOLE FARCI AUX EPINARDS, BEURRE BLANC SAFRANÉE

FILLET OF SOLE STUFFED WITH SPINACH IN A SAFFRON BEURRE BLANC

How fitting for a whimsical bistro called La Giraffe to be having such fun with fish. The coils of spinach-stuffed sole (their assembly is surprisingly straightforward) contain inner swirls of green set again the beurre blanc's saffron yellow.

MAKES 4 SERVINGS

10 tablespoons butter
1½ pounds spinach, washed and tough stems removed
Salt
Freshly ground black pepper
4 sole fillets, about 6 ounces each
2 tablespoons finely chopped shallots
¼ cup white wine vinegar
¼ cup dry white wine
1 pinch saffron threads, crumbled

1. Heat 2 tablespoons butter in a saucepan over moderately high heat. Add the spinach, season with salt and pepper, and cook, tossing the spinach with a fork, until wilted, about 2 minutes.

2. Preheat the oven to 350 degrees. Butter a 9 by 13-inch metal roasting pan.

3. Season the sole fillets lightly with salt and cover each completely with a very thin layer of spinach, not letting the spinach overlap the fillets. Roll the fillets over the spinach.

Cut each bundle widthwise with a very sharp knife into half-inch slices. Place these sole-and-spinach coils flat in a single layer on the bottom of the prepared pan. Bake until the fish is cooked through, about 5 minutes.

4. To prepare the saffron beurre blanc: Place the shallots, white wine vinegar, and white wine in a saucepan over moderately high heat, season with salt, and heat until most of the liquid has evaporated, about 5 minutes. Turn down the heat to very low. Cut the remaining 8 tablespoons (1 stick) butter into tiny cubes and whisk a little of the butter at a time into the shallots. Just as each piece of butter dissolves add another. As the last piece of butter disappears into the sauce whisk in the crumbled saffron threads. Remove from the heat, whisk a few more times, and serve immediately, spooning the sauce on the center of each plate and topping it with the spinach-stuffed sole fillets.

SAUMON EN PEAU DE COURGETTE ET CHÈVRE FRAIS, ET COULIS DE TOMATES

ZUCCHINI-WRAPPED SALMON FILLETS WITH GOAT CHEESE AND TOMATO SAUCE

Olivier Vettorel normally wraps his goat cheese–stuffed salmon fillets handkerchief style in ultra-thin slices of eggplant. But he is proposing zucchini as a more practical substitute.

MAKES 4 SERVINGS

1 cup Provençal Tomato Sauce (page 68) or any
    tomato sauce
4 salmon fillets, 5 to 6 ounces each and at least ½
    inch thick
12 ounces goat cheese, thinly sliced
3 zucchini
Salt
Freshly ground black pepper
¼ cup olive oil
¼ cup chopped fresh basil

1. Heat the tomato sauce in a saucepan, remove from the heat, and cover to keep warm.

2. With a very sharp knife, make a deep horizontal cut through the side of each salmon fillet, making sure you do not cut all the way through to the other side. Working with one fillet at a time, lift its top, lay a quarter of the goat cheese slices across the middle, and then close the top half of the fillet over the cheese.

3. Using a mandoline, vegetable slicer, or cheese slicer, cut the zucchini lengthwise into long, very thin slices. Season on both sides with salt and pepper.

4. Place 3 or 4 zucchini slices together like the fingers of your hand, sides touching, over a clean work surface. Lay a stuffed salmon fillet perpendicular over the middle of the zucchini slices. Repeat with the remaining zucchini and salmon fillets.

5. To sauté the salmon bundles: Heat the olive oil in a large skillet over moderately high heat. Working with one fish bundle at a time, fold the zucchini from top and bottom over the fish fillet to completely envelop it. Ideally, the zucchini slices should just meet or slightly overlap on the top side of the fish. (If they're too long, snip them down to size.) Holding the zucchini in place, invert the fish bundles and place in the skillet, seam side down, and cook until golden, about 3 minutes. Turn and cook until golden, about 3 minutes. Drain over paper towels.

6. Add the basil to the tomato sauce, spoon over the zucchini-salmon bundles, and serve.

FILET DE SAUMON FARCI DE FENOUIL, GRATINÉ À LA CONFITURE D'OIGNON

FENNEL-STUFFED SALMON FILLET WITH ONION JAM

Giselle Philippi of the restaurant Le Sud en Haut just won't compromise. Instead of choosing between caramelized fennel and onion jam to sweeten her salmon fillets she uses them both. To prevent this from being cloying, she relies on lemon juice to offset the sweetness. The smell as the honey cooks and caramelizes makes me downright dizzy. Later, it has a similar effect on the salmon.

MAKES 4 SERVINGS

3 fennel bulbs, peeled and halved
4 tablespoons unsalted butter
1 tablespoon honey
1 tablespoon lemon juice
1½ pounds salmon fillet, at least ½ inch thick
Salt
Freshly ground black pepper
1 tablespoon olive oil
½ cup Onion Jam (page 64)
½ cup bread crumbs

1. Place the fennel in a steamer over an inch or two of lightly salted water, cover, bring the water to a boil, and cook over medium heat for 15 minutes. Remove from the heat, let cool, and cut into slices.

2. Heat 2 tablespoons butter over moderately high heat. Place the fennel, honey, and 2 teaspoons lemon juice in the pan and cook, stirring occasionally, until the fennel turns golden and caramelizes, about 5 minutes. Reduce the heat to very low and cook gently until the fennel is soft and melted, 10 to 15 minutes.

3. Preheat the oven to 350 degrees. Oil a 9 by 13-inch metal roasting pan. Using a very sharp knife, make a deep horizontal cut through the side of the salmon fillet, making sure you do not cut all the way through to the other side. Lift the top, season the middle with salt and pepper, drizzle with olive oil and the remaining lemon juice. Lay the caramelized fennel in an even layer across the middle, lay the top flap of the salmon back over the fennel, and place the salmon on the prepared pan. Spoon the onion jam over the fish as evenly as possible and dust the top with bread crumbs. Cut the remaining 2 tablespoons butter into small cubes, scatter over the fish toppings, season with salt and pepper, and bake for 30 minutes. Serve immediately.

TRUITE À LA TOMATE
FILLET OF TROUT WITH TOMATO

As improbable as it sounds, there are many Marseillais—and not all of them "émigrés" from Paris, as locals are wont to believe—who have no idea what to do with a piece of fish. Fishmonger Neige Perez advises dozens of them, often young professionals entertaining their in-laws for the first time, in her tiny shop in the affluent Bompard quarter.

This trout recipe could be page 1 of Neige's Workbook for Cooking Fish 101. There are no fish bones to fillet, no tomatoes to peel, and no saucepans to clean. Cooked together in a single roasting pan, the capers, olives, onions, tomatoes, garlic, olive oil, white wine, and trout fillets conspire to create a wonderful, unmistakably Mediterranean ensemble sure to entice even Marseillais who were scaling and gutting fish—or so they say—before they could walk.

MAKES 4 SERVINGS

4 trout fillets, about 6 ounces each
Salt
1 tablespoon capers
2 tablespoons green olives, pitted
8 to 10 pearl onions, chopped
1 pound ripe plum tomatoes, chopped
1 tablespoon chopped parsley
1 clove garlic, chopped
1 cup dry white wine
3 tablespoons olive oil
Freshly ground black pepper

1. Preheat the oven to 425 degrees.
2. Place the trout fillets on an oiled baking dish and season with salt.
3. Combine the capers, green olives, pearl onions, tomatoes, chopped parsley, and chopped garlic and spoon the mixture over the trout fillets.
4. Pour the white wine over the fillets and vegetables, drizzle with olive oil, season with salt and pepper, and bake until the fillets are just cooked through, about 20 minutes.

FILET DE POISSON AU BEURRE DE COLOMBO

FISH FILLETS WITH CARIBBEAN CURRY BUTTER SAUCE

You may be wondering what Colombo spice powder and Caribbean curry butter sauce are doing in a Marseille cookbook. But considering the mania for Colombo, a staple of the French West Indies, with Marseillais from Guadeloupe, Martinique, and Senegal, its exclusion would have been more glaring. A cornerstone of Antillaise cuisine, the traditional blend of spices originated in Sri Lanka and was brought to the French Antilles by migrant laborers. It was renamed Colombo after the capital of Sri Lanka.

Similar to a hot curry powder, Colombo may contain coriander, cumin, cinnamon, nutmeg, cayenne pepper, mustard powder, turmeric, fenugreek, garlic powder, ground clove, and black pepper. It's used in this straightforward recipe from Gilles Garnier, a French chef who cooked in Guadeloupe for eight years before returning to France with his wife, Karine, and opening the mostly Provençal bistro L'Oliveraie at Marseille's Place aux Huiles.

MAKES 4 SERVINGS

1½ cups long grain white rice

2 ripe plantains, peeled and cut into ½-inch slices

1 tablespoon chopped shallots

½ cup dry white wine

¼ cup heavy cream

12 tablespoons (1½ sticks) unsalted butter

2 tablespoons Colombo powder (substitute spicy curry powder)

¼ cup all-purpose flour

4 skin-on firm-fleshed whitefish fillets, about 6 ounces each (red snapper, sea bass, cod)

1. In a saucepan bring 2½ cups of salted water to a boil. Slowly add the rice and return to a boil. Lower the heat, cover, and cook until the water is absorbed and the rice is soft, about 15 minutes.

2. In a separate saucepan bring 1 quart of salted water to a boil, add the sliced plantains, and cook at a boil until softened but not mushy, 6 to 10 minutes (semi-ripe plantains will take up to 30 minutes to cook).

3. Preheat the oven to 350 degrees.

4. Combine the shallots and white wine in a saucepan and cook over moderately high heat until most of the liquid has evaporated, about 5 minutes. Add the cream and cook

until its volume is reduced by half, 3 to 4 minutes.

5. Turn down the heat to very low. Cut 10 tablespoons of the butter into small chunks and whisk into the shallots a little at a time. Just as each piece of butter dissolves add another. As the last piece of butter disappears into the sauce, whisk in most of the Colombo powder, mix well, cover, and keep warm.

6. Heat the remaining 2 tablespoons butter in a skillet over high heat.

7. Place the flour in a shallow dish. Dip the fillets skin side down in the flour to coat their skin side only, place them skin side down in the skillet, and cook until well seared, 2 to 3 minutes. Transfer to a baking or roasting pan, uncooked side down, and cook in the oven until opaque all the way through, about 5 minutes.

8. TO SERVE, place a mound of rice in the middle of 4 plates, top each mound with some plaintain slices, and spoon Colombo butter around the rice and plantains. Place a fish fillet skin side up on top of each mound of rice and plantains, and dust all with the remaining Colombo powder. Serve immediately.

MILLEFEUILLE DE LOUP EN CROUSTILLANT DE TAPENADE, TOMATES CONFIT ET POÊLÉE DE DIFFÉRENTS POIS

NAPOLEON OF SEA BASS AND TAPENADE WITH TOMATO CONFIT AND PEAS

From the restaurant Le Charles Livon comes Christian Ernst's napoleonic tower of sautéed sea bass fillets layered with tapenade-filled phyllo rectangles and ornamented with tomato red and pea green.

SERVES 4

1 cup shelled peas or frozen peas

1½ cups snow peas or snap peas

1 cup shelled fava beans

12 tablespoons (1½ sticks) unsalted butter

4 sheets phyllo dough

1½ cups Tapenade (page 55)

Tomato Confit (page 67)

4 tablespoons olive oil

Coarse salt

1½ pounds striped bass fillets, cut into 8 evenly sized fillets

Salt

Freshly ground black pepper

1. Bring a pot of salted water to a boil. Drop in the shelled peas and boil for 2 to 3 minutes. Remove the peas with a slotted spoon and plunge in ice water to cool. Repeat the same for the snow peas or snap peas and then the fava beans.

2. To clarify the butter, place in a small saucepan and melt over low heat. Remove from the heat, skim off the foam, and set aside until the solids have settled to the bottom. Carefully pour off and reserve the clear fat, discarding the residue.

3. Preheat the oven to 350 degrees. Butter a 9 by 13-inch metal roasting pan.

4. Unravel the thawed sheets of phyllo dough and cover with a damp kitchen towel so they don't dry out. Place a sheet of phyllo on a dry work surface and brush with clarified butter. Top with a second sheet and brush with clarified butter. Spoon the tapenade over the second layer and, using a spatula, spread it out into a thin even layer. Top with a third sheet and brush with clarified butter.

Top with a fourth sheet and brush with clarified butter. Using a sharp knife, cut the phyllo-layered tapenade into 8 small rectangles or squares roughly the same size as the small fish fillets. Delicately transfer these rectangles to a buttered baking sheet and bake in the oven until crisp and golden, 10 to 12 minutes.

5. Lower the oven temperature to 250 degrees. Place the tomato confit in a small roasting pan and place in the oven.

6. Heat 1 to 2 tablespoons olive oil in a saucepan over moderately high heat. Drain and pat dry the peas and fava beans, place in the saucepan, and sauté, stirring occasionally, for 3 minutes. Remove from the heat and cover to keep warm.

7. Heat 2 tablespoons olive oil in a large skillet over moderately high heat. Sprinkle the bottom of the pan with a little coarse salt. Season the fish fillets with salt and pepper, place as many of them as will fit in the skillet, skin side down, and cook for 2 to 3 minutes, depending on the thickness of the fillet. Turn and cook for 2 minutes more. Remove the fillets from the pan. Repeat with the remaining fish.

8. To assemble the napoleons, place one sea bass fillet in the center of each of 4 plates. Top each with a tapenade rectangle, then another fish fillet, and finally a second tapenade rectangle. Decorate each side of the four-sided napoleons with the garnishes, alternating between the tomato confit and the peas.

FILET DE POISSON AUX AROMATES DANS SON FUMET DE CHAMPIGNON

NUT-ENCRUSTED STRIPED BASS FILLET WITH ASIAN SPICES AND SOY MUSHROOM CONSOMMÉ

So as not to shock his conservative Marseillais clientele with his Asian-Mediterranean fusion cuisine, chef Florent Saugeron of Lemon Grass always gives them some familiar tastes or elements to lean on. In this dish it is the peanuts, almonds, hazelnuts, and anise seeds that encrust the fish fillets, the honey that caramelizes the mushrooms, and the fresh lime juice that offsets their sweetness in the soy consommé. Don't be afraid of the relatively large quantity of soy sauce (¼ cup) in the consommé, as I initially was—it works fine.

MAKES 4 SERVINGS

3 tablespoons unsalted butter

¾ pound white mushrooms, halved

1 tablespoon honey

Juice of 1 lime

2 cups water

¼ cup soy sauce

1 teaspoon Chinese five spice powder

¼ teaspoon aniseed

3 tablespoons chopped peanuts

2 tablespoons chopped blanched almonds

2 tablespoons chopped blanched hazelnuts

Salt

Freshly ground black pepper

2 tablespoons heavy cream

4 striped bass fillets (6 to 8 ounces each), preferably with the skin on

¼ cup olive oil

1. Melt the butter in a saucepan over moderately high heat. Add the mushroom halves and cook until their color deepens and most of the liquid evaporates, about 5 minutes. Add the honey, lower the heat to medium, and cook until the mushrooms begin to caramelize, about 4 minutes. Add the lime juice to deglaze the pan. Add the water and soy sauce and bring to a boil. Remove from the heat, cover, and set aside.

2. Preheat the oven to 400 degrees. Combine the Chinese five spice powder, aniseed, peanuts, almonds, and hazelnuts in a shallow dish. Season with salt and pepper. In a separate shallow dish pour in the heavy cream.

3. Dip the striped bass fillets skin side down in the heavy cream, letting the excess liquid

drip off, and dredge the striped bass fillets skin side down in the spice-and-nut mixture.

4. Heat the olive oil in a skillet over moderately high heat. Place the striped bass fillets in the skillet skin side down and cook for 1 minute.

5. Transfer the fillets, flipping them so they are skin side up, to a nonstick baking pan, place in the oven, and cook for 2 to 3 minutes.

TO SERVE, pour the mushroom soup through a strainer to remove the mushrooms. Ladle the soup into 4 shallow soup bowls and top each with a fish fillet. Serve immediately.

BOULETTES DE POISSON À LA SAUCE TOMATE

FISH BALLS IN TOMATO SAUCE

This dish is a specialty of Marseille's Jews of North African origin. In Tunisia and Morocco, the *boulettes de poisson* are usually prepared in a tomato sauce or as part of a fish couscous. Benjamin Zuili, a Jew of Italian origin who immigrated to Marseille from Tunisia in 1983, serves his fish balls on a whim at L'Art et Les Thés. His café/tea salon and exhibition space is tucked beneath the arcades of the Vielle Charité. The pronounced cumin in the tomato sauce makes it clear that the dish reflects Zuili's Tunisian and not Italian roots. But figuring out whether his *gnocchi au pistou* is Provençal or Italian is more problematic.

MAKES 4 SERVINGS

1 pound white-fleshed fish fillets

3 to 4 slices bread

1 onion, finely chopped

1 egg, beaten

1 tablespoon chopped fresh mint

¼ cup chopped fresh parsley

Salt

Freshly ground black pepper

½ cup flour

3 tablespoons olive oil

1 teaspoon cumin

¼ teaspoon cayenne

2 cups Provençal Tomato Sauce (page 68) or
  any tomato sauce

Cooked couscous, optional

1. Place the fish fillets in a food processor and pulse just until the fish is ground but not pulverized to a mush. Place in a large mixing bowl.

2. Place the bread slices in a large mixing bowl, cover with water, and let soak for 30 seconds. Lift the bread from the bowl with your hands and squeeze out the water. Pour out the remaining water in the bowl and return the bread to the bowl. Add the fish along with the onion, egg, mint, and parsley. Season with salt and pepper and mix thoroughly with your hands into a smooth paste.

3. Place the flour in a shallow bowl. Moisten your hands and shape the fish mixture into smooth balls, about 1½ inches in diameter. Roll each fish ball in the flour to coat on all sides and place on a platter. Heat the olive oil in a large saucepan over moderately high heat. Place the fish balls in the saucepan and cook on all sides until golden, about 5 minutes. Stir the cumin and cayenne into the tomato sauce, pour over the fish balls, lower the flame, cover, and simmer for 25 minutes. Serve over cooked couscous, rice, or pasta.

POISSON GRILLÉ À L'ESCALE
WHOLE FISH GRILLED IN THE STYLE OF L'ESCALE

L'Escale, French for "the port of call," can easily be applied to any one of many so-named restaurants, bars, and hotels that dot French shores. Prior to the modern era of cell phones, fewer romantic seaside trysts were frustrated by jealous spouses than by heedless paramours who left word for their lovers to meet them at the Restaurant L'Escale without specifying which one. Therefore, let's be clear exactly which *escale* and which L'Escale we're talking about: The port of call is of course Marseille or, as it was known to the Greeks who founded it, Massalia. The restaurant is the one perched over the fishing village of Les Goudes at the southern end of the Marseille coastline, where I first came to understand how a town's fabled fish could reverse the course of a Greek proverb, a French novel, or this American's culinary education.

That this discovery could have transpired at another dining terrace in the same village—Chez Aldo or Le Tiboulen de Maïre—proves only that this fish mastery is more about a bond between a people and their fish than any single chef or personality. Nevertheless, it was the passion of L'Escale's Serge Zarokian and, more precisely, his response to my ambivalence about grilled fish that put me in the same boat as those awestruck Greeks. I was tempted to order a whole loup cooked on the grill, but expressed concern that its delicate flavors might be compromised by the dryness or excessive charred taste. While cooking fish whole with its bone structure intact helps to retain moisture and flavor, grilling can have the opposite effect.

"Our origins are Greek, but we don't eat like Greeks," said Zarokian, poking fun at the Greek penchant for well-done fish and meats.

He keeps his whole fish moist by limiting their stay on the hot grill to 3 minutes a side, just long enough to mark the skin with dark stripes. He then lays the fish on a protective mattress of sliced potatoes seasoned with wild fennel picked from the nearby hills and oven-roasts it just until the fish's fin detaches easily from its body. The fin test is a surefire indicator of when a white-fleshed fish is "rose," meaning there remains some pale pinkness around the bones. If this Marsellais preference for slightly underdone fish is not yours, 3 to 5 minutes more of roasting will ensure completely white but not dry flesh.

2 pounds potatoes (preferably Yukon Gold), peeled and cut into ¼-inch slices

2 teaspoons pastis (Ricard or Pernod)

1 cup olive oil

One 3-pound whole red snapper, striped bass, or grouper, scaled and gutted with head and fins left on

Coarse salt

Freshly ground black pepper

1 handful fresh herbs and stems (rosemary, thyme, parsley)

1 lemon, cut into wedges

1. Cook the potato slices in a pot of boiling salted water for 5 minutes. Drain well, pat dry, and then place the slices in even layers on the bottom of a roasting pan large enough to hold the entire fish. Drizzle the potatoes with the pastis and about 3 tablespoons of the olive oil.

2. Heat the gas or charcoal grill until very hot. Rub the grill with an oil-dampened towel (be careful of flames produced by any oil dripping through) to prevent the fish from sticking.

3. Preheat the oven to 450 degrees.

4. Season the cavity of the fish with the coarse salt and pepper and then stuff the cavity with the herbs. Brush olive oil on the outer skin. (You do not need to score the fish, which allows grilled fish to cook more evenly, since it will be doing most of its cooking in the oven.) Lay the fish on the grill and leave it in

place, letting the sear set in for 2½ to 3 minutes, depending on how hot the grill is. Use your tongs to turn the fish and let sear for 2½ to 3 minutes on the other side.

5. With a pair of tongs and a metal spatula, lift the fish off the grill and lay it on its side (its belly facing you) over the potatoes in the roasting pan. Brush the fish again with olive oil. Cook on the lowest shelf in the oven until the fin becomes brittle and detaches easily from the fish body, 25 to 30 minutes (shorter for smaller whole fish). Remove from the oven.

6. To fillet the whole fish: Place on a serving platter. Using a large serving spoon and fork, separate the head and tail from the body and ease the fin bones away from the side of the fish. Carefully peel back the skin from the tail to the head and remove. Divide the upper side of the fish into two fillets by using the side of the spoon to cut along the line down the center of the fish. Gently ease the two fillets off the bone and transfer to the side of the platter. Lift the backbone from the side nearest the head and pull gently back toward the tail to expose the other side of the fish. Carefully lift and turn over this bottom side of the fish and peel off the skin, if desired. (In most cases the skin is edible.)

7. Divide the fillets into 4 portions and serve with potatoes, lemon wedges, coarse salt, and olive oil.

RAGOÛT DE LOTTE ET GAMBAS AU JUS DE BANDOL

MONKFISH AND PRAWN STEW WITH BANDOL WINE JUS

The craggy hills overlooking the port and resort town of Bandol, situated twenty miles east of Marseille, soak in some three thousand hours of sun exposure per year. Blessed with such persistent Mediterranean rays, Bandol's tiered vineyards are exceptionally hospitable to Mourvèdre, the principal grape variety in the appellation's red wines. But because the very traits—full-bodied, earthy, tannic, peppery, gamey—that distinguish Bandol among the best reds of Provence are ones that immediately suggest pairings with red meats or game but certainly not fish, it's unusual to find a red Bandol admitted to the same dinner, much less saucepan, as monkfish. A Marseillais would intuitively match a fresh and fruity white or rosé wine from Bandol with seafood.

Anyone open to if not yet prepared to embrace the idea of subjecting the delicate flavors of seafood to a robust red wine sauce can see the merits of Serge Zarokian's Monkfish and Prawn Stew with Bandol Wine Jus. The intense, blackberry-like fruit that is characteristic of Bandol, coupled with the oft-present aroma of fresh herbs, bestows a quality of Provençal freshness to the jus and therefore the fish. And Bandol's velvety texture and deep, garnet color generates a sensual dressing for the firm prawns and monkfish chunks and give the dish the impression of a rich ragout.

Such outstanding Bandol reds as Domain Tempier, Château Pibarnon, and Domaine Terrebrune are in limited distribution throughout the U.S. Even if you can find one of these wines at a local merchant, it may seem extravagant to use a $20 or $25 bottle as a cooking wine. You may wish instead to set it aside for drinking and seek out a less costly Bandol, a Mourvèdre wine from another region (Australia, Spain, California), or a robust red of your choosing (I suggest a California Zinfandel below, which, like Bandol, is often berrylike and spicy).

MAKES 4 SERVINGS

6 tablespoons olive oil

1 large onion, minced

¼ cup red wine vinegar

2 cups red Bandol wine (or California Zinfandel)

1 bouquet garni (thyme, bay leaf, parsley)

1 small pinch cayenne

Salt

Freshly ground black pepper

1 teaspoon unsalted butter (for the rice), plus 2 tablespoons unsalted butter, cut into cubes (for the sauce)

1 cup Basmati rice, washed under running water, soaked in cold water, and drained

¼ cup golden raisins

3 tablespoons pine nuts

1 pound monkfish fillet, cut into chunks between ¾ and 1 inch thick

16 prawns or jumbo shrimp, peeled with tails left on

2 teaspoons cornstarch, optional

½ cup chopped fresh parsley

1. Heat 3 tablespoons of the olive oil in a saucepan over medium heat. Add the onion and cook until translucent but not yet golden, about 5 minutes. Pour in the red wine vinegar and heat to a boil. Add the red wine, bouquet garni, and cayenne, season with salt and pepper, raise the heat to high, and cook until reduced by half and the alcohol is burned off (you can no longer smell the alcohol in its vapors), about 20 minutes. Drain through a fine sieve to remove the onion and bouquet garni and set aside.

2. Put 1½ cups of water in a saucepan, add 1 teaspoon butter, and bring to a rapid boil.

Slowly add the rice and raisins, cover, reduce the heat to very low, and simmer until all of the water has been absorbed, about 15 minutes. Remove from the heat, mix in the pine nuts, fluff with a fork, and season with salt and pepper. Cover with a dish towel to keep warm.

3. Season the monkfish chunks and prawns with salt and pepper.

4. Heat the remaining 3 tablespoons olive oil in a skillet over moderately high heat. Add the monkfish and prawns and cook until almost cooked through, 1½ to 2 minutes on each side for the monkfish, about 1 minute on each side for the prawns. Some traces of rawness should remain. (The hot sauce draped over the monkfish and prawns will finish off their cooking.) Remove from the heat and cover to keep warm.

5. Place the cornstarch, if desired, in a small cup or bowl, pour about 3 tablespoons of cold water over the starch, and stir until dissolved. Pour this mixture into the wine jus and heat over moderately high heat, stirring with a wooden spoon, until the mixture thickens, 4 to 5 minutes. Remove from the heat. Add the butter cubes to the wine sauce, one at a time, and beat with a whisk until emulsified before adding each additional cube.

6. TO SERVE, For each serving, spoon a mound of rice on the center of 4 plates. Arrange 4 prawns and a quarter of the monkfish chunks around each rice mound. Spoon the wine jus over and around the prawns and monkfish. Garnish with the chopped parsley.

MARMITE DU PÊCHEUR

FISHERMAN'S STEW

Neige Perez's Marmite du Pêcheur is not, as the chef-turned-fishmonger insists, truly superior to bouillabaisse. Yet for those occasions when you don't have all the time, fish varieties, seasonings, or hungry eaters needed for an authentic bouillabaisse, the garlicky, fifteen-minute fisherman's stew is a remarkably easy and satisfying—I hate to use the word—alternative. The pitfall in thinking of this dish as a simplified bouillabaisse is that it might encourage you to add some of the flavors—saffron, fennel, tomatoes—closely associated with Marseille's great classic. It is exactly this sort of improvisation that Marseille mentors like Neige, Marion Nazet, and Renée Brunet cautioned me against. In Provence, where the same ingredients show up again and again, everything should not be prepared to taste like everything else. That is not to indicate the stew would be hurt by a pinch of saffron or a teaspoon of pastis any more than I will be when Neige, Marion, and Renée discover what I just wrote. But it is an important principle to keep in mind.

The Marmite du Pêcheur can be assembled entirely with fish readily available in U.S. markets. Ingredients are carefully layered into the pot according to how they cook: potatoes on the bottom, then firm-fleshed fish varieties such as monkfish, then thinner fish fillets, then shellfish. Don't be concerned by the small quantity of water. You'll get plenty of broth from the shellfish, especially the mussels.

This is a perfect dish to bring to the table in the pot in which it was cooked, or a tureen.

MAKES 4 SERVINGS

4 potatoes, peeled and cut into ¼-inch slices
1 to 1½ pounds white-fleshed fish fillets or chunks (monkfish, cod, red snapper, sea bass, halibut, turbot)
12 raw shrimp, peeled
2 squid, cleaned and rinsed, the bodies cut in rings, the tentacles, in smaller pieces
12 to 16 mussels

Salt
Freshly ground black pepper
Cayenne, optional
6 cloves garlic, chopped
¼ cup chopped parsley
¼ cup olive oil
Baguette or country bread, cut into ½-inch slices and lightly toasted

1. Place the potato slices into the bottom of a large pot, 4 to 5 quarts, to cover the bottom.
2. Top with the fish fillets or chunks as evenly as possible, starting first with the monkfish on the bottom layer and then proceeding with the firmest to the least firm varieties.
3. Place the shrimp, squid, and mussels atop the fish and season with salt, pepper, and a tiny pinch of cayenne, if desired. Add the garlic, parsley, olive oil, and $\frac{1}{4}$ cup cold water, cover tightly, and cook over moderately high heat for about 15 minutes. Make sure that the fish fillets are cooked through and the potatoes are tender. If necessary, cook for 5 minutes more.
4. Place the baguette slices on the bottom of 4 large soup bowls and ladle the fish and broth over the bread.

NOIX DE SAINT JACQUES POÊLÉES AUX LÉGUMES, PANISSES AU BASILIC ET TAPENADE AVEC TOMATES CONFITES

SEA SCALLOPS WITH SAUTÉED VEGETABLES, BASIL PANISSES, TAPENADE, AND TOMATO CONFIT

For his sautéed scallops and vegetables, chef Christian Ernst of Le Charles Livon has assembled a wonderful ensemble of traditional Marseillais flavors: chickpea flour and basil in the panisses; black olives and capers in the tapenade; tomato, garlic, and olive oil in the tomato confit.

Take note of Christian's amusing and effective technique for melting garlic into the spinach. He spears a clove of garlic with a fork and then uses that fork to stir and toss the spinach as it wilts in the saucepan.

MAKES 4 SERVINGS

¾ cup snow peas or snap peas

20 asparagus tips

2 tablespoons butter

2 pounds fresh spinach, trimmed and washed

1 clove garlic

4 tablespoons olive oil

1½ pounds large sea scallops

Salt

Freshly ground black pepper

Tomato Confit (page 67)

16 to 20 Basil Panisses (page 74)

¼ cup Tapenade (page 55), warmed or at room temperature

1. Bring a pot of salted water to a boil. Drop in the snow peas and boil for 2 minutes. Remove the snow peas with a slotted spoon and plunge in ice water to preserve their color. Repeat with the asparagus tips.

2. Melt the butter in a saucepan over medium heat. Add the spinach. Spear a garlic clove with a fork and use that fork to stir (and thus melt garlic throughout) the spinach until it has wilted, about 3 minutes. Cover and set aside.

3. Preheat the oven to 350 degrees. Heat 2 tablespoons olive oil in a skillet, preferably ovenproof, over high heat. Season the scallops with salt and pepper, place in the skillet, and sear on both sides, about 30 seconds on each side. If not using an

ovenproof skillet, transfer to an oiled roasting pan and cook in the oven for 4 to 6 minutes. At the same time you can also reheat the panisses and tomato confit in the oven.

4. Heat the remaining 2 tablespoons olive oil in a skillet at moderately high heat, add the snow peas, asparagus tips, and spinach, season with salt and pepper, and sauté for 2 minutes.

5. TO SERVE, arrange the panisses in a circle on 4 dishes and season with salt and pepper. Inside each of these circles place a quarter of the vegetables in a mound and top that mound with a quarter of the scallops. Arrange the sections of tomato confit around the panisse and dot with tapenade.

COQUILLES SAINT-JACQUES AU SEL D'ORANGE, ENDIVE CARAMELISÉE

SAUTÉED SEA SCALLOPS WITH CARAMELIZED ENDIVE AND ORANGE SALT

At the restaurant Une Table au Sud, the discovery within Lionel Lévy's scallop dish is the *sel d'orange,* his seasoning of grated and dried orange peel blended with salt. It is a novel and colorful way to apply the flavor that is so much a part of Marseillaise cuisine. There are certainly many other possibilities for its application. Just think: orange salt. You could sprinkle it on fish, grilled shrimp, roast chicken, duck, carrots, goat cheese and walnut salad, cranberry relish, or even to salt the rim of a margarita glass.

The recipe also merits notice for the contrast between the sweetness of its long-cooked, lightly caramelized endive and the mild sourness of its orange butter sauce. The scallops aren't bad either.

MAKES 4 SERVINGS

2 oranges
Salt
Sugar
8 small endives
10 tablespoons unsalted butter
1½ pounds large sea scallops
Freshly ground black pepper

1. The day before: Grate the oranges, reserving the orange sections in the refrigerator to make a juice the following day. Set aside the zest in a warm place and let it dry out overnight.

2. Mix some salt (fine, not coarse) into the dried orange zest (about ¼ teaspoon salt for each teaspoon of dried orange zest) and set aside. This is your orange salt.

3. Combine 1 quart water, ½ teaspoon salt, and ½ teaspoon sugar in a pot and bring to a boil. Add the endives to the pot of water, lower the temperature to medium, and cook at a boil for 45 minutes. Drain the endives and let cool.

4. Squeeze the oranges, pour the juice into a saucepan, set over moderately high heat, and

cook until reduced by half, about 5 minutes. Remove from the heat.

5. Heat about 4 tablespoons butter in a large skillet over moderately high heat. Split the endives in half lengthwise and sprinkle the flat sides with a little sugar, salt, and pepper. Place the endive halves in the pan, flat side down, and cook until the bottoms begin to brown and caramelize, about 5 minutes.

6. Heat a nonstick skillet over high heat and sear the scallops, about 2 minutes on each side.

7. Just before serving, quickly reheat the reduced orange juice, gradually stirring in 5 or 6 tablespoons of butter to make an orange butter sauce.

8. TO SERVE, Place the scallops and endives on each plate. Pour a little of the orange butter sauce on top and sprinkle with orange salt.

Lionel Lévy prepares his scallops.

The presentation
of the lunch specials.

GAMBAS ROTIS AU MIEL ET GINGEMBRE

GINGER HONEY SHRIMP

The buzz of ginger, aided by the bite of lemon, cuts through the sweetness of the marinade's honey. Served over semolina grains, this shrimp dish, like the probable reaction it would likely elicit from traditionalists dining at Chez Fonfon in the quaint fishing village of Vallon des Auffes, is both sweet and sour.

MAKES 4 SERVINGS

2 pounds jumbo shrimp
2 tablespoons honey
1 tablespoon chopped ginger
1 cup lemon juice
9 tablespoons olive oil
Freshly ground black pepper
2/3 cup milk
1/2 cup semolina grains
1/4 cup raisins
2 tablespoons unsalted butter
Salt
Coarse salt

1. Six hours before you plan to serve: Peel the shrimp, place in a large bowl with the honey, ginger, lemon juice, and 7 tablespoons olive oil, and mix well. Season with pepper (but not salt), place in the refrigerator, and let marinate for at least 6 hours.

2. Heat the milk in a saucepan to a boil. Add the semolina grains, raisins, butter, and the remaining 2 tablespoons olive oil, mix well, season with salt and pepper, cover, and set aside for at least 5 minutes.

3. Heat a nonstick skillet over high heat. Sprinkle the bottom of the skillet with coarse salt. Remove the shrimp from the marinade, reserving the marinade, and season with fine salt. Place half of the shrimp in the skillet and cook for about 2 minutes. Flip the shrimp and cook the other side for 1 minute. Repeat with the remaining shrimp and set aside.

4. To prepare the sauce, heat the marinade and 2 tablespoons water over medium heat. Season to taste with salt.

5. TO SERVE, spoon a quarter of the semolina grains in the center of 4 plates. Surround each mound of semolina with a quarter of the shrimp and top with the honey-ginger marinade.

BROCHETTE DE LANGOUSTINES AUX SAINT JACQUES, BISQUE DE CRUSTACÉS

PRAWN AND SCALLOP BROCHETTE WITH SEAFOOD BISQUE

Rosemary stems serve as the skewers in Christian Ernst's prawn and scallop brochettes. The seafood bisque gets its rich sweetness from prawn (or shrimp) heads that are flambéed in Cognac.

MAKES 4 SERVINGS

3 tablespoons unsalted butter

8 Dublin bay prawns or jumbo shrimp, with heads on

2 teaspoons Cognac or other brandy

5 tablespoons olive oil

1 onion, chopped

2 carrots, diced

Salt

Freshly ground black pepper

1 cup dry white wine

1 cup shellfish stock (substitute fish stock or clam juice)

1 bouquet garni (thyme, rosemary, bay leaf)

4 rosemary stems (as thick as you can find), leaves removed

8 bay scallops

1 cup heavy cream

½ cup Shallot and Red Wine Jam, optional (page 65)

1. To make the bisque: Melt the butter in a saucepan over high heat. Remove the heads and the shells from the prawns, setting the prawn bodies aside. Place the heads in the saucepan and sear, tossing once or twice, for 2 minutes. Pour the Cognac over the prawn heads and set aflame with a match. When the flames have died down, set aside.

2. Heat 3 tablespoons of the olive oil in a saucepan over moderately high heat. Add the onion and carrots and cook until the onion is translucent and the carrots have softened a little, 5 to 6 minutes. Season with salt and pepper and pour in the white wine, shellfish stock, and 1½ cups cold water. Add the prawn heads and the bouquet garni and cook until reduced by half, about 30 minutes. Pour through a fine sieve to remove the vegetables and prawn heads (discard them) and set aside the bisque broth.

3. Preheat the oven to 350 degrees.

4. Spear each rosemary stem with two scallops and two prawns, alternating between them. Season with salt and pepper.

5. Heat the remaining 2 tablespoons olive oil in an ovenproof skillet. Over high heat sear the brochettes until the scallops begin to brown, 30 to 45 seconds on each side. Transfer to the oven for about 2 minutes for medium-rare scallops and prawns, 3 to 4 minutes for well-cooked ones.

6. Immediately before serving, combine the bisque broth and the heavy cream in a saucepan over moderately high heat and stir until hot but not boiling. Correct the seasoning. Place the brochettes in shallow soup bowls, top with the bisque, and serve with shallot and red wine jam, if desired.

Meats

Couscous Fassi
CHICKEN COUSCOUS WITH CHICKPEAS, ONIONS, AND RAISINS

Fillet de Volaille au Pain d'Epice et Crème de Reglisse
GINGERBREAD-CRUSTED CHICKEN BREASTS WITH
LICORICE SAUCE

Cigares de Pastilla MOROCCAN CHICKEN ROLLS

Médaillon de Veau et Sa Semoule aux Huit Saveurs
MEDALLION OF VEAL WITH AN EIGHT-SPICE SEMOLINA PILAF

Gigot d'Agneau aux Parfums de Garrigue
ROAST LEG OF LAMB WITH THYME AND ROSEMARY

Tagine d'Agneau aux Pruneaux et Amandes
LAMB STEW WITH PRUNES AND ALMONDS

Pieds et Paquets Marseillais
STUFFED MUTTON TRIPE WITH SHEEP'S TROTTERS

Bacon Laitue Tomate Marseillais
OPEN-FACED MARSEILLE-STYLE BLT

Daube Provençale PROVENÇAL BEEF STEW

Cannelloni de Daube BRAISED BEEF CANNELLONI

Dafina SEPHARDIC SABBATH STEW

Kouclas GROUND BEEF CROQUETTES FOR DAFINA

Alouettes sans Tête PROVENÇAL BEEF ROLLS

Filet de Boeuf Poêlé au Poivre Concassé
sur Échalotes Confites
STEAK AU POIVRE WITH CARAMELIZED SHALLOTS

Côte de Boeuf et Frites à l'Ail
RIB STEAK WITH GARLIC FRIES

I F A MODERN MARSEILLAIS consumes less beef, veal, pork, duck, cheese, and chicken than do inhabitants of most French cities, it probably has more to do with Mediterranean customs than geographic restrictions. A large variety of meats, poultry, and cheeses from other regions of France have long been available from local markets.

But living so close to the sea (and some of the world's best seafood) in a region where lamb and mutton constitute the primary livestock has had a lasting impact on the Marseille diet. As such, this section contains only two indigenous beef specialties: *daube* (Provençal beef stew) and *alouettes sans tête* (beef rolls). Both are slow-cooked dishes designed for modest cuts of beef.

The Marseille appetite is, however, also a product of the city's multicultural traditions. Appropriately, this section features North African, Southeast Asian, Sephardic, and classic French origins. Yes, newcomers from other regions of France enrich the melting pot.

COUSCOUS FASSI

CHICKEN COUSCOUS WITH CHICKPEAS, ONIONS, AND RAISINS

One of the best Moroccan restaurants in Paris is named after the 404, a Peugeot car model that was introduced in 1960 and is still spotted today on the roads of Morocco. A newer Marseille restaurant takes its name from a later Peugeot model, the 504, which, though unrelated to the Parisian eatery, was obviously inspired by it. As proof, they hired one of its former chefs, Karim Iala, who moved to France from Casablanca.

The 504 recipe for couscous fassi is a glorious merger of sweet and savory elements. I adore the softened texture of the sweet onions, which are melted but not browned in sugar and olive oil and then simmered in a little water to create a sweet but not cloying broth. The fassi is but one of six couscous varieties at the 504. And those are but six of many regional Moroccan, Algerian, and Tunisian couscous varieties prepared in the kitchens of Marseille.

MAKES 6 TO 8 SERVINGS

1 cup golden raisins
5 cups raw couscous (about 2 pounds)
Salt
1 tablespoon olive oil, plus ¼ cup
4 large onions, sliced
1 chicken (about 5 pounds), cut into 8 pieces
2½ teaspoons ground cinnamon
2 teaspoons sugar plus ⅓ cup
1 cup flour
1 cup drained cooked chickpeas

1. Place the raisins in a bowl and cover with hot water. Cover and set aside for 20 minutes. Drain the raisins.

2. Spread out the couscous on a large platter. Gradually moisten the couscous with 2 cups warm water. Add a pinch of salt and a tablespoon of olive oil. Rub the couscous with the palms of your hands to separate and moisten all the grains and remove any lumps. Cover and set aside for 20 minutes.

3. Heat ¼ cup olive oil in the bottom of a couscous steamer (*couscoussière*) or large pot over moderately high heat. Add a quarter of the sliced onions, chicken pieces, 1 teaspoon cinnamon, 2 teaspoons sugar, 2 teaspoons salt, and sauté, stirring frequently and moving the chicken pieces around until they begin to brown, 12 to 15 minutes.

4. Cover the chicken with 4 cups cold water and bring to a boil.

5. Combine the flour with ½ cup water and mix into a thick dough. Roll out into a thick rope long enough to fit around the perimeter of

the couscous steamer (or large pot) and apply it to the rim. This will help seal the seam between the two parts of the couscous steamer (or the large pot and its lid).

6. Cover the holes of the top part of the couscous steamer (or a shallow metal colander that will fit inside a large pot) with cheesecloth and add the couscous. Place over the bottom part of the couscous steamer, cover tightly, lower the heat to medium, and cook at a simmer for 1 hour.

7. In a separate saucepan combine the remaining $\frac{1}{4}$ cup olive oil, the remaining onions, 1 teaspoon cinnamon, $\frac{1}{3}$ cup sugar, and the chickpeas, season with salt, and cook over moderately high heat, stirring frequently, until most of the liquid has

evaporated, about 10 minutes. Add 1 cup cold water, heat to a boil, cover, lower the heat to medium, and simmer for 15 minutes. Set aside.

8. Fluff the couscous with a fork, mix in the golden raisins, and sprinkle with $\frac{1}{2}$ teaspoon cinnamon.

9. TO SERVE, Bring the entire couscous steamer to the table. Place the onion-and-chickpea mixture in a bowl and bring to the table. Spoon some of the couscous on each plate and make a shallow well in the center. Place a piece of chicken in the well and spoon a little chicken broth over the chicken and couscous. Spoon some of the onion-and-chickpea mixture over the chicken and serve.

FILLET DE VOLAILLE AU PAIN D'EPICE ET CRÈME DE REGLISSE

GINGERBREAD-CRUSTED CHICKEN BREASTS WITH LICORICE SAUCE

Rather than dredging the chicken cutlets with bread crumbs or rubbing them with dry spices, Florent Saugeron merges the benefits of both in a single coating of pain d'épice (gingerbread) crumbs. Moreover, the cinnamon and ginger you might find in gingerbread are a nice complement for the (real) licorice sauce. Saugeron picked up the licorice idea working for Jean-Georges Vongerichten at Vong in London and concluded that its similarity to anise, a flavor adored in Southeast Asia and Southeast France, made it a fitting ingredient for his Marseille fusion restaurant.

In place of gingerbread, you can get good results using a combination of crumbled ginger snaps (break the snaps into pieces and pulse in a food processor) and bread crumbs. In place of real licorice you can use licorice candy. Really!

MAKES 4 SERVINGS

3½ tablespoons butter

2 shallots, minced

1 cup dry white wine

1 cup chicken stock

1 stick licorice root or 1 black licorice stick candy

2 tablespoons heavy cream, plus ½ cup

Three 1-inch-thick slices of Gingerbread (page 229)

Salt

Freshly ground black pepper

4 boneless skinless chicken cutlets (about 1½ pounds)

1½ tablespoons olive oil

Ricotta Sesame Rolls, optional (page 80)

1. Preheat the oven to 350 degrees.
2. Melt 2 tablespoons butter in a saucepan over moderately high heat. Add the shallots and cook for 2 minutes.
3. Add the wine and chicken stock and reduce the liquid by a third, 10 to 15 minutes. Add the licorice and 2 tablespoons heavy cream, lower the heat, and cook for 5 minutes more. Pass through a fine sieve to remove the shallots and licorice.
4. Place the gingerbread slices on a baking sheet and heat in the oven to dry out, about 10 minutes. Place pieces in a blender or food processor and blend or pulse to make crumbs.

5. Season the gingerbread crumbs with salt and pepper and transfer to a shallow dish. In a separate shallow dish pour in $\frac{1}{2}$ cup heavy cream. Dip the chicken cutlets in the heavy cream, letting any excess liquid drip off, and dredge the cutlet in the gingerbread crumbs to coat both sides. Transfer to a platter.

6. Heat the remaining $1\frac{1}{2}$ tablespoons butter and olive oil in a skillet over medium heat. Add the cutlets and cook for about 2 minutes on each side. Spoon the licorice sauce over the cutlets and serve with ricotta sesame rolls, if desired.

CIGARES DE PASTILLA

MOROCCAN CHICKEN ROLLS

For Fatima Rhazi, preparing a pastilla in little rolls rather than as one large pie facilitates her serving the sweet-and-savory chicken pastry as an hors d'oeuvre, a finger food, or a light meal at the various functions the sisterhood she founded, Femmes D'Ici et D'Ailleurs, caters. For novice or hurried cooks unversed in this classic Moroccan dish, the principal advantage of the rolls is simplicity. Putting together the pastry for a large pie according to Fatima's directions is a complicated process involving the layering and tucking of overlapping Tunisian brick pastry sheets. There are many golden opportunities along the way to go wrong. To assemble the rolls, all you are required to do is roll the chicken-and-egg filling as you would a cigar in a single brick or, as suggested below, a spring roll wrapper and then either fry or bake. Baked rolls are less crisp and greasy than fried ones and take longer to prepare.

MAKES 10 APPETIZER SERVINGS OR 6 MAIN-COURSE SERVINGS

1 pound blanched almonds

½ cup confectioners' sugar, plus more for garnish

3 tablespoons butter

One 4-pound chicken, cut into parts and reserving giblets

Salt

Freshly ground black pepper

1 onion, finely chopped

4 threads saffron, crumbled

1 teaspoon turmeric

2 tablespoons chopped parsley

1 teaspoon ground cinnamon, plus more for garnish

3 tablespoons sugar

2 cups chicken broth

5 eggs, beaten

4 egg yolks, lightly beaten

Vegetable oil for frying, optional

1. Place the almonds in a skillet over medium heat and toast, stirring often, until golden brown, about 5 minutes. Chop the toasted almonds (or grind them in a food processor), combine with the confectioners' sugar, and mix well. Set aside.

2. Melt the butter in a large casserole over moderately high heat. Season the chicken parts with salt and pepper, place in the casserole, and brown on all sides, 8 to 10 minutes. Remove from the casserole and set aside.

3. Place the onion and giblets in the skillet and cook, tossing occasionally, until the onion is soft but not browned and the giblets are browned on all sides, 3 to 4 minutes. Add the

saffron, turmeric, parsley, cinnamon, and sugar. Cook, stirring occasionally, for 2 minutes.

4. Pour in the chicken broth and bring to a boil. Add the chicken parts and return to a boil. Cover, lower the heat, and simmer until the chicken is extremely tender, 50 minutes to 1 hour. Remove the chicken parts and giblets with a slotted spoon and set aside.

5. Increase the heat to high and cook, stirring constantly with a wooden spoon to prevent burning, until the liquid is reduced in half, about 10 minutes. Exchange the wooden spoon for a wire whisk, and gradually beat in the eggs and 2 of the egg yolks, reserving 2 to seal the rolls. Remove from the heat and set aside.

6. Remove the chicken from the bones and chop or shred into small pieces. Finely chop the giblets. Add the chicken pieces and chopped giblets to the sauce and mix well.

7. If baking, preheat the oven to 350 degrees. Butter a cookie sheet.

8. Place a spring roll wrapper on a work surface, with one corner facing you, and sprinkle with the almond-sugar mixture. Place 2 tablespoons of the chicken-egg mixture in a compact log diagonally across the bottom third of the wrapper. Fold the bottom corner of the wrapper over the chicken mixture and tuck it under. Roll once to enfold the chicken, fold in the sides of the wrapper, and continue rolling almost to the end. Brush the top corner with the remaining beaten egg and press to seal the roll. Repeat with the remaining wrappers.

9. If baking, place the rolls on a buttered baking sheet and bake until lightly crisp and golden, about 25 minutes. If frying, pour enough oil into a large skillet to a depth of about $1/4$ inch. Heat over high heat. Fry the rolls until golden on all sides, 3 to 4 minutes in all. Drain on paper towels.

10. Dust the rolls with confectioners' sugar and cinnamon and serve immediately.

MÉDAILLON DE VEAU ET SA SEMOULE AUX HUIT SAVEURS

MEDALLION OF VEAL WITH AN EIGHT-SPICE SEMOLINA PILAF

A slightly simplified version of chef Florent Saugeron's Marseille excursion from the Middle to the Far East.

MAKES 4 SERVINGS

5 tablespoons butter
1 shallot, finely chopped
2 leeks (whites only), sliced
1/3 cup raisins
1 small pinch cayenne
1 teaspoon Chinese five spice powder
2 teaspoons turmeric
1 cup semolina grains
1 tablespoon olive oil
1 1/2 to 2 pounds veal loin, cut into 4 medallions
28 to 30 pearl onions, peeled
1 teaspoon sugar
Salt
Freshly ground black pepper

1. Preheat the oven to 400 degrees. Boil 1 1/2 cups water.
2. Heat 2 tablespoons butter in a saucepan over moderately high heat. Add the shallot and leeks and cook for 2 minutes. Add the raisins and cook for 1 minute. Add the cayenne, Chinese five spice powder, 1 teaspoon turmeric, and semolina. Sauté, stirring once or twice, for 1 minute. Remove from the heat, stir in 1 1/4 cups boiling water, cover, and set aside.
3. Heat 1 tablespoon butter and the olive oil in a skillet over moderately high heat. Add the veal medallions and cook for 1 minute on each side. Transfer to a roasting pan and cook in the oven for 10 to 12 minutes.
4. Combine 2 tablespoons butter, onions, sugar, and 1 teaspoon turmeric in a saucepan. Season with salt and pepper, add enough water to cover the onions, cover the saucepan, and cook slowly over a low flame until the liquid is almost evaporated, about 10 minutes. Remove the lid and shake the pan to distribute the glaze evenly over the onions.
5. TO SERVE, reheat the semolina in a microwave. Spoon a mound of the semolina in the center of each dish. Top each mound of semolina with a veal medallion and surround with a quarter of the pearl onions.

GIGOT D'AGNEAU AUX PARFUMS DE GARRIGUE

ROAST LEG OF LAMB WITH THYME AND ROSEMARY

A roast leg of lamb or an entire *baron* (large joint of two legs and the saddle) of lamb is a traditional Easter dish. The word *garrigue* ("scrubland") refers to the local source of wild thyme and rosemary. The outer coats of olive oil, chopped thyme, and chopped rosemary result in the meat having a crisp, beautifully perfumed crust. Your guests will likely fight over pieces carved from the exterior.

MAKES 6 SERVINGS

1 leg of lamb, 5 to 6 pounds
2 cloves garlic, thinly sliced
¼ cup olive oil
1 tablespoon chopped fresh thyme
2 teaspoons chopped fresh rosemary leaves
1 teaspoon salt
1 teaspoon freshly ground black pepper

1. Preheat the oven to 425 degrees. Use the point of a sharp knife to cut 8 to 10 small slits on the surface of the lamb. Insert the garlic slivers into the slits.

2. Brush or rub the olive oil over the surface of the lamb. Combine the thyme, rosemary, salt, and pepper and spread out the mixture on the bottom of a large plate. Roll the lamb in this mixture to coat with the spices. Place the lamb in a shallow open roasting pan, top with any of the spice mixture that didn't stick to the meat, and roast for 25 minutes. Reduce the oven temperature to 350 degrees and roast for 40 minutes to 1 hour more, depending on how you want the meat cooked. Insert a meat thermometer in several places to gauge its doneness: 130 degrees for medium rare, 140 degrees for medium, 150 degrees for medium well. Remove from the oven and let rest for 15 minutes.

3. TO CARVE, transfer the meat to a cutting board. Grab the shank bone with a kitchen towel and lift to tilt the leg. Start carving from the rounded side of the leg, keeping the knife blade almost parallel to the bone. After you have carved down to the bone, turn the leg over, and carve thin slices from the opposite side.

TAGINE D'AGNEAU AUX PRUNEAUX ET AMANDES

LAMB STEW WITH PRUNES AND ALMONDS

Tagine refers both to the traditional Moroccan-style stew and to the conically shaped earthenware pot in which it is slow-cooked and served. While chefs throughout the south of France experiment with Provençal–North African fusion tagines, the classic already has a local feel. Zohra Sahnoune and her tagine recipe may be Algerian-born, but there is no ingredient in her lamb stew that would seem foreign or exotic to her Marseille neighbors. With savory lamb, sweet prunes, and freshly toasted almonds, a tagine contains these three essentials of the Provençal Christmas table.

2 tablespoons vegetable oil

2 tablespoons butter

3 pounds boneless lamb shoulder or lamb neck, cut into 1½-inch chunks

1 onion, chopped

1 cinnamon stick

5 to 6 saffron threads, crumbled

Salt

Freshly ground black pepper

1½ cups (about 8 ounces) pitted prunes, halved

½ cup sugar

½ teaspoon ground cinnamon

½ cup blanched almonds

1. Heat the oil and 1 tablespoon butter in a large casserole over low heat. Add the lamb chunks, onion, cinnamon stick, and saffron, season with salt (about ½ teaspoon) and pepper, and cook, tossing occasionally, until the meat is golden on all sides, 6 to 8 minutes.

2. Pour 3 quarts water into the casserole, raise the heat to high, and bring to a boil. Cover, reduce the heat to low, and simmer until the meat is very tender, about 30 minutes.

3. Combine the prunes, sugar, cinnamon, the remaining tablespoon butter, and 1 cup water in a saucepan and cook over low heat, stirring occasionally, for 15 minutes. Add the prune mixture to the meat and simmer for 5 minutes more.

4. Immediately before serving, place the almonds in a skillet over high heat and toast until golden, about 5 minutes.

5. TO SERVE, cover the lamb with the prunes and juices and sprinkle with toasted almonds.

PIEDS ET PAQUETS MARSEILLAIS

STUFFED MUTTON TRIPE WITH SHEEP'S TROTTERS

Any compilation of Marseille recipes would be unthinkable without *pieds et pacquets*, "feet and packets," a specialty in which little bundles of stuffed mutton tripe are slow cooked with sheep's trotters in white wine and tomato. Admittedly, you may find the suggestion of preparing the dish that, in the annals of Marseille gastronomy, is second in importance only to bouillabaisse unthinkable too. First, it's virtually impossible to find an American butcher that sells cleaned sheep's feet. Second, the combination of intestines and feet is not likely to entice most American palates.

Interestingly, the dish was apparently a favorite of African-American longshoremen and sailors on leave in Marseille between the First and Second World Wars. In *Banjo*, Claude McKay's 1929 novel about a group of Old Port drifters from Africa, the West Indies, and the American South, the title character craves *pieds et paquets* because the long-simmered mutton intestines remind him of chitterlings. The only throat-tickling cooking like French cooking, concludes Banjo, "is black folks' cooking back in Dixie."

No butter or flour is added to the thick, rich-flavored sauce that distinguishes *pieds et paquets*. It is enriched with the gelatinous juices of the *pieds*. The slow cooking softens the tripe's rubbery texture to the point where the *paquets* are wonderfully tender but not mushy.

Although I was unable to find sheep's feet in New York, I did manage to prepare a credible and delicious version of *pieds et paquets* using lamb's feet and lamb tripe purchased from a Greek butcher. Pigs trotters are not a suitable substitution, as the sauce becomes too gooey and sticky.

The difficult art of *pieds et paquets* is in the assembly of the packets. Many Marseillais buy their *paquets* ready-made. Filled with garlic, parsley, and bacon lardon, these little bundles are enclosed by passing them though a buttonhole (essentially a 1-inch slit) that you cut into a 6-inch square or triangular piece of the tripe. If you can't execute, much less master, the technique, the bundles can easily be secured with string or toothpicks.

MAKES 6 SERVINGS

4 pounds lamb tripe

2 pounds lamb's feet, cleaned and cut into pieces (between 1½ and 2 inches long) by the butcher

¼ cup chopped parsley

6 cloves garlic, chopped

¼ pound bacon lardon, diced

Salt

Freshly ground black pepper

1¼ cups olive oil

1 large onion, chopped

1 leek (white part only), chopped

2 carrots, peeled and sliced

One 28-ounce can plum tomatoes, drained

2 tablespoons tomato paste

2 bay leaves

1 pinch nutmeg

3 cups white wine

1. Use a scissor to cut open the tripe and soak the tripe in cold water for 1 hour.

2. Place the lamb's feet in a pot of boiling lightly salted water and boil for 3 minutes. Drain and set aside.

3. Drain the tripe and cut it into squares (roughly 6 by 6 inches). Thoroughly wash each square in cold water, drain, pat both sides dry with a paper towel, and place on a platter.

4. Chop the parsley and 1 tablespoon chopped garlic together and combine in a bowl with the bacon lardon. Season with salt and pepper and mix well. This will be the stuffing.

5. To form the packets: Lay a tripe square on a work surface with one of its corners pointing toward you. Use the point of a sharp knife to make a 1-inch horizontal slit just below the top corner. Place a little of the stuffing (not more than ½ teaspoon) on the middle of the square. Lift the bottom corner and fold it over the stuffing. Then fold over the right and left corners to cover and enclose the stuffing. Roll this bundle up toward the top corner. Lift the top corner, fold it over the bundle, and pass the bundle through the slit as you would a large button through a buttonhole. Place on a platter. Repeat with the remaining tripe squares.

6. Heat the olive oil in a large casserole over medium heat. Add the onion, leek, and carrots, and cook until softened, stirring occasionally and not letting the onion brown, about 10 minutes. Add the tomatoes, tomato paste, bay leaves, and the remaining chopped garlic, season with nutmeg, salt, and pepper, and cook for 3 to 5 minutes more.

7. Add the lamb's feet. Delicately place the tripe packets over the feet. Pour the wine over all, season with salt and pepper, cover, reduce the flame to very low, and simmer for 4 to 5 hours.

8. TO SERVE, place 3 packets and 3 feet pieces on each plate and spoon the thick sauce over all.

BACON LAITUE TOMATE MARSEILLAIS

OPEN-FACED MARSEILLE-STYLE BLT

Lionel Lévy prepared his first BLT, or at least Alain Ducasse's glorification of that great sandwich trio, working for the famous French chef at the Paris restaurant Spoon Food & Wine. Lévy's Marseille-style rendering of a Parisian take on an American classic veers still farther from the original BLT and thus could disappoint purists barely able to recognize an old standby. There are no strips of bacon and no mayonnaise.

Still, to BLT or not to BLT is not the question. This open-faced sandwich is better relished as an ensemble of favorite Provençal tastes—basil, garlic, black olives, olive oil, tomato—on a single piece of toast. More significant, it's constructed to let you sample some of its most dynamic components both together and apart. While the bottom layer of olive oil, garlic, and basil-powered pistou extends over the entire piece of toast, the next layer's two toppings, tapenade and tomato-pepper compote, are limited to opposite halves of the sandwich. This means that, depending on how the sandwich is cut, no more than a few mouthfuls contain both the pungent tapenade, with its crushed black olives, capers, and anchovies, and the sweeter, gentler, mildly peppery tomato compote.

MAKES 4 MAIN-COURSE SERVINGS OR 6 TO 8 APPETIZER SERVINGS

4 pieces sun-dried tomato
½ cup olive oil
1 tablespoon balsamic vinegar
Salt
Freshly ground black pepper
6 to 8 plum tomatoes
1 onion, finely chopped
1 small bell red pepper, seeded and chopped
1 teaspoon sugar
1 pinch cayenne

4 slices country bread, cut from a large round loaf
1 clove garlic
½ cup Pistou (page 61)
¼ cup Tapenade (page 55)
1 small head Romaine lettuce
8 thin slices Canadian bacon or pancetta

1. Chop the pieces of sun-dried tomato and soak in warm water for 15 minutes.

2. To prepare the vinaigrette: Combine 3 tablespoons of the olive oil with the balsamic vinegar and $\frac{1}{4}$ teaspoon salt and beat with a whisk. Season with freshly ground pepper.

3. To prepare the tomato-pepper compote: First peel the tomatoes: Cut a small X in their smooth ends and plunge in boiling salted water for 30 seconds. Peel the tomatoes, remove the seeds, and then chop.

4. Heat 2 tablespoons of the olive oil in a saucepan over moderately high heat. Add the onion and cook until golden, 5 to 6 minutes. Add the red pepper and cook, stirring occasionally, for 5 minutes. Add the chopped tomatoes and sugar, season with salt, pepper, and cayenne and mix well. Cover, lower the heat to low, and cook gently until the mixture thickens into a compote, 8 to 10 minutes. Set aside.

5. Toast or grill the bread slices until golden brown on both sides. While still hot, rub each slice on one side with the garlic. Drizzle olive oil over each slice.

6. Cover each slice with a thin even layer of pistou. Spoon a tablespoon of tapenade over one half of each slice and spoon 1 tablespoon of the tomato-pepper compote on the other half (one half of each slice should be olive black and the other tomato red).

7. Cover each with some Romaine lettuce and a few pieces of the chopped sun-dried tomato and drizzle with the vinaigrette.

8. Place the Canadian bacon or pancetta slices in a nonstick skillet over medium heat and cook for 1 minute. Place 2 slices of bacon atop each open-faced sandwich, season with freshly ground pepper, slice the sandwiches in half or quarters, and serve.

DAUBE PROVENÇALE

PROVENÇAL BEEF STEW

There are only two worthy arguments against designating daube as Provence's national dish: (1) Provence is not a country; (2) bouillabaisse.

Renditions of the classic vary according to many factors, including the cut of stew beef employed; the assortment of vegetables, herbs, and seasonings used in both the marinade and the stew itself; the cooking vessel and time; and the type of wine in which the whole shebang simmers. Although food historians cite examples of eighteenth-century Provençal daubes cooked in white wine, almost all of today's versions are prepared with a red wine, preferably one that is full-bodied, tannic, and, because it is advisable to drink the same wine with a daube as you used to marinate it, of good quality.

This is the recipe of Renée Brunet or, to be more precise, Renée Brunet's grandmother. It is preferable to prepare her daube the day before you plan to eat it so that, after a night of refrigeration, the fat can be lifted off its top before eating. It may be served over pasta (elbow macaroni or noodles), polenta, or boiled potatoes. Leftover daube may be used as a stuffing for pasta (see page 192). It is also terrific when served cold and congealed.

MAKES 6 TO 8 SERVINGS

4 pounds boneless stew beef (chuck roast, beef shank, rump roast, bottom round, shoulder pot roast, beef cheek)

1 celery stalk, chopped

3 carrots, peeled and sliced

4 cloves garlic

3 onions, cut into small chunks

2 cloves

1 strip dry orange peel, about 3 inches long and ½ inch wide

Bouquet garni (thyme, bay leaf, parsley)

2 teaspoons salt

½ teaspoon freshly ground black pepper

6 tablespoons olive oil

1 bottle full-bodied, good quality red wine (Côte du Rhône, Bandol)

½ pound salt pork, diced

1 cup marc de Provence (substitute grappa or brandy)

1. The day before you plan to serve: Cut the beef into 2½- to 3-inch cubes. Place the cubes in a large bowl with the celery, carrots, garlic, onions stuck with the cloves, orange peel, bouquet garni, salt, pepper, and 3 tablespoons olive oil. Pour the wine over all, mix well, and let marinate in the refrigerator overnight, stirring two or three times.

2. Drain the meat cubes, reserve the marinade, and pat dry.

3. Heat the remaining 3 tablespoons olive oil in a very large casserole or stew pot over medium heat, add the salt pork, and cook, stirring occasionally, until the fat is rendered, about 5 minutes. Remove the diced pieces of salt pork with a slotted spoon and discard.

4. Add the meat and cook, turning once or twice, until its purplish color deepens, about 5 minutes. Pour in the marc and cook until evaporated (you'll know when the vapors no longer smell of alcohol), 5 to 7 minutes.

5. Lift the vegetables from the marinade with a slotted spoon and add to the casserole. Raise the heat to moderately high, slowly pour in three-quarters of the liquid from the marinade, and bring to a boil. Reduce the heat to very low, cover with a tight-fitting lid, and simmer gently until the meat is very tender, at least 3 hours. The remaining marinade should be kept warm in a covered saucepan over very low heat and added to the daube as needed.

6. Serve hot over pasta (elbow macaroni or noodles), polenta, or boiled potatoes. Transfer the contents immediately to a loaf pan or other mold and chill for several hours. To unmold the chilled daube, set the mold in a bath of hot water, turn it over a serving dish, and tap the bottom. A chilled daube is sliced and served as you would a terrine or layer cake.

CANNELLONI DE DAUBE

BRAISED BEEF CANNELLONI

In shaping a Provençal specialty to an Italian format, pasta stuffed with left-over daube can be as popular in many Marseille homes as the celebrated braised beef dish itself. It's a rare instance in which kids and grown-ups alike may beg for rather than bemoan a dinner of leftovers.

In lieu of stuffing it into cannelloni, manicotti, or perhaps jumbo pasta shells, the shredded daube mixture can be layered with sheets of lasagna.

MAKES 4 TO 6 SERVINGS

12 cannelloni shells or manicotti shells

1 pound Swiss chard

2 to 3 slices bread

10 to 12 ounces beef chunks from leftover daube (page 190), minced or shredded (yields about 1½ cups)

1 onion, finely chopped

2 cloves garlic, minced

¼ cup chopped parsley

1 egg, beaten

2 cups sauce from leftover daube

½ teaspoon salt

½ teaspoon freshly ground black pepper

½ cup (2 ounces) freshly grated Parmesan cheese or shredded Gruyère

1. Boil the cannelloni shells according to the directions on the package, being careful not to overcook. Drain the shells.

2. Remove and discard the stalks from the Swiss chard. Wash the leaves thoroughly and blanch them in boiling salted water just

until softened, about 1 minute. Drain, rinse in cold water, press or squeeze out the water, and finely chop the leaves.

3. To prepare the stuffing: Soak the bread slices in water for 10 seconds. With your hands, squeeze out the water from the bread slices. Combine in a large mixing bowl with the Swiss chard, beef chunks, onion, garlic, parsley, egg, and 2 tablespoons of the daube sauce. Season with salt and pepper and mix well.

4. Preheat the oven to 350 degrees. Butter a 9- by 9-inch metal baking dish.

5. Use a pastry bag or your longest, skinniest spoon to fill the pasta shells with the stuffing mixture. Arrange the filled shells in the prepared baking dish, top with the remaining daube sauce, and sprinkle with grated Parmesan. Bake until the cheese is melted and just begins to turn golden, about 25 minutes. Serve immediately.

DAFINA

SEPHARDIC SABBATH STEW

On Friday afternoons, Marseille reunites the great diaspora of dafina, the traditional stew originated by observant Spanish Jews forbidden to kindle fires on the Sabbath day. In perhaps no other large city outside of Tel Aviv, Jerusalem, and Paris will you find so wide and international a variety of the stew that by custom simmers from sundown on Friday until it is served on Saturday as the midday meal.

The term *dafina*, from the Arabic meaning "covered" (presumably because it is slow-cooked in a covered pot), was adopted by descendants of Sephardic Jews who were expelled from Spain in 1492 and settled in North Africa. Interpretations of the dish vary from country to country and, within the diverse immigrant Jewish community of Marseille, house to house. Moreover, Marseille Jews of Central and Eastern European origin prepare another version of the Sabbath stew called cholent.

Although the city's Middle Eastern specialty markets carry just about every type of bean, pea, grain, dried fruit, dried spice, or green vegetable any dafina devotee could possibly need, most stock their pot according to long-standing family recipes shaped by the limited ingredients available to their ancestors in different areas of Morocco, Algeria, Tunisia, and Egypt.

The family saga behind the recipe that follows is hardly atypical. It comes from Jäelle Amouyal, an interior designer who, at the age of eleven, was among some 130,000 Algerian Jews who emigrated to France after Algeria was granted independence in 1962. The daughter of Moroccan-born parents, Jäelle lived in a Spanish-speaking household in the northwest Algerian city of Oran. With no stoves in their homes, residents of Oran's Jewish quarter would leave their dafina pots in public ovens to simmer overnight. The Amouyal family dafina pot was painted white and marked with the letter A to distinguish it from the twenty or so others sharing the same oven. Such precautions did not always prevent the odd case of mistaken dafina identity and, to the horror of those left holding the wrong pot, the unthinkable: a Sabbath without their beloved "daf."

You will understand such concerns once you try the Amouyal "daf," which is prepared, like many classic renditions, with stew beef (Jäelle prefers the gelatinous but not excessively fatty meat from beef shins and knuckles), chickpeas, potatoes, eggs, and a little honey. The eggs are cooked in their shells, absorbing some of the maroon color of the stew and much of its beefy, garbanzo-garlicky flavors. This prized method of slow boiling hard-boiled eggs is known as *huevos haminados*. You may also add to the pot the sausage-shaped ground meat patties called *kouclas* (page 196). Jäelle's one concession to modern tastes is the use of the French product Ebly, a parboiled durum wheat now sold in some U.S. markets—in place of barley. You are not discouraged from turning back the clock and reinstating barley.

A dafina is in all instances a thick, leaden stew best consumed during winter months. The great challenge in preparing it for the first time is achieving a consistency that is neither dry nor liquid. This requires regular surveillance of the pot and, should it be drying out, the addition of some water. If prepared overnight according to custom, a vigilant dafina cook might even set the alarm at 4:00 A.M. to check on its progress and liquidity. A perfect dafina is said to be "oiled," meaning most of the liquid has disappeared and a little oil has risen from the bottom to the top of the pot.

MAKES 6 TO 8 SERVINGS

1 pound (about 2½ cups) dried chickpeas

1 teaspoon baking soda

3 tablespoons vegetable oil

2½ pounds boneless stew beef (beef shins, beef knuckles, chuck roast, beef shank, rump roast, bottom round, shoulder pot roast), cut into large pieces

1 head garlic

6 medium potatoes, peeled

6 eggs

1 tablespoon honey

1 tablespoon mild paprika

Salt

2 tablespoons olive oil

1 cup Ebly wheat or barley

1 recipe Kouclas, optional (page 196)

1. The day before starting to cook: Combine the chickpeas and baking soda in a pan or large bowl, cover with cold water to a level several inches over the chickpeas, and let soak overnight. Drain the chickpeas and rinse well in cold water.

2. Heat the vegetable oil in a large casserole over moderately high heat. Add the meat pieces and cook until browned on all sides, about 5 minutes.

3. Use a sharp knife to make several gashes in the head of garlic. Add the unpeeled head of garlic to the casserole along with the potatoes, eggs (in their shells), honey, and paprika, and season with salt. Add enough water to cover all (roughly 1 quart) and bring to a boil.

4. Meanwhile, heat the olive oil in a skillet over moderately high heat. Add the Ebly wheat or barley and cook, stirring occasionally, until lightly toasted, 2 to 3 minutes.

5. Once the liquid in the pot reaches a boil, add the kouclas patties, if desired, making sure they are fully submerged in the liquid. (The kouclas will absorb a good deal of liquid and thus will require you to add more water as the dafina simmers than you would without them.) Tightly cover the pot, reduce the heat to very low, cover, and simmer gently, adding more water when necessary, until the chickpeas, potatoes, and meat are all tender, at least 3 hours. After 2 hours or so, taste and correct the seasoning, adding more salt and paprika as needed. (If cooking overnight you may wish to use a stovetop diffuser so that the stew neither burns nor overcooks.)

6. Immediately before serving, peel the eggs and, if you've added the kouclas, slice into small chunks.

KOUCLAS

GROUND BEEF CROQUETTES FOR DAFINA

A dafina is often accompanied by sausage-shaped patties of ground meat, bread crumbs, rice or other grains that are cooked with the other dafina ingredients. Its name varies according to a family's country of origin: *coura* or *kora* in parts of Morocco, *l'asban* or *coukla* in Tunisia, *coklo, couklou,* or *kouclas* in Algeria. The preference for first preparing these patties as croquettes, as in the semolina-dredged kouclas of Jäelle Amouyal's recipe, crosses many boundaries within Marseille's Sephardic Jewish community. The semolina coating effectively seals the patties, thus avoiding the need to wrap them in cheesecloth or aluminum foil before they are dipped into the dafina pot for an overnight Sabbath simmer.

There is no law, religious or culinary, against serving kouclas outside of a dafina. You might simmer them in tomato sauce as you would meatballs and then serve them with pasta or rice.

MAKES 6 SERVINGS

5 to 6 slices baguette or country bread

1 pound ground beef

3 eggs, beaten

1 onion, finely chopped

1/4 cup chopped fresh parsley

1/2 teaspoon salt

1/4 teaspoon cumin

1/4 teaspoon nutmeg

1/4 cup semolina grains

Oil for frying

1. Soak the baguette slices in water for 1 minute and squeeze out the water with your hands. Combine in a large mixing bowl with the ground beef, 2 beaten eggs (reserve the third to dredge the patties), onion, parsley, salt, cumin, and nutmeg. Mix thoroughly with your hands into a smooth paste. Moisten your hands and use them to shape the mixture into tightly packed, sausage-shaped patties about 4 inches long and 1 inch thick.

2. Place the semolina grains in one shallow dish and the beaten eggs in another. Roll the patties in the semolina to coat on all sides and then roll in the beaten egg to seal.

3. Pour the frying oil into a large skillet to a depth of about 1/4 inch and heat over moderately high heat. Drain any excess egg from the patties and then fry until golden brown on all sides, about 5 minutes. Add the patties to the dafina and cook according to the directions in the recipe. (If serving instead in a tomato sauce, simmer the kouclas in 2 cups tomato sauce for 45 minutes.)

Chef Guillaume Sourrieu in the kitchen of L'Epuisette.

ALOUETTES SANS TÊTE

PROVENÇAL BEEF ROLLS

One of the few beef dishes in the traditional Marseillais repertoire, *alouettes sans tête*—"headless larks"—are so-named because these beef rolls are sort of shaped like the bodies of those larks. Comparable to Italian braciole, they are known elsewhere in France as *oiseaux* ("birds") *sans tête* or *paupiettes* and may be prepared with veal, turkey, lamb, fish fillets, or even cabbage in place of beef. My friend Bernard Loubat suggests serving them with boiled potatoes first halved and then drizzled with olive oil. The snack bar O' Stop, a late-night institution that commingles patrons and performers from the nearby opera house with those from the adjacent red-light district, serves its surprisingly good alouettes with pasta and tomato sauce (see instructions).

MAKES 4 SERVINGS

5 ounces slab bacon, chopped (about 1 cup)

6 cloves garlic, chopped

1/4 cup chopped fresh parsley

Salt

Freshly ground black pepper

2 pounds beef steaks, cut 1/4 inch thick from chuck or top round

2 tablespoons butter

2 tablespoons olive oil

1 1/2 cups dry white wine

1/4 cup whole black olives

1 bouquet garni (thyme, rosemary, bay leaf)

2 tablespoons tomato paste

1. To prepare the stuffing: Combine the bacon, garlic, and parsley in a bowl, season with salt and pepper, and mix well.

2. Place the beef on a work surface and flatten any thick parts by pounding on them with a cleaver or your fist. Cut the meat into smaller 3 by 4 by 1/4-inch slices (20 to 24 pieces in all), and season lightly with salt.

3. Working with one slice of meat at a time, place the meat slice so that the longer, 4-inch side is facing you. Place a heaping teaspoon of the stuffing mixture on the lower half of the slice and roll it from the bottom over itself to fully enclose the stuffing. Tie with kitchen twine, twice or three times around, or secure with toothpicks, so the beef rolls keep their shape while cooking.

4. Heat the butter and olive oil in a heavy-bottomed pot or flameproof casserole over moderately high heat. Place the meat rolls against each other in the pot and cook until the meat browns and begins to stick to the pot, 2 to 3 minutes on each side. Pour the white wine into the pot, add the olives and bouquet garni, cover, lower the flame to very low, and cook gently for 2 hours.

Check every so often that the liquid and juices have not completely evaporated. If they have, add ¼ cup or so of beef stock or water.

5. Just before serving, combine the tomato paste with 1 teaspoon warm water and stir it into the meat juices. Use this as a sauce to top the beef rolls (5 to 6 to a serving).

6. TO SERVE WITH A CHUNKY FRESH TOMATO SAUCE, omit the tomato paste. When the beef rolls are done cooking, remove from the pot and set aside. Peel, seed, and chop 2 pounds of ripe plum tomatoes, place in the pot, and cook with the meat juices over a medium flame, stirring occasionally, for 15 minutes. Immediately before serving, place the beef rolls into the tomatoes, correct the seasoning, and serve.

FILET DE BOEUF POÊLÉ AU POIVRE CONCASSÉ SUR ÉCHALOTES CONFITES

STEAK AU POIVRE WITH CARAMELIZED SHALLOTS

On French menus it is common to find steaks prepared either *au poivre* (encrusted in cracked peppercorns) or *aux échalotes* (with shallots). Giselle Philippi, however, does not respond well to either-or propositions. "I have no need to do one or the other," says the chef-owner of Le Sud en Haut. "That would bore me. I do both."

I was skeptical about this needless merger of two steak styles, but nevertheless gave it a try. Afterward, I took out my menu pad and wrote out a brief note that I left on my cleared plate for the waiter to take back to the kitchen. It read: "I tried the steak au poivre without the shallots and then the shallots without the steak. First I was missing the steak. Then I was missing the shallots. One without the other was intolerable."

Giselle's written reply was a message of love: *Ils étaient fait pour se rencontrer*—they were made to meet each other.

She uses a fillet of beef for her steak au poivre, but you don't have to. A sirloin, T-bone, rib steak, ribeye, or hanger steak will do. A crucial element in the shallot preparation is the lemon juice, which cuts through the sweetness of the honey and the caramelization.

MAKES 4 SERVINGS

4 filet mignon steaks, 6 to 7 ounces each
2 tablespoons unsalted butter
4 to 5 shallots, peeled and thinly sliced
2 teaspoons honey
1 teaspoon lemon juice
½ cup white wine
Salt
Cracked black pepper
Herbes de Provence

2 tablespoons olive oil
Coarse salt, optional

1. Heat the butter in a saucepan over medium heat. Add the shallots and cook, stirring occasionally, until they begin to turn golden, 4 to 5 minutes. Add the honey and lemon juice, raise the heat to moderately high, and cook until it turns deep brown, about 4

minutes. Add the wine and cook until two-thirds of the liquid has evaporated and you can no longer smell the wine in the vapors, about 3 minutes. Season with salt and pepper, cover, and remove from the heat. (If it looks dry, add a little water.)

2. Pat dry the steaks. Rub and press the cracked pepper into both sides of the meat. Sprinkle both sides with herbes de Provence.

3. Heat the oil in a heavy-bottomed skillet over moderately high heat. Cook the steaks to desired doneness, about 3 to 4 minutes on each side for medium rare.

4. TO SERVE, spoon a heaping tablespoon of the caramelized shallots in the middle of 4 dishes. Top each with a steak. If desired, place $1/2$ teaspoon or so of coarse salt in a pile on each plate next to the steak.

CÔTE DE BOEUF ET FRITES À L'AIL

RIB STEAK WITH GARLIC FRIES

Wistful habitués of the dearly departed Le Panier des Arts will be delighted to see that its thrice-fried garlic frites live on with the publication of this recipe. (The recipe for the bistro's beloved *soupe au chocolat* appears on page 236.) The frites accompany a rib steak that, seared in a frypan and then roasted in the oven, is the perfection of pinkness. The dish's third component, as prepared by chef Eric Boiron, is marrowbones. The marrow inside the bones is scooped out by the diner, spread over toast, and sprinkled with coarse salt. If you want to include the marrowbone option, ask your butcher to cut a beef bone or bones into 2-inch pieces that still have marrow.

MAKES 4 SERVINGS

1 tablespoon olive oil

2 tablespoons vegetable oil

2½ pounds rib of beef

5 large Yukon Gold or Idaho russet potatoes, peeled

Vegetable oil for deep frying

6 cloves garlic, coarsely chopped (if too fine, the garlic will burn)

Salt

Coarse salt

Cracked black pepper

Grain mustard

Four 2-inch pieces marrowbone, scraped clean, optional

1 baguette or country bread, sliced and lightly toasted, optional

1. Preheat the oven to 370 degrees.

2. Heat the olive oil and vegetable oil in a large saucepan over high heat until hot but not smoking. Place the meat in the pan and sear on all sides, 2 to 3 minutes on each side. Reserve the juices in the saucepan. This will be used later for the garlic fries.

3. Transfer the meat to a roasting pan, insert a meat thermometer into the thickest part of the meat, making sure that the tip of the thermometer is not resting in fat or touching bone, and roast to the desired level of doneness, first checking the thermometer after 25 minutes of cooking: 125 degrees for rare, 130–135 degrees for medium rare, 135–140 degrees for medium, 155 degrees for well done.

4. Cut the potatoes into strips 1 inch wide and ½ inch thick. Slender frites about ⅓ inch wide and thick will work just as well, only the cooking time will be slighter shorter. Rinse the potatoes in water and pat dry.

5. Pour enough frying oil into a deep fryer or

heavy skillet to reach a little over halfway up the sides of the pan and heat to 300 degrees. Plunge one-third of the potatoes into the hot oil and cook until they stiffen and start to color, 7 to 8 minutes. Lift out the fries and drain on paper towels. Repeat with the second and final batches of the fries.

6. Increase the oil temperature to 360 degrees. Drop in all the fries at once and cook until crisp and golden, about 3 minutes. Lift out and drain on paper towels.

7. Heat the saucepan containing the beef juices over low heat. Add the chopped garlic and cook, stirring occasionally, until golden, 4 to 5 minutes. Toss in the fries and sprinkle with salt. Stir with the garlic and beef juices for 1 minute. Transfer to a serving plate.

8. Once the beef has reached the desired temperature, remove it from the oven, place it with the rib pointing up on a carving board, and using a fork to steady the meat without piercing it, cut along the contour of the bone to separate it from the meat. Turn the meat on its side and carve relatively thick slices (about ¾ inch) across the grain. Arrange the slices and the rib bone on a wooden board and serve with the garlic fries and ramekins filled with coarse salt, cracked black pepper, and grain mustard.

To prepare marrowbones:

Place in an ovenproof pot, cover with water, filling the pot three-quarters full, and cook in a 375-degree oven for 10 minutes. Remove from the oven and, immediately before serving, drain. The diners scoop out the marrow themselves with a small spoon or knife and spread it on toast.

PRODUITS EXOTIQUES
TEL.91.54.00.86
Hàng
Thực phẩm
á Đông
Và hàng
Spécialités
Fruits
&
Légumes

Vegetables

Ragoût de Carottes et Olives de Nyons
GLAZED CARROTS WITH BLACK OLIVES
AND CUMIN

Purée de Pommes de Terre au Fondant
de Citron et Oignon MASHED POTATOES
WITH LEMON AND ONION CONFIT

Pommes de Terre Fourées au Basilic
BASIL POTATO CHIPS

Beignets de Courgettes ZUCCHINI FRITTERS

Terrine de Cougette ZUCCHINI TERRINE

Petits Légumes Farcis au Caviar
Aubergine STUFFED VEGETABLES WITH
EGGPLANT CAVIAR

La Bohémienne
EGGPLANT AND TOMATO STEW

Ragoût d'Aubergines à l'Anchois
EGGPLANT STEW WITH ANCHOVIES

Cocotte de Légumes
YVON'S VEGETABLE CASSEROLE

Gratin de Blettes à la Provençale
PROVENCE-STYLE SWISS CHARD GRATIN

*The tropical produce
market of Tam Ky.*

IN THE MEDITERRANEAN KITCHEN, vegetables are not instantly relegated to the status of side courses. Rather, they are first and foremost the crucial elements in a number of Marseille's "national" dishes, be it Provençal daube, Armenian dolma, Algerian chorba, Moroccan couscous, or *la bouillabaisse marseillaise*. And even when the vegetables are cooked apart from the meats or fish, the instinct is to combine them into something bigger. This is reflected in several mixed vegetable dishes—stuffed vegetables with eggplant caviar, vegetable casserole, eggplant and tomato stew—that can easily be served as main courses.

Although I have included such main-course complements as the glazed carrots with black olives and cumin and the mashed potatoes with lemon and onion confit, the overall intention has been to do as the Marseillais do and not push beloved vegetables, especially zucchini, eggplant, and the all-important tomato, to the side.

RAGOÛT DE CAROTTES ET OLIVES DE NYONS

GLAZED CARROTS WITH BLACK OLIVES AND CUMIN

Though glazed, cumin-scented carrots are now prepared everywhere, the addition of black olives tips the dish's origins from Morocco to Provence and stamps a Marseille address on the version Lionel Lévy serves with a filet mignon of veal. A versatile side course, the sweet carrot ragoût may accompany any number of veal, beef, pork, or poultry dishes.

MAKES 6 SERVINGS

3 pounds carrots

2 tablespoons olive oil

1 onion, chopped

1 teaspoon cumin

2 cups chicken stock

2 teaspoons sugar

½ cup pitted black olives

Salt

Freshly ground black pepper

1. Peel the carrots and cut them diagonally into ½-inch slices.

2. Heat the olive oil in a saucepan over moderately high heat. Combine the carrots, onion, and cumin in the saucepan and cook, stirring frequently, until the onions turn golden and the carrots begin to brown, 8 to 10 minutes.

3. Pour in the chicken stock and sugar and cook until all the liquid has evaporated, about 10 minutes.

4. Stir in the olives, season with salt and pepper, and cook, stirring occasionally, for 2 minutes. Correct the seasoning, adding more sugar if necessary.

PURÉE DE POMMES DE TERRE AU FONDANT DE CITRON ET OIGNON

MASHED POTATOES WITH LEMON AND ONION CONFIT

This is Serge Zarokian's perfect potato pairing for fish. At first the combination seems ideal: lemon, onion, olive oil, potatoes, fish—what could be wrong with that? But the potatoes are so yummy and the sweet bits of lightly caramelized lemon peel such a revelation that this side course is usually eaten long before the main course it was intended to support.

1½ pounds Yukon Gold or Idaho Russet
    potatoes
½ cup olive oil
1 onion, finely chopped
2 small lemons (as thin-skinned as you can find),
    washed thoroughly, diced, and pitted
Salt
Freshly ground black pepper
1 cup dry white wine
4 tablespoons unsalted butter
½ teaspoon lemon juice

1. Scrub the potatoes, place in a large pot, cover by at least 1 inch with cold salted water (2 teaspoons salt per quart water), and bring to a boil. Lower the heat to medium and cook the potatoes uncovered until tender, about 25 minutes.

2. Heat 3 tablespoons olive oil in a saucepan over moderately high heat. Add the onion and cook just until translucent, about 5 minutes. Add the lemons (leaving the peel on), season with salt and pepper and cook, stirring occasionally, until the lemon peel begins to turn golden, about 7 minutes. Add the white wine to deglaze the pan and cook, stirring occasionally, until most of the wine has evaporated, about 15 minutes.

3. Drain the potatoes and while still warm (but not too hot to handle), peel, place in a large saucepan, and mash with a potato masher.

4. Heat the potatoes over medium heat and gradually whisk in the butter until fully melted. Slowly whisk in ¼ cup olive oil.

5. Add the lemons and onion to the potatoes and whisk together until fully incorporated and evenly distributed through the mashed potatoes. Correct the seasoning. Immediately before serving, drizzle the potatoes with 1 tablespoon olive oil and the lemon juice.

POMMES DE TERRE FOURÉES
AU BASILIC

BASIL POTATO CHIPS

At the restaurant Le Charles Livon, chef Christian Ernst serves these basil potato chip sandwiches as part of an entree of daurade fillets and ratatouille. But they can be served with most meat and fish entrees, the Marseille-Style BLT (page 188), or as a snack.

MAKES 4 SERVINGS

2 pounds Yukon gold or Idaho russet potatoes
24 to 30 basil leaves
$1/4$ cup olive oil
Salt

1. Peel the potatoes and slice with a vegetable slicer as thinly as possible, about $1/16$ inch thick. Separate the chiplike slices into matched pairs and make a tiny sandwich by filling each pair with 1 basil leaf.
2. Heat the olive oil in a skillet over high heat. Delicately place the basil-filled potato sandwiches in the skillet and fry until golden brown on bottom, 2 to 3 minutes. Turn and fry on the other side, 2 to 3 minutes. Delicately transfer to paper towels to drain. Sprinkle with salt to taste and serve.

BEIGNETS DE COURGETTES
ZUCCHINI FRITTERS

Beignets are a passion shared by the Marseillais of Provençal, Corsican, and, in this instance, Armenian origin. Although Berte Baghtchejian would not dream of doing so, you can serve her beignets with the tomato-ginger jam (page 66) Olivier Vettorel prepares to accompany his zucchini blossom fritters. The more traditional Provençal accompaniment is tomato sauce.

MAKES 4 SERVINGS (ABOUT 12 FRITTERS)

2 pounds zucchini
½ cup all-purpose flour
½ teaspoon baking powder
1 onion, finely chopped
2 tablespoons chopped parsley
2 eggs
Salt
Frying oil

1. Peel the zucchini (or, if you intend to use the zucchini shells for stuffed vegetables, cut the zucchini and scoop out the pulp), cut into chunks, place in a pot of boiling salted water, and cook for 15 minutes; drain and let cool. Wrap the zucchini in a dishcloth and squeeze out the juices.
2. Combine the flour and baking powder in a bowl. Add the zucchini, onion, parsley, and eggs. Season lightly with salt and mix well.
3. Heat a good ½ inch of the frying oil in a skillet over moderately high heat. Working in batches, scoop out a heaping tablespoonful of the mixture, drop it into the skillet, flatten it just slightly with a spatula, and fry until golden, about 2 minutes on each side. Drain on paper towels, sprinkle with salt, and serve.

TERRINE DE COURGETTE

ZUCCHINI TERRINE

This dish is wonderful when served as a tricolored ensemble with Giselle Philippi's salmon (page 90) and chicken liver terrines (page 93).

MAKES 4 SERVINGS

2 tablespoons olive oil

¾ pound zucchini, partially peeled in alternating lengthwise strips and cut into ½-inch slices

1 tablespoon chopped fresh basil or 1 tablespoon chopped fresh mint

1¾ cups evaporated milk

4 egg yolks, beaten

1 teaspoon salt

1 teaspoon white pepper

Tomato Confit (page 67)

1 baguette or country bread, sliced and lightly toasted

1. Heat the olive oil in a saucepan over moderately high heat. Add the zucchini and basil and cook, stirring occasionally, for 5 minutes. Drain the liquid from the zucchini.

2. Preheat the oven to 250 degrees.

3. Combine the zucchini with the remaining ingredients, except the tomato confit and toast, in a blender and puree until smooth, 3 to 5 minutes. Pour the mixture into a buttered 1-quart terrine or loaf pan or 4 8-ounce baking dishes and cook in a bain-marie for 90 minutes. To check if the terrine is cooked throughout, insert a knife into the terrine. If it comes out dry and hot, it's done. Remove from the oven and let cool. Pass a knife around the perimeter to unmold. Serve warm or cold, whole or cut into slices, with the tomato confit and slices of toasted bread.

PETITS LÉGUMES FARCIS AU CAVIAR AUBERGINE

STUFFED VEGETABLES WITH EGGPLANT CAVIAR

Chef Olivier Vettorel describes this dish from the bistro La Giraffe as a *farandale*—a Provençal folk dance—of vegetables stuffed with eggplant caviar. His puree of roasted eggplant is transformed into a smooth, fluffy mousse through the addition of instant mashed potato powder. The number of eggplants will depend on their size and whether or not you want to remove the bitter seeds. Leftover eggplant caviar can be served alone as a spread or dip.

MAKES 4 SERVINGS

2 to 3 eggplants
½ cup heavy cream
1 tablespoon plus 1 teaspoon mashed potato mix
½ cup olive oil
2 cloves garlic, crushed
Salt
Freshly ground black pepper
4 medium onions, peeled
4 ripe tomatoes
4 large white mushrooms

1. Preheat the oven to 500 degrees.
2. Pierce the eggplants several times with a knife, place in a baking dish, and roast, turning once, for 5 minutes. Remove from the oven and let cool for 5 minutes.
3. Lower the oven temperature to 375 degrees. Heat the heavy cream in a saucepan until hot but not boiling. Remove from the fire, stir in the mashed potato mix and the olive oil, and let cool for 5 minutes.
4. Cut the eggplants in half, scoop out the pulp, and transfer to the mixing bowl of a food processor. Add the cream mixture and the garlic, season with salt and pepper, and process until smooth and fluffy, about 2 minutes. This is the eggplant caviar that will be used to stuff the vegetables.
5. Hollow out the onions with the aid of a knife and spoon, being careful not to remove too much onion (the hollowed cups should be at least two layers thick). Place the hollowed onions in boiling salted water and blanch for 5 minutes. Rinse and set aside.
6. Cut the tops off the tomatoes. Scoop out the tomato pulp with a spoon, being careful not to pierce the skin.
7. Cut the stems off the mushrooms. Scoop out the interior of the mushrooms.
8. Fill the hollowed onions, tomatoes, and mushrooms with the eggplant mixture, place on a buttered baking dish, and bake until the stuffing starts to turn golden, 20 to 25 minutes. Remove from the oven and let cool.
9. Serve at room temperature or slightly chilled.

LA BOHÉMIENNE

EGGPLANT AND TOMATO STEW

Everyone agrees on one thing: The *bohémienne* referred to in the name of this ratatouille-like stew is a Gypsy and not a poet/musician/nomad living in Marseille's Cours Julien. What isn't sure about this is if it was first prepared by Gypsies living in Provence or if it was simply named after the colorful Gypsy skirts the stew resembles after it's been cooked for an hour or so and the tomato can no longer be distinguished from the eggplant.

This sweet, delectably mushy stew is terrific when served cold the following day. Renée Brunet, who provided me with this recipe, suggests spooning it over a thick slice of crusty country bread. "Next to that," she says, "pizza is nothing."

MAKES 4 SERVINGS

¼ cup olive oil

2 onions

2 pounds ripe tomatoes, chopped

3 cloves garlic, chopped

¼ cup chopped parsley

Salt

Freshly ground black pepper

3 pounds eggplant, peeled and cut into cubes

1 tablespoon flour

¼ cup grated Parmesan or Gruyère cheese

1. Heat the olive oil in a large saucepan over moderately high heat. Add the onions and cook, stirring occasionally, until golden, 8 to 10 minutes.

2. Add the tomatoes, garlic, and parsley, season with salt and pepper, lower the heat to medium, and cook, stirring occasionally, until all the liquid from the tomatoes has evaporated, about 20 minutes.

3. Add the eggplant cubes and cook, stirring occasionally, until the eggplant and tomatoes have blended together into a smooth paste and all the liquid has evaporated, 45 to 60 minutes.

4. Add the flour and stir well.

5. Just before serving, remove from the heat and stir in the grated cheese.

RAGOÛT D'AUBERGINES À L'ANCHOIS

EGGPLANT STEW WITH ANCHOVIES

At first glance, this will look like a ratatouille or *bohémienne* with the addition of anchovies. In fact, many classic versions of *la bohémienne* consider the anchovies a nonnegotiable ingredient. What makes this rustic stew truly special is the slow cooking of the tomatoes and eggplant, first apart and then together. With a good amount of olive oil assisting this meltdown, the result is wonderfully sweet, rich, and, yes, creamy.

MAKES 4 SERVINGS

1 cup olive oil
2 pounds eggplant, peeled and cut into 1-inch cubes
2 pounds tomatoes, quartered and partly seeded
3 cloves garlic, chopped
¼ cup chopped parsley
Salt
Freshly ground black pepper
10 salted anchovies, rinsed, filleted, and dried (substitute 20 canned anchovy fillets, drained and dried)
½ pound Gruyère cheese, shredded

1. Pour half of the olive oil in one large saucepan and the other half in a second large saucepan or casserole and heat both over moderately high heat. Put the eggplant cubes into the first saucepan, cover and cook for 15 minutes, stirring frequently. Put the tomatoes in the second saucepan or casserole and cook uncovered for 15 minutes, stirring frequently.

2. Add the eggplant to the tomatoes, stir in the garlic and parsley, season with salt (not too much; you will be adding anchovies and can add more salt later) and pepper, cover, lower the temperature, and let slowly stew for at least 45 minutes.

3. Meanwhile, chop the anchovies and then crush in a mortar into a paste. When the eggplant and tomatoes have stewed for at least 45 minutes stir in the anchovies and let stew for 5 minutes. Correct the seasoning. The eggplant stew may be served now or prepared as a gratin by transferring it to a large baking dish or 4 small ones, topping with shredded Gruyère, and baking it in a 400-degree oven until golden, about 15 minutes.

COCOTTE DE LÉGUMES

YVON'S VEGETABLE CASSEROLE

Midway through lunch at his makeshift flea-market restaurant tucked into a storehouse otherwise occupied by antiques dealers, Yvon Cadiou would occasionally pop out of his tiny kitchen, dash through a bazaar-like maze of junk dealers to the vast food hall, stop at a produce stand, and buy more vegetables and herbs to replenish his *cocotte de légumes.* This purchase was typically made with money earned from the day's first paying customers. His cocotte is essentially a chunky ratatouille enriched with the crunch and perfume of fennel and imparted, like the flea market itself, with the spices—cumin, curry, chile pepper—of a North African souk.

MAKES 4 SERVINGS

3 tablespoons olive oil

4 cloves garlic, chopped

2 onions, chopped

4 carrots, peeled and cut into ¾-inch slices

1 large fennel bulb, discolored parts removed and cut into 4 pieces

1 large red bell pepper, chopped

1 eggplant, cubed

1 zucchini, cut into ½-inch slices

4 plum tomatoes, quartered

1 branch rosemary

1 branch thyme

4 bay leaves

1 pinch cayenne

Pinch cumin

1 pinch curry powder

Salt

Freshly ground black pepper

GARNISHES

¼ cup shaved Parmesan cheese

Fresh basil leaves

1 tablespoon olive oil

1. Heat the olive oil in a casserole over moderately high heat. Add the garlic, onions, carrots, and fennel and cook, stirring occasionally, for 10 minutes.

2. Add all the remaining ingredients, except the garnishes, season with salt and pepper, cover, and cook for 10 minutes. Stir the vegetables, reduce the heat to low, cover, and cook for 20 minutes. Remove from the heat and set aside, covered, for 10 minutes to let the flavors stew.

3. TO SERVE, top each serving with shaved Parmesan, adorn with fresh basil, and drizzle with olive oil.

GRATIN DE BLETTES À LA PROVENÇALE

PROVENCE-STYLE SWISS CHARD GRATIN

Not all of the outside influences in Marseille cooking are foreign. Dishes like this Swiss chard gratin were introduced by Provençal highlanders who moved to the seaport, usually for economic reasons.

MAKES 4 TO 6 SERVINGS

3 pounds Swiss chard

Salt

3 cloves garlic, chopped

3 tablespoons chopped parsley

3 slices white bread

1 cup milk

½ cup (about 2 ounces) shredded Gruyère cheese

½ cup cooked white rice

2 eggs, beaten

3 tablespoons olive oil

Freshly ground black pepper

2 teaspoons bread crumbs

1. Preheat the oven to 425 degrees. Separate the Swiss chard leaves from the stalks, thoroughly wash the leaves, and drain. Place the leaves in a pot with ½ teaspoon salt, cover, and heat over moderately high heat for 15 minutes. Transfer the leaves to a strainer to drain out the liquid. When the leaves have cooled, squeeze out any remaining liquid with your hands, chop the leaves coarsely (this should produce about 3 cups chopped Swiss chard), and place in a large mixing bowl.

2. Chop the garlic with the parsley and add to the Swiss chard.

3. Place the bread slices in a shallow bowl and cover with milk. Let stand for 1 minute. Squeeze out the milk from the bread slices with your hands and combine with the Swiss chard, garlic, and parsley. Add the Gruyère, rice, eggs, and olive oil, season with salt and pepper, and mix well.

4. Place the mixture in a 9 by 9-inch baking pan, casserole, or gratin dish, sprinkle with bread crumbs, and bake in the oven for 15 minutes.

SARDINE AND SWISS CHARD GRATIN: Grease the bottom of the baking pan or casserole with olive oil. Place 6 to 8 split fresh sardine fillets on the bottom of the pan, skin side down. Drizzle with olive oil and top with half the Swiss chard mixture. Top with another layer of 6 to 8 split sardine fillets, this time skin side up. Drizzle with olive oil. Top with the remaining Swiss chard mixture, sprinkle with bread crumbs, and bake in a 425-degree oven for 20 minutes. Makes 4 main-course servings.

**To fillet and split fresh
sardines:** Hold the fish with its head to
the right. Hold the head between your thumb
and index finger and tear it off, pulling toward
the belly. Run your thumb along the belly flap,
tearing open the fish down to the tail, and
removing any remaining innards. Grab the
backbone between your thumb and forefinger
and gently pull it out. Drop each fish into ice
water. Rinse the sardines and dry with paper
towels.

Desserts

Poêlé de Royal Gala au Pain d'Epice
FLAMBÉ OF PAN-FRIED APPLES WITH GINGERBREAD CRUMBS

Raviolis Comme les Auraient Aimés les Soeurs Tatin CARAMELIZED APPLE RAVIOLI

Pommes au Four et Son Caramel aux Fruits Secs et aux Épices, Brioche
Perdue BAKED APPLES WITH A CARAMEL OF NUTS AND SPICES AND BRIOCHE FRENCH TOAST

Tomates de Pays Farcies Caramelisées
TOMATOES STUFFED WITH CARAMELIZED FRUITS AND NUTS

Cake à la Banane et Basilic BANANA BASIL CAKE

Pain d'Épice GINGERBREAD

Compote de Mangue au Miel HONEY MANGO COMPOTE

La Pompe à l'Huile PROVENÇAL ROUND SWEET BREAD

Pouding à la Semoule SEMOLINA PUDDING

Claufoutis aux Olives Noires Confites BLACK OLIVE CLAFOUTIS

Soupe au Chocolat CHOCOLATE "SOUP"

Brownie "Dakatine"

Beignets de Truffes au Chocolat Gianduja CHOCOLATE HAZELNUT TRUFFLE BEIGNETS

Chichi-Fregi L'ESTAQUE-STYLE FUNNEL CAKES

Figues Rôties en Papillote, Caramel au Vin Rouge
ROASTED FIG DUMPLINGS WITH A RED WINE CARAMEL SAUCE

Poires Pochées au Vin Rouge POACHED PEARS IN RED WINE

Navettes Marseillaises MARSEILLE CANDLEMAS COOKIES

Canistrelli CORSICAN COOKIES

Griouch ALGERIAN HONEY FRITTERS

Glace aux Amandes ALMOND CUSTARD ICE CREAM

Glace au Basilic BASIL ICE CREAM

Glace aux Capucins CURRY ICE CREAM

ESSENTIALLY THERE ARE TWO WAYS to give a dessert a Marseille accent: You can prepare or garnish it with one or more of Marseille's traditional dessert flavors—honey, orange zest, lemon zest, figs, almonds, hazelnuts, pine nuts, dried fruits, anise, cinnamon—or you can introduce regional ingredients ordinarily used in savory Provençal dishes, among them basil, tomato, curry powder, and olives. No such manipulation is necessary with native sweets like *navettes* (Candlemas cookies) and *la pompe à l'huile* (round Christmas sweet bread), which are tied, like many traditional desserts, to religious feasts.

PAGE 218: *The Café Samaritaine.*

POÊLÉ DE ROYAL GALA
AU PAIN D'EPICE

FLAMBÉ OF PAN-FRIED APPLES WITH GINGERBREAD CRUMBS

Gingerbread may not in itself be a Provençal specialty, but its crumbs do constitute the ultimate spice mix for Marseille's collective dessert palate. Gingerbread crumbs also have savory applications, as in chef Florent Saugeron's gingerbread-crusted chicken breasts, page 179. Within those crumbs can be found many of the flavors and spices Marseillais of varying Mediterranean origins mix into their traditional desserts: honey, cinnamon, orange zest, lemon zest, and star anise. In addition, the somewhat coarse crumbs add a texture that ground spices lack. Here, Lionel Lévy uses the crumbs as well as dried gingerbread crisps to garnish flambéed apple sections. (Royal Gala is an excellent dessert apple chosen here for the beauty of its red-streaked yellow skin.) Gingersnaps, half of them crumbled and half left intact, serve as a satisfactory substitute for the gingerbread crumbs and crisps.

MAKES 4 SERVINGS

½ loaf Gingerbread (page 229)

4 Royal Gala apples

4 tablespoons unsalted butter

1 tiny pinch (scant ¼ teaspoon) salt

⅔ cup light brown sugar

½ cup Calvados (substitute apple brandy, cider brandy, or applejack)

1. Preheat the oven to 250 degrees.
2. Slice the gingerbread as thinly as possible. Place the slices on a cookie sheet and dry in the oven for 1 hour. Once done, set aside half the gingerbread slices. Place the remaining slices and pieces in a blender or food processor and blend or pulse to make crumbs.
3. Wash the apples well and pat dry, but do not peel them. Core the apples and slice into sections. (Alternatively, you may use a small melon ball scooper to scoop out as many balls from the apples as possible.)
4. Combine the butter and salt in a saucepan over moderately high heat and cook,

stirring with a wooden spoon once or twice, until the butter turns a medium brown color.

5. Stir in the apple sections. Gradually pour the sugar over the apples and cook, stirring continuously, for 5 minutes.

6. TO FLAMBÉ THE APPLES, douse them with the Calvados (you may do this at the table, warming the Calvados beforehand to ensure they don't catch fire).

7. TO SERVE, spoon the apple sections and their sauce into 4 dessert dishes. Sprinkle liberally with gingerbread crumbs and serve with the reserved gingerbread slices. (Unused gingerbread crumbs should be stored in a tight-lidded jar.)

RAVIOLIS COMME LES AURAIENT AIMÉS LES SOEURS TATIN

CARAMELIZED APPLE RAVIOLI

My English translation of Chez Fonfon chef Alexandre Pinna's recipe title is obviously not the literal one. Were that the case it would read: "Ravioli as the Tatin Sisters Would Have Loved Them." The Tatin sisters Pinna is referring to are Stephanie and Caroline, the innkeepers in Lamotte-Beuvron (some 360 miles northwest of Marseille) who in 1888 or so inadvertently inverted their apple tart and thus upended the course of French dessert history. Pinna's caramelized apple ravioli, made by folding the filling into boiled wonton skins, is an homage to Stephanie and Caroline and their famous caramelized apple tart. Sprinkled with dark chocolate, the ravioli may be served right side up or, in a gesture of pure empathy, upside down.

MAKES 4 SERVINGS

4 golden delicious apples
1¼ cups sugar
4 tablespoons unsalted butter
16 wonton skins
1½ ounces dark chocolate, grated
1 pint vanilla ice cream

1. Peel, core, and dice the apples.
2. To prepare the caramel: Combine the sugar and ⅓ cup water in a small saucepan over moderately high heat and stir for a few seconds with a wooden spoon. Continue to heat, tilting the saucepan from time to time to evenly distribute its color, until the liquid has a deep golden color, 5 to 7 minutes. Stir in the butter and apples, raise the heat to high, cover, and cook for 8 minutes more. Remove from the heat and set aside.
3. Bring a large pot of lightly salted water to a boil and, working in batches of 4 to 6, cook the wonton skins for 20 seconds. Remove the wonton skins with a slotted spoon and plunge in cold water.
4. Preheat the oven to 350 degrees. Butter a 9 by 13-inch metal roasting pan or baking dish.
5. Drain the wonton skins and lay them out in the prepared pan. Top the center of each with a tablespoon of the caramelized apple, sprinkle with grated chocolate, and fold the ravioli over the fillings. Heat in the oven for 5 minutes.
6. TO SERVE, delicately lift the ravioli with a spatula and place 4 on each plate. Top each serving with a scoop of vanilla ice cream.

POMMES AU FOUR ET SON CARAMEL AUX FRUITS SECS ET AUX ÉPICES, BRIOCHE PERDUE

BAKED APPLES WITH A CARAMEL OF NUTS AND SPICES AND BRIOCHE FRENCH TOAST

Chef Christian Ernst of Le Charles Livon first gives his baked apples a Provençal treatment with a caramel of pine nuts, pistachios, walnuts, almonds, and allspice and then takes the fruit and nut dessert over the top with brioche French toast and vanilla ice cream. Yum!

MAKES 4 SERVINGS

4 golden delicious apples, peeled and cored

4 tablespoons unsalted butter, cut into smaller pieces

1⅓ cups sugar

1 teaspoon vanilla extract

1 cup milk

2 egg yolks, beaten

4-inch-thick slices brioche, preferably one or two days old (substitute challah or another eggy bread)

½ cup shelled pistachio nuts

½ cup pine nuts

½ cup shaved almonds

¼ cup chopped walnuts

1 teaspoon ground allspice

1 pint vanilla ice cream

1. Preheat the oven to 350 degrees.
2. Place the apples upright in a baking pan with half of the butter pieces, sprinkle the apples with ⅓ cup sugar, drizzle with the vanilla extract, cover with foil, and bake until just tender, about 30 minutes.
3. Place the milk and egg yolks in separate shallow bowls. Soak each slice of brioche on both sides in the milk and then dunk each on both sides in the egg yolks.
4. Heat the remaining butter in a skillet over moderately high heat. Cook the brioche until golden, 2 to 3 minutes a side.
5. Combine the remaining 1 cup sugar and ⅓ cup water in a small saucepan over moderately high heat and stir for a few seconds with a wooden spoon. Continue to heat, tilting the saucepan from time to time to evenly distribute its color, until the liquid has a deep golden color, 5 to 7 minutes. Turn off the flame and slowly stir in ½ cup cold water to stop the cooking. Stir in the nuts and the allspice.

6. TO SERVE, reheat the apples and the French toast in the oven (they can be made several hours in advance). Place a slice of French toast in the middle of 4 dishes and top with a baked apple. Spoon the caramel-nut mixture over, inside, and around the apples, and serve with a scoop of vanilla ice cream.

Nuts sold by the kilo at the flea market bazaar.

TOMATES DE PAYS FARCIES CARAMELISÉES

TOMATOES STUFFED WITH CARAMELIZED FRUITS AND NUTS

Lionel Lévy turns Provence's adored stuffed tomato on its top by replacing the love apple's usual savory filling of chopped vegetables, meats, and herbs with a sweet one of caramelized fruits and nuts. But devising a convincing dessert out of a stuffed tomato, which is, after all, a fruit, has proven a lesser challenge than convincing skeptical Marseille diners to try it. When he first introduced the dish, Lionel counted on there being one daring diner at a table to share its pleasures with his or her cautious companions. Later he resorted to serving it gratis to those he viewed as potential converts. This patient, piecemeal approach reflected Marseille's gradual but sure acceptance of his restaurant, Une Table au Sud.

No sugar is added to the stuffed tomato. It gets all its sweetness from the slowly caramelized fruits. A great advantage of preparing it at home is that you get to experience this slow transformation from savory to sweet through the heady aroma emanating from the oven. Most impressively, the sweet and increasingly pronounced notes of tomatoes, orange, and nuts constitute a distinctly Provençal orchestration.

MAKES 4 SERVINGS

4 large ripe tomatoes
1 Granny Smith apple
7 dried apricots
1 orange
1 vanilla bean
¼ cup shelled pistachio nuts
¼ cup pine nuts
¼ cup blanched almonds
¼ cup blanched hazelnuts
12 cardamom seeds, crushed
Fresh mint
1 pint vanilla ice cream

1. Slice or cut a round lid out of the top of each tomato as you would with a pumpkin when carving a jack-o'-lantern. Scoop out the seeds and pulp, being extra careful not to pierce the skin of the hollowed tomatoes. Reserve the tops.
2. Peel and core the apple and cut into a fine dice.
3. Cut the apricots into a fine dice.
4. Peel the orange and chop the peel into a fine dice. Squeeze the orange, remove the pits, and reserve the juice.

5. Slit the vanilla bean lengthwise down the center and scrape out the seeds.
6. Chop the pistachios, pine nuts, almonds, and hazelnuts. Combine with the diced apple, diced apricots, chopped orange peel, orange juice, seeds from the vanilla bean, and cardamom seeds in a saucepan and cook over moderate heat, stirring occasionally and ensuring that the bottom does not burn, for 15 minutes.
7. Preheat the oven to 300 degrees. Butter a 9 by 9-inch ovenproof baking dish.
8. Carefully fill the hollowed tomatoes with the fruit and nut stuffing, put the tops on the tomatoes, place in a buttered baking dish, and cook for $2\frac{1}{2}$ hours. Serve the tomatoes warm with a small scoop of vanilla ice cream and fresh mint garnish.

CAKE À LA BANANE ET BASILIC

BANANA BASIL CAKE

Two tablespoons of chopped basil do not make this banana cake a Provençal treat any more than do two glasses of pastis turn an American into a Marseillais, but both do come off smelling like the genuine article. In planting the region's beloved herb in such comfy confines, Yvon Cadiou has found a subtle and harmless way to introduce it as a sweetly fragrant, vaguely minty dessert flavor. And when the banana basil cake is paired with his basil ice cream, Cadiou transforms the dessert appeal of basil from "thinkable" to "unthinkably good."

MAKES ONE 9 BY 5 BY 3-INCH LOAF, 6 SERVINGS

3 ripe bananas
2 eggs, beaten, at room temperature
1 teaspoon baking soda
¾ cup sugar
1½ cups flour
1 pinch salt
2 tablespoons chopped fresh basil
3 tablespoons chopped blanched almonds
½ teaspoon ground cinnamon
1 sliced ripe banana, optional, as garnish
Maple syrup, optional
Basil Ice Cream (page 253), optional

1. Place the bananas in a mixing bowl and mash with a potato masher. Add the beaten eggs and mix well.
2. In a separate bowl combine the baking soda, sugar, flour, and salt. Add to the banana-egg mixture and mix well. Stir in the basil and chopped blanched almonds.
3. Preheat the oven to 350 degrees.
4. Dust a buttered 1-quart loaf pan with flour and fill with cake batter. Sprinkle the top with cinnamon and set aside in a warm place for 20 minutes.
5. Place the cake in the oven and bake for about 45 minutes, or until a toothpick comes out clean. Remove from the oven and let cool for at least 5 minutes. Serve plain, topped with sliced banana and maple syrup, or with a scoop of basil ice cream.

PAIN D'ÉPICE

GINGERBREAD

French *pain d'épice*, though common in Marseille and throughout Provence, is not counted among the region's specialties. The two principal prototypes come from Dijon, where it is made with wheat flour, and Reims, where it is made with rye flour. This recipe lets you choose between the two. Nevertheless, having come to Dijon and Reims from China via North Africa, it seems as though *pain d'épice* should have passed into France through Marseille via the traditional trade routes and spice trails. Its spices are certainly not foreign to the Marseillais palate.

From this recipe come the gingerbread crumbs required in the flambé of pan-fried apple balls (page 221) and the gingerbread-crusted chicken breasts (page 179). Those are the convenient excuses to enjoy this wonderful cake on its own.

MAKES 2 CAKES, EACH CAKE SERVES 4 TO 6

3½ cups rye flour or all-purpose flour
2 cups honey
2 eggs
3 teaspoons baking soda
1 pinch ground cloves
1 pinch ground ginger
½ teaspoon ground cinnamon
¼ cup chopped candied orange (you may use half-candied orange and half-candied lemon)

1. The day before you plan to serve, place the flour in the bowl of an electric mixer.

2. Place the honey in a saucepan over medium heat and heat, stirring continuously with a wooden spoon, for 2 minutes. Pour the honey over the flour and beat at a low speed until thoroughly combined.

3. Add the eggs and mix at low speed until smooth.

4. Add all the remaining ingredients and beat until fully incorporated and smooth. Set aside the batter for one hour.

5. Preheat the oven to 350 degrees. Grease two 5-cup loaf pans (8 by 4 by 2½ inches).

6. Spoon the batter into the pans, smoothing the top with the back of the spoon. Place a rack one-third up from the bottom and bake until deep brown or when a tester comes out clean and dry, about 1 hour. Unmold each pan and transfer the cakes to a cooling rack. Once cool, wrap each in plastic and let stand at room temperature or in the refrigerator for at least 24 hours.

COMPOTE DE MANGUE AU MIEL

HONEY MANGO COMPOTE

Great either as a stand-alone dessert, as the filling for a fruit tart or crumble, or as a hot topping for either a toasted slice of banana basil cake (page 228), a wedge of *Pain d'épice* (page 229), or curry ice cream (page 254).

MAKES 4 TO 6 SERVINGS

4 very ripe mangos
1 vanilla bean
3 tablespoons honey
¼ teaspoon sesame oil
3 tablespoons olive oil

1. Carefully peel and halve the mangos, remove the pits, cut into small chunks, and place in a bowl. Slit the vanilla bean lengthwise down the center and scrape out the grains onto the mango chunks. Add the honey and sesame oil and toss well without mashing the mango.

2. Heat the olive oil in a saucepan over high heat. When the pan is very hot add the mangos and cook, stirring occasionally and scraping the bottom, for 5 to 7 minutes. Remove with a slotted spoon and serve. (It may also be refrigerated and served cool or at room temperature).

LA POMPE À L'HUILE

PROVENÇAL ROUND SWEET BREAD

Throughout Provence, the honored place reserved for La Pompe à l'Huile among the celebrated *treize desserts*—thirteen desserts—of Christmas Eve supper is indisputable. On December 24 no mantel timepiece could be relied upon to tick past 11:59 P.M. without the appearance and consumption of that round, sweet, orange- or lemon-scented cake. The *pompe à l'huile* can be traced back to the Middle Ages. What is much less clear is the exact origin, significance, and symbolism of the number thirteen which, by coincidence or not, is the code number for the French administrative *département*—Bouches-du-Rhône—with Marseille as its capital. Thirteen is also the winning score in a match of pétanque.

The prevailing view, that the *treize desserts* is a centuries-old tradition serving to symbolize Christ and his twelve apostles, is difficult to prove through existing historical accounts. Though François Marchetti, a monk at Marseille's Saint Victor Abbey, writes of "thirteen breads" in his 1683 account of Marseille customs, the first mention of thirteen desserts does not appear until the nineteenth century. Furthermore, admiring accounts of this custom by such prominent writers of that era as Mistral and Lazarine Négremany speak of multiple sweets without any mention of a symbolic number. Others put the holiday dessert count at "no less than fourteen" and, in one instance, thirty-three to commemorate the age of Christ. It is therefore possible that the number thirteen is not so much unlucky as it is an under-count.

According to Marseillaise tradition, the auspicious dessert lineup is structured around nuts, dried fruit, and candied fruit and may feature raisins, dried figs, almonds, hazelnuts or walnuts, prunes, pears or apples, dates, oranges, quince jam, white nougat or dark nougat, melon, fougasse, and *la pompe à l'huile*. Outside the holidays, Enzo Fassone's *pompe* may be served as a bread, coffee cake, dessert, or, once stale, for French toast.

MAKES TWO 10-INCH CAKES, 10 TO 12 SERVINGS

3 tablespoons dry active yeast

¾ cup warm water

3 cups flour

3 tablespoons cold water

¼ cup olive oil

1¾ teaspoons salt

3 eggs

½ cup plus 1 tablespoon sugar

Zest of 1 orange

Zest of 1 lemon

1. Pour ¾ cup warm water in a measuring cup, stir in the yeast, and let stand for 5 minutes, until the yeast dissolves and turns creamy.

2. In the bowl of a heavy-duty mixer combine 1 cup flour, 3 tablespoons cold water, and the dissolved yeast and mix at low speed for 1 minute and then at medium speed for 2 minutes. If the dough is wet, add 1 teaspoon flour and mix for 30 seconds. Gather up the dough, transfer to a lightly floured work surface, and shape into a ball. Dust the ball with flour, place in a bowl, cover with plastic, and let rise until doubled in bulk, 10 to 15 minutes. This is the levain.

3. Meanwhile, combine 2 cups flour, olive oil, salt, eggs, sugar, grated orange zest, and grated lemon zest in the bowl of the mixer and mix at slow speed until the dough comes together, about 2 minutes. Increase the speed to medium and mix for 8 minutes more. Remove the levain from the bowl where it has been rising, punch it down, add it to the other dough in pieces, and mix at medium speed until the levain is fully incorporated, about 5 minutes.

4. Transfer the dough to a lightly floured surface and shape into a ball. Dust with flour, place in a bowl, cover with plastic, and let rise until doubled in bulk, about 1 hour.

5. Punch down the dough, cut into two equal parts, and form each part into a smooth ball. Cover the balls with plastic and let them relax for 15 minutes.

6. Preheat the oven to 400 degrees.

7. Transfer the balls to a lightly floured work surface and, with the aid of a rolling pin, spread out each ball into a round roughly 10 inches in diameter and not more than ¾ inch thick. Place each round on the bottom of 2 oiled, 10-inch cake pans. Using a round, 1-inch cookie cutter or a small spice jar of a similar diameter, cut and scoop out 4 rounds from the dough, leaving 4 holes. Position these disks of dough atop the cake between or around the holes. Cover with plastic and leave in a warm place (perhaps near the oven as it preheats) to puff out for 30 minutes.

8. Sprinkle the top of each *pompe* with ½ tablespoon sugar. Bake on the medium rack until lightly golden, 15 to 16 minutes. Unmold and transfer to a cooling rack for 20 minutes. Serve immediately, cutting the cake into wedges, or wrap in plastic to store for up to 24 hours. One- or two-day-old *pompe* may be used in your favorite bread pudding or French toast recipe.

POUDING À LA SEMOULE

SEMOLINA PUDDING

A French classic of English ancestry, *pouding à la semoule* easily assumes a Mediterranean identity and Marseille footing if thought of as couscous pudding. Home cook Janine Palazzolo, a Corsican-born Marseillaise, begins the preparation of her lemon-scented semolina pudding in the manner of a quick couscous. After stirring semolina grains into boiling milk, Janine does not put the mixture in a low oven, as suggested by both Escoffier and *Larousse Gastronomique*. Rather, she removes the mixture from the heat and lets it stand for several minutes. The result is a fluffier pudding which, baked in a ring mold lined with lemon caramel, has a sweet sheen that needs no cream or dessert sauce.

SERVES 6 TO 8

1 quart milk
1 teaspoon grated lemon zest
1⅓ cups semolina grains
1½ cups sugar
1 pinch salt
1 tablespoon lemon juice
5 eggs, well beaten

1. Pour the milk into a large saucepan, add the lemon zest, and bring to a boil. Stir in the semolina, ⅔ cup sugar, and salt. Remove from the heat, cover, and let stand for 8 minutes.

2. Preheat the oven to 400 degrees. Place a nonstick ring mold (9 to 10 inches in diameter) in the oven.

3. Prepare the caramel: Combine ⅔ cup sugar, lemon juice, and 2 tablespoons water in a small saucepan and heat over moderately high heat and stir for a few seconds with a wooden spoon. Continue to heat, tilting the saucepan from time to time to evenly distribute its color, until the liquid has a deep, caramel color, 5 to 8 minutes. Remove the ring mold from the oven, pour the lemon caramel into the mold, and tilt and turn it to completely cover its sides and bottom. Let cool.

4. Pour the beaten eggs into the semolina-and-milk mixture, mix well, and turn into a caramel-coated ring mold. Bake in a bain-marie for 30 minutes. Insert a knife into the pudding. If it comes out wet with batter, bake for 5 minutes more. Transfer to a cooling rack.

5. To unmold the pudding, let the mold sit in cold water for a few seconds. Then top with a serving plate and flip over. Serve plain or with a marmalade, fruit topping, whipped cream, or sabayon.

CLAUFOUTIS AUX OLIVES NOIRES CONFITES

BLACK OLIVE CLAFOUTIS

Do you find it hard to think of black olives as an integral part of any dessert, much less taking the place of cherries, the traditional filling in the pancake-battered fruit flan known as clafoutis? Would it help if you were reminded that olives are a fruit roughly the same size as cherries? Would it make a difference if I told you Lionel Lévy's black olive clafoutis is that rare sort of sweet revelation that can transform a merely agreeable dinner into an "unforgettable" event?

Perhaps the most effective way to get you to take the olive clafoutis plunge is to suggest you serve it at brunch in place of pancakes, waffles, or French toast. In that case, I would suggest you serve it with a salad. Since sweetening the olives into a confit requires slow cooking them in syrup for 6 hours, I encourage you to at least quadruple the quantity of black olives to 2 cups and refrigerate the unused olives in a tight-lidded jar.

MAKES 4 TO 6 SERVINGS

½ cup pitted black olives

1 cup sugar

¾ cup blanched almonds

8 tablespoons unsalted butter (1 stick)

3 eggs, beaten

4 egg yolks

¼ cup flour

¼ teaspoon salt

1 cup milk

FOR SIDE SALAD (IF SERVING AT A BRUNCH)

¼ cup olive oil

2 tablespoons lemon juice

½ teaspoon honey

¼ teaspoon sugar

Salt

Lamb's lettuce

1. The day before you plan to serve, place the black olives in a pot of boiling water and blanch for 5 minutes.

2. In a separate saucepan combine ½ cup sugar and 2 cups water and bring to a boil. Add the blanched black olives to this syrup solution and heat covered over a very low flame, using a flame tamer, if necessary, for 6 hours. Transfer the olives and syrup to a lidded jar or container and refrigerate.

3. Preheat the oven to 350 degrees. Butter a 9- or 10-inch-round ovenproof baking dish.

4. Place the almonds in a grinder or food

processor and grind or pulse until a coarse powder is produced. Do not overmix, as this will extract the oils in the almonds.

5. Melt the butter, combine with the almond powder and eggs, and mix well.

6. In a separate bowl, beat the egg yolks into the remaining $\frac{1}{2}$ cup sugar, gradually add the flour and salt, and mix until smooth. Pour in the milk and mix until fully incorporated.

7. Combine the two mixtures and mix to a smooth consistency. Drain the olives from their syrup, add them to the clafoutis batter, and mix just enough to ensure that they are evenly distributed throughout the mixture. Pour the batter into the prepared pan and bake until golden on top and firm in center, 15 to 20 minutes. Bring the whole clafoutis to the table and serve warm, cutting it into slices or wedges. (If serving for brunch with a side salad: To prepare the honey-lemon salad dressing, whisk together the olive oil, lemon juice, honey, and sugar. Season with salt and drizzle over the lamb's lettuce.)

SOUPE AU CHOCOLAT

CHOCOLATE "SOUP"

Despite its name, this molten-centered flourless chocolate soufflé cake is not quite thin enough to really be mistaken for a soup, even if it is sufficiently liquid to assume the contours of any container. The dessert followed chef Eric Boiron from the much missed bistro Le Panier des Arts in the Panier quarter all the way downtown to a charming new New York–style French-Asian fusion restaurant called Charbone with such ease that it never experienced a single lunch or dinner as the second most popular dessert.

MAKES 6 SERVINGS

8 ounces dark chocolate, broken into small
    pieces
2 tablespoons unsalted butter
¾ cup heavy cream
⅓ cup lowfat milk
3½ tablespoons cocoa powder
3 eggs
2 tablespoons pine nuts
Confectioners' sugar

1. Preheat the oven to 400 degrees.
2. In the top of a double boiler set over simmering water, melt together the chocolate, butter, heavy cream, lowfat milk, and cocoa powder and stir with a wooden spoon until smooth. Remove from the heat and set aside to cool.
3. Separate the eggs. Add the yolks to the chocolate mixture and whisk until fully incorporated.
4. Beat the whites until foamy. Using a wooden spoon, fold delicately into the chocolate mixture.
5. Place a dozen or so pine nuts on the bottom of 6 ramekins or small baking dishes. Pour the chocolate mixture into the ramekins, filling them about three-quarters to the top. Store in the refrigerator for 2 hours.
6. Place the ramekins on the middle rack in the oven and bake until puffed out and golden in tone, about 6 minutes (a little less for shallow baking dishes, a little more for deeper ones). Remove and let cool for 1 minute. Dust with confectioners' sugar and serve.

BROWNIE "DAKATINE"

Chef Yvon Cadiou named his ultra-rich, molten-centered chocolate brownie in honor of Dakatine, the brand of concentrated peanut butter that has a staunch following at African, Asian, and Creole markets throughout Marseille. Short of O.M., the beloved home soccer team, few commercial institutions ignite so passionate and so universal a following among Marseille's immigrant communities as yummy Dakatine.

Even so, Cadiou's brownies owe their wonderfully gooey stickiness not to the addition of Dakatine or any substitute peanut butter but rather to another secret ingredient: instant mashed potatoes. A tablespoon of *mousseline*, as the packaged mix is known in France, gives the brownies a lighter, creamier texture than you would get from such other thickening agents as cornstarch or potato starch. Chef Olivier Vettorel of the fashionable bistro La Giraffe obtains a comparable result by using the potato granules in his superbly fluffy eggplant caviar (page 212). The success of these two courageous chefs with this prefab product could signal the beginning of a new culinary trend, if not the outright reinvention of instant mashed potato mix from lowly processed potato powder to gourmet nonfat-style mousse mix.

MAKES 6 SERVINGS

8 ounces dark chocolate, broken into small pieces

3 tablespoons peanut butter

12 tablespoons butter (1 1/2 sticks)

8 egg yolks

1 cup sugar

1 tablespoon mashed potato granules

1/4 teaspoon salt

1/4 to 1/2 cup chopped walnuts

1 pint vanilla ice cream, optional

1. Preheat the oven to 350 degrees. Butter an 8-inch-square baking pan.

2. In the top of a double boiler set over simmering water, melt together the chocolate, peanut butter, and butter and stir with a wooden spoon until smooth. Remove from the heat and set aside to cool.

3. Beat the egg yolks and sugar. Stir in the chocolate mixture, add the mashed potato granules and salt and stir until blended. Stir in the walnuts.

4. Spread this mixture in the prepared pan and bake until the brownie puffs up a little and appears dry on the surface, 25 to 30 minutes. Remove from the oven and submerge the pan immediate in cold water to stop the cooking. Let stand several minutes to allow the brownie to solidify. Serve warm or at room temperature with a small scoop of vanilla ice cream, if desired.

BEIGNETS DE TRUFFES AU CHOCOLAT GIANDUJA

CHOCOLATE HAZELNUT TRUFFLE BEIGNETS

These fritters were not on the menu on any of the three occasions I dined at L'Epuisette. But pastry chef Guy Condroyer insisted I consider them for this book, knowing full well I would fall victim, as you are about to do, to the sensuous pleasures of these molten-centered pastries. The chocolate-hazelnut truffles are first frozen, then batter-dipped, and finally fried in oil until the exterior is crisp and the hidden interior becomes as liquid as hot fudge and twice as dangerous.

4 TO 6 SERVINGS, 18 TO 20 BEIGNETS

1 cup toasted hazelnuts
10 ounces dark chocolate, cut into small pieces
5 ounces milk chocolate, cut into small pieces
1$\frac{1}{4}$ cups heavy cream
$\frac{3}{4}$ cup all-purpose flour
3 tablespoons cocoa powder
$\frac{1}{4}$ teaspoon salt
1 egg
1 tablespoon plus 1 teaspoon sugar
1 cup Champagne (substitute dry sparkling wine
   or sparkling water)
1$\frac{1}{2}$ tablespoons butter, melted
Frying oil
Confectioners' sugar
Fresh mint, optional

1. To prepare the truffles: Grind the toasted hazelnuts in a spice grinder or food processor. Combine with the dark chocolate and milk chocolate in the top of a double boiler set over simmering water and stir with a wooden spoon until melted and smooth.

2. In a separate saucepan bring the heavy cream to a boil. Gradually pour the cream over the melted chocolate mixture and stir with a wooden spoon until smooth. Refrigerate for at least 2 hours.

3. Remove the chocolate mixture from the refrigerator. Using either the large side of a melon ball scooper or a spoon, scoop out small balls of the chocolate hazelnut mixture no larger than 1$\frac{1}{4}$ inches in diameter. Place these rough balls on a work surface and roll them under the palm of your hand to make them smooth. Transfer to a tray or pan lined with parchment paper and place in the freezer for at least 2 hours.

4. To prepare the beignet batter: Combine the flour, cocoa powder, and salt in a mixing bowl. Beat the egg into the sugar and slowly incorporate into the flour mixture. Add the Champagne and beat the mixture with a whisk. Add the melted butter and beat with a whisk until smooth.

5. Heat the oil in a deep fryer or heavy-bottomed saucepan to 360 degrees.

6. Working in small batches, dunk the frozen truffle balls into the beignet batter until fully coated, lift out with a spoon, drop delicately into the oil, and fry until crisp, about 2 minutes. (Frying for less time may leave the center of the truffle cool.) Remove with a slotted spoon, drain on paper towels, and remove any loose ends or fry scraps attached to the beignets. Sprinkle lightly with confectioners' sugar and garnish with fresh mint, if desired.

CHICHI-FREGI

L'ESTAQUE-STYLE FUNNEL CAKES

There are probably hundreds of Marseillais who can spend a very happy Sunday in the old fishing village L'Estaque without indulging in *chichi-fregi*. That there are rarely more than thirty-five people on line at each of the three kiosks where those sugar-dipped spirals of fried dough are prepared and dispensed is proof of this assertion. But the idea of a weekend at L'Estaque without at least the temptation of this local, cruller-style counterpart to Spanish churros or Pennsylvania funnel cakes—not to mention the off-color jokes about it—is unthinkable.

Once fried, the long coils of crisp, golden dough are cut into pieces roughly 6 inches in length and 1 inch in diameter that are then rolled in sugar and served in a paper bag. The shape of these pieces may have something to do with the name of this folkloric specialty of Marseille. *Chichi* is Provençale for small bird or, in the slang, penis; *fregi* means fried.

Fashioning a *chichi-fregi* recipe for this book was no easy affair. It took me weeks to hunt down Aldo-Christian and Renée Rozzonelli, whose stand, Chez Magali (named after their daughter), makes L'Estaque's best *chichi-fregi,* but just seconds for them to turn down my request for the recipe made famous by the kiosk's prior owner, a certain Monsieur Cruciani. Most alternative recipes call for you to somehow squeeze the dough out of a pastry bag in a spiral motion to make concentric circles from the middle toward the outer rim of the deep fryer. (The Rozzonellis have a big machine to do it.) Baker Enzo Fassone helped me devise the alternative of rolling and stretching out his bread dough into long cords. With either technique it really does not matter if the shape is a perfect spiral. This will not be noticed after the *chichi-fregi* are cut into smaller pieces.

MAKES 6 TO 8 SERVINGS

Vegetable oil for frying
Bread dough (page 97), remembering to add
   grated orange zest
¾ cup sugar

1. Heat about 3 to 4 inches of oil in a deep fryer or heavy-bottomed saucepan to between 370 and 385 degrees.
2. To form the spirals of bread dough: If using

a pastry bag, fit it with a #9 or #10 tip (or cut an opening about ¾ inch in diameter), fill the bag with a ball of dough, press the dough out into the center of the deep fryer and, using a spiral motion, make concentric circles from the middle toward the outer rim of the deep fryer. If forming the spirals by hand, place the dough ball on a lightly floured surface and stretch it out into a flattened sausage. Fold the dough in two lengthwise by pinching along the middle of the sausage with your thumb, folding the dough over itself, and then pressing down on the open seam with the heel of your hand. Roll out the dough using the palms of both hands and then pull at each end to stretch it into a long cord about ½ inch in diameter. Cover with plastic and let rise for 10 minutes. Repeat with the other dough balls. Lower the end of this dough into the center of the deep fryer and wind it around the center in concentric circles to create a spiral.

3. Fry the dough, turning when golden brown on one side, about 5 minutes. Drain, cut the spiral into 6-inch lengths, roll in sugar, and serve warm.

Chez Magali makes L'Estaque's best chichi-fregi.

FIGUES RÔTIES EN PAPILLOTE, CARAMEL AU VIN ROUGE

ROASTED FIG DUMPLINGS WITH
A RED WINE CARAMEL SAUCE

A lush fruit gets a voluptuous packaging in chef Dominque Frérard's roasted fig dumplings with red wine caramel sauce, and, taken to the limit, almond custard ice cream. And though the construction is a modern one, Frerard uses several of Marseille's indelible dessert tastes—honey, bitter orange, red wine, allspice—to accessorize a historic fruit and important local commodity. One of the sweetest and most prized French fig varieties is known as the Marseillaise and is cultivated east of Marseille in the Var department of Provence.

Frérard wraps the figs in leaves of Tunisian brick pastry, a North African accent now common in Marseille's French Provençal restaurants. I propose bundling them in spring roll wrappers, a reflection both of the growing Southeast Asian influence in the seaport's markets and kitchens and its wider availability in the United States.

MAKES 4 SERVINGS

8 fresh figs

3 tablespoons honey

1 cup red wine

1 cinnamon stick, broken in two

Zest of 1 orange

2 teaspoons allspice

6 tablespoons butter

4 spring roll wrappers

2 tablespoons sugar plus ½ cup

1 pint Almond Custard Ice Cream (page 251)
   or vanilla ice cream, optional

1. The day before serving, make an incision in the stem of each fig, open slightly using the point of the blade, and pour a little honey inside the fig.

2. Combine the red wine, cinnamon, grated orange zest, allspice, and the figs in a bowl and let the figs marinate in the refrigerator overnight. Drain the figs, discarding the cinnamon, and reserving half the red wine marinade for the sauce.

3. Preheat the oven to 350 degrees.

4. Heat 4 tablespoons butter in a saucepan until melted.

5. Cut the spring roll wrappers in half, creating 8 small wrappers. Brush butter on both sides of each and sprinkle with sugar (using not more than 2 tablespoons). Roll each fig in a wrapper. Fold the overlapping sides of the wrapper over the fig and secure both sides in place with 2 toothpicks. Place the fig

dumplings in a buttered baking dish and bake until crisp and golden, 12 to 15 minutes.

6. Meanwhile, to make the caramel: Combine $\frac{1}{2}$ cup sugar and 3 tablespoons water in a small saucepan, place over moderately high heat, and stir for a few seconds with a wooden spoon. Continue to heat, tilting the saucepan from time to time to evenly distribute its color, until the liquid has a light caramel color but does not harden, 4 to 5 minutes. Slowly add half the red wine marinade to deglaze the pan and stir with a wooden spoon. Gradually add the remaining 2 tablespoons butter and stir until the mixture is smooth.

7. Remove the toothpicks from the fig dumplings, place 2 on each of 4 dessert dishes, and surround with the red wine caramel sauce and a small scoop of almond ice cream, if desired.

POIRES POCHÉES AU VIN ROUGE
POACHED PEARS IN RED WINE

The November appearance of this classic dessert coincides with the first arrival of winter pears. In keeping with that spirit, I propose the use of Anjou, Bosc, or Comice pears. And to position these pears as close as possible to Marseille, I suggest poaching them in red wine from Bandol. The full-bodied and peppery Bandols produce a wonderful syrup.

MAKES 4 SERVINGS

2 cups Bandol red wine (substitute full-bodied red)
1 cup water
½ peel of 1 lemon
1 cinnamon stick
1 pinch nutmeg
1 cup sugar
4 small reasonably firm pears (Anjou, Bosc, or Comice), peeled

1. Combine all the ingredients except the pears in a saucepan and heat to a rapid boil.
2. Add the peeled pears to the liquid, cover, reduce the heat to medium, and boil the pears until soft, about 30 minutes. Remove the pears and set aside. Raise the heat to moderately high and cook the liquid until reduced to the consistency of a syrup, 15 to 20 minutes.
3. TO SERVE, place each pear in a dessert bowl and spoon red wine syrup over it.

NAVETTES MARSEILLAISES

MARSEILLE CANDLEMAS COOKIES

According to Provençal legend, the cylindrical, boatlike shape of this cookie symbolizes the miraculous *navette* (small boat) which, without sail, oar, or supplies, safely carried Lazarus, Mary Magdalene, Mary Salome, and Martha from Jerusalem to the Provençal fishing village of Saintes-Maries-de-la-Mer around the year A.D. 40. Navettes are traditionally consumed during Candlemas, the February 2 feast commemorating the presentation of Christ in the temple. In Marseille, the Candlemas procession begins before sunrise at Saint Victor Abbey, which was founded beside the Old Port in the fifth century. The nearby Four de Navettes, the oldest bakery in Marseille, has been baking navettes continuously since 1781. Its recipe for these pale, faintly orange-scented, yeast-free cookies is a closely guarded secret.

A cross between a biscotto and a butter cookie, navettes may be dunked in coffee, tea, milk, wine, or jam.

MAKES 10 TO 14 COOKIES

1 cup sugar
4 tablespoons unsalted butter
1 pinch salt
2 eggs
2 cups flour
1 teaspoon grated orange zest

1. Combine the sugar, butter, and salt in the bowl of a standing, heavy-duty mixer and mix at a moderately high speed to a crumbly consistency, about 1 minute. With the motor running, add the eggs and then very gradually the flour. Mix until the flour is fully incorporated, about 2 minutes. Add the orange zest and mix for 20 seconds more. (To mix the dough by hand: Cream the butter with the sugar and salt. Beat in the eggs, very gradually stir in the flour and orange zest, and mix thoroughly.)

2. Place the dough hook on the mixer and mix the dough at medium speed for 1 minute. (Or transfer the dough to a flouring work surface and knead for a few minutes.) Form the dough into a ball, place in a bowl, cover with plastic, and leave in a warm place for 1 hour.

3. Preheat the oven to 350 degrees. Butter a large cookie sheet. Separate the dough into about a dozen small balls roughly the size of walnuts. Place each on a lightly floured work surface and roll under the palm of your hand into a cylinder about 3 inches long. Pinch the ends of the cylinder so that it has a boat shape, and place on a cookie

sheet at least $\frac{1}{2}$ inch apart from the other navettes. Flatten each navette slightly by pressing down lightly with a spatula.

4. Make a lengthwise slit (about $\frac{1}{4}$ inch deep) down the middle of the top side of each cookie to just within $\frac{1}{2}$ inch of each end. Use a spatula or the stem of a fork to pry open the middle of this slit. Bake in the oven for 25 minutes. (The navettes should be cooked through but not turn golden.) Remove from the oven and slide a metal spatula under the cookies to make sure they don't stick.

5. Serve warm or let cool and then store in a tightly lidded cookie jar or cookie tin for up to 6 months. Reheat the navettes in the oven before serving.

CANISTRELLI

CORSICAN COOKIES

Should you ever be fortunate enough to visit his biscuiterie in the Marseille quarter of La Blancarde, José Orsoni will happily give you a vivid demonstration of what a strain it is on his body to shape his biscuits by hand. It's as if you need to feel his acute lower back pain to truly appreciate the specialties honoring the two places he calls home, the navettes (Candlemas cookies) of his native Marseille and the canistrelli of his family's native land, Corsica. The canistrelli are square-shaped Corsican cookies which, in their standard variety, bear the scent and, for Marseille's transplanted Corsicans, the memory of that island's incomparable lemons. They are halfway between an Italian biscotto and a butter cookie.

I would not acknowledge Orsoni's back woes with anything other than a sympathetic ear, if only to get him to throw in an extra handful of canistrelli with my order. Regardless, they sell easily without the sob story. Available in lemon, orange, anise, almonds, chocolate chip, raisins, or white wine, these canistrelli make me nostalgic for Corsica even though I've never visited the island.

Honestly, I think Orsoni gave me his closely guarded canistrelli recipe only because he was sure I wouldn't be able to reproduce it with American products in my New York kitchen. Happily, he was dead wrong.

MAKES ABOUT 40 BISCUITS

2 sticks butter
1 cup sugar
4 eggs, beaten
Juice and grated zest of 2 lemons
$3\frac{1}{2}$ cups all-purpose flour
1 teaspoon baking soda
$\frac{1}{4}$ teaspoon salt

1. Preheat the oven to 325 degrees. Butter a baking sheet.
2. Cream the butter, add the sugar, and beat until smooth and creamy. Add the beaten eggs, lemon juice, and the grated lemon zest until the mixture has a smooth and even consistency. Mix in the flour, baking soda, and salt and beat until fully incorporated.
3. Transfer the dough to a lightly floured work surface, divide the dough in two, and roll out each half into a rectangle just over $\frac{1}{2}$ inch in thickness. Cut the dough into squares, roughly $1\frac{1}{2}$ by $1\frac{1}{2}$ inches.
4. Set the biscuits on the baking sheet at least $\frac{1}{2}$

inch apart and bake until lightly golden, 30 to 35 minutes. Cool on a rack and store in a tightly covered cookie jar.

ANISE CANISTRELLI. Substitute 2 teaspoons aniseeds for the lemon juice and lemon zest.

ORANGE CANESTRELLI. Substitute the grated zest and juice of 1 orange for the lemon juice and lemon zest.

CHOCOLATE CHIP CANESTRELLI. Substitute $\frac{3}{4}$ cup semisweet chocolate chips for the lemon juice and lemon zest, adding the chips after the flour has been incorporated into the mixture.

RAISIN CANESTRELLI. Substitute $\frac{1}{2}$ to $\frac{3}{4}$ cup raisins for the lemon juice and lemon zest, adding the raisins after the flour has been incorporated.

GRIOUCH

ALGERIAN HONEY FRITTERS

Known alternatively as *mahalkra*, *shebbakia*, or, in French, *oreillettes*, these crunchy, honey-dipped fritters are traditionally served in Algerian homes to family, neighbors, and friends at the conclusion of Ramadan. But for Zohra Sahnoune their sweetness has an additional purpose. She prepares her griouch throughout the year so that she can proudly offer them to guests in the small, vine-shaded Mediterranean patio that is symbolic of the happiness and relative calm she has found in Marseille.

"I used to live in the country in the Var so coming to the city was very hard," recalls Zohra, who lived in some of Marseille's most notoriously troubled *cités* (housing projects). "When we moved to this house it was like a dream. I felt like I was living again."

MAKES 20 FRITTERS

3½ cups flour
½ teaspoon baking powder
1 teaspoon vanilla sugar (substitute 1 teaspoon sugar and ¼ teaspoon vanilla extract)
1 tablespoon white vinegar
1 egg, beaten
4 tablespoons butter, melted and cooled
½ cup vegetable oil, preferably sunflower oil
Vegetable oil for frying
1 pound honey, warmed to liquefy
2 ounces (about ½ cup) sesame seeds

1. Combine the flour, baking powder, and sugar in a bowl and mix well. Form a well in the center, pour in the vinegar, egg, butter, and oil and gradually stir into the flour mixture until thoroughly blended. The dough should be smooth and elastic. If it is not, add up to ½ cup water.

2. Divide the dough into five equal pieces and form each into a smooth ball. Working with one ball of dough at a time, place on a lightly floured surface and, using a rolling pin, spread out the dough into a very thin (no more than ⅛ inch thick) square, 8 by 8 inches. Cut this into 4 smaller squares and then slice each smaller square into 5 bands by making 4 parallel, evenly spaced slits starting ½ inch from the bottom of the square and ending just within ½ inch of the top. To braid the bands, loop every other band in your fingers and, seizing the bottom of the last band with your other hand, tuck it under the loop toward the bottom of the first band. Release your fingers and press down on the bands to seal. Repeat with the remainder of the dough.

3. Fill a deep fryer or heavy-bottomed saucepan halfway with frying oil and heat to between 360 and 375 degrees. Fry several of the fritters at a time, turning once, until golden on both sides, about 3 minutes. Drain on paper towels.

4. Heat the honey in a saucepan over low heat just to make it more liquid. Place the sesame seeds in a shallow bowl.

5. Dunk the fritters in the honey, letting any excess honey drip off, and then dip in sesame seeds to coat both sides. Once cooled, the fritters can be stored in a tightly lidded cookie jar for up to 4 weeks.

Malika and Virgil at a café on the Cours Julienne.

GLACE AUX AMANDES

ALMOND CUSTARD ICE CREAM

Although rival Aix-en-Provence is widely recognized as Provence's great almond capital, Marseille has played a crucial role in the history of the region's beloved nut. Because the earliest almond varieties were carried from China to Greece by traders along the ancient silk road, it is thought that the nuts, like bouillabaisse, were first introduced to Provence by the Greeks who settled in Marseille. In later years, the city was a major importer and later exporter of almonds. More recently, Marseille became the "birthplace" of chef Dominique Frérard's almond ice cream. Frérard may live in Aix, but he cooks at Marseille's Les Trois Forts and thus his city of employment must be recognized as the ice cream's rightful place of origin.

Smooth and custardy rather than nutty in texture, the ice cream was designed as the accompaniment for his dessert dumplings filled with figs (page 242), a fruit with a storied Marseille heritage not even a chauvinistic Aixois nut case could dismiss as a figment of a Marsellais' imagination. But be forewarned: The ice cream, when consumed with nothing other than a spoon, is virtually impossible to stop eating. You make a quart, you eat a quart.

MAKES 1 QUART

1 quart milk
½ cup chopped blanched almonds
8 egg yolks
¾ cup sugar
1 teaspoon cornstarch

1. The day before serving: Pour the milk in a saucepan and bring to a boil. Remove from the heat, add the chopped almonds, cover, and let stand for 90 minutes so that the almond flavor is absorbed. Pass the milk through a fine sieve to remove the chopped almonds.

2. Place a large stainless steel bowl in the freezer to chill.

3. To make a crème anglaise: Place the egg yolks in a large mixing bowl and gradually beat the sugar into the yolks with a whisk or an electric beater until the mixture turns frothy and pale yellow and forms a ribbon, 2 to 3 minutes. Slowly beat in the cornstarch, which will prevent the custard from clotting if allowed to overheat.

4. Reheat the milk to a boil. Gradually add in the boiling milk, drop by drop, so that the eggs heat slowly.

5. Transfer this mixture to a saucepan and heat over medium heat, stirring constantly with a wooden spoon, until the froth on the top

disappears and the mixture thickens just enough to coat the spoon, 6 to 8 minutes. Pour the entire mixture into the chilled stainless steel bowl, beat it with a whisk for 1 minute to put some air into it, and place in the freezer overnight.

6. Remove the mixture from the freezer and let stand for 5 minutes. Cut the frozen mixture into chunks roughly the size of large ice cubes, add these chunks a few at a time to the bowl of a food processor, and process until smooth with no remaining hard chunks. Return the mixture to the stainless steel bowl and freeze for at least 3 hours.

GLACE AU BASILIC

BASIL ICE CREAM

Those opposed to the trend of using aromatic herbs and savory spices in desserts should not use Yvon Cadiou's basil ice cream to bolster their argument. The sweet, mintlike quality of the basil makes it a legitimate dessert flavor. I love it.

MAKES 1 QUART

8 egg yolks
3/4 cup sugar
1 teaspoon cornstarch
1 quart boiling milk
1/2 cup basil leaves

1. The day before you plan to serve: Place a large stainless steel bowl in the freezer to chill.
2. To make a crème anglaise: Place the egg yolks in a large mixing bowl and gradually beat the sugar into the yolks with a whisk or an electric beater until the mixture turns frothy and pale yellow and forms a ribbon, 2 to 3 minutes. Slowly beat in the cornstarch, which will prevent the custard from clotting if allowed to overheat. Gradually add in the boiling milk, drop by drop, so that the eggs heat slowly.
3. Transfer this mixture to a saucepan and heat over medium heat, stirring constantly with a wooden spoon, until the froth on the top disappears and the mixture thickens just enough to coat the spoon, 6 to 8 minutes.
4. Combine the mixture with the basil leaves in a blender, working in two batches if necessary, and puree until the mixture has an even green color with few if any specks of green, about 3 minutes. Pour the entire mixture into the chilled stainless steel bowl and place in the freezer overnight.
5. Remove the mixture from the freezer and let stand for 5 minutes. Cut the frozen mixture into chunks roughly the size of large ice cubes, add these chunks a few at a time to the bowl of a food processor, and process until smooth with no remaining hard chunks. Return the mixture to the stainless steel bowl and freeze for at least 4 hours.

GLACE AUX CAPUCINS

CURRY ICE CREAM

Yvon Cadiou's curry ice cream has nothing to do with Capuchin monks. It was named after the rue Longue-des-Capucins and the Marché des Capucins, respectively the street and the food market that together mark the final stop on the wondrous spice trails leading from the Middle East, Far East, North Africa, sub-Saharan Africa, and the Caribbean to Marseille. If Marseille is the Mediterranean's great melting pot, then the exotic produce stands, spice shops, pastry shops, and grocery stores clustered around the Marché des Capucins constitute its multiethnic pantry.

Remembering that curry is not a single spice but rather a variable blend of many spices (Yvon has you adding anise seeds to the mix), the intensity and character of your ice cream's curry flavor will reflect the makeup and the freshness of the curry powder you are using. If your curry powder has been unsealed within the last week or two and is therefore at its most potent, you may wish to reduce its quantity by as much as half. If, however, the curry powder is several months old, you'll need the full teaspoon and perhaps even a pinch more. The turmeric gives the ice cream the deep yellow-orange color that is a perfect visual match for Yvon's honey mango compote.

MAKES 1 QUART

1 vanilla bean
1 quart milk
1 teaspoon curry powder
1 teaspoon turmeric
½ teaspoon anise seeds
2 tablespoons honey
8 egg yolks
¾ cup sugar
1 teaspoon cornstarch
Honey Mango Compote, optional (page 230)

1. The day before you plan to serve: Place a large stainless steel bowl in the freezer to chill.

2. The next day: Slit the vanilla bean lengthwise down the center. Combine with the milk, curry powder, turmeric, anise seeds, and honey in a saucepan and bring to a boil. Pass the mixture through a fine sieve to remove the aniseed and vanilla bean (but not the tiny vanilla seeds).

3. To make a crème anglaise: Place the egg yolks in a large mixing bowl and gradually beat the sugar into the yolks with a whisk or an electric beater until the mixture turns frothy and pale yellow and forms a ribbon, 2 to 3 minutes. Slowly beat in the cornstarch,

which will prevent the custard from clotting if allowed to overheat.

4. Gradually add the boiling flavored milk to the egg mixture, drop by drop, so that the eggs heat slowly.

5. Transfer this mixture to a saucepan and heat over medium heat, stirring constantly with a wooden spoon, until the froth on the top disappears and the mixture thickens just enough to coat the spoon, 6 to 8 minutes. Pour the entire mixture into the chilled stainless steel bowl and place in the freezer overnight.

6. Remove the mixture from the freezer and let stand for 5 minutes. Cut the frozen mixture into chunks roughly the size of large ice cubes, add these chunks a few at a time to the bowl of a food processor, and process until smooth with no remaining hard chunks. Return the mixture to the stainless steel bowl and freeze for at least 4 hours. Top with honey mango compote, if desired.

Marseille Restaurants

LES ARCENAULX
25, cours d'Estienne d'Orves
13001 Marseille
04 91 59 80 30

CARBONE
22, rue Sainte
13001 Marseille
04 91 55 52 73

LE CHARLES LIVON
89, boulevard Charles Livon
13007 Marseille
04 91 52 22 41

LE 504
34, place des Huiles
13001 Marseille
04 91 33 57 74

CHEZ ETIENNE
43, rue Lorette
13002 Marseille
No telephone

CHEZ FONFON
140, rue Vallon des Auffes
13007 Marseille
04 91 52 14 38

LES ECHEVINS
44, rue Sainte
13001 Marseille
04 96 11 03 11

L'ESCALE
4, boulevard Alexandre Delabre
chemin Les Goudes
13008 Marseille
04 91 73 16 78

L'EPUISETTE
156, rue Vallon des Auffes
13007 Marseille
04 91 52 17 82

LA GIRAFE
8, rue Sainte
13001 Marseille
04 91 33 21 43

LEMON GRASS
8, rue Fort Notre Dame
13007 Marseille
04 91 33 97 65

LE LUNCH
Calanque Sormiou
13009 Marseille
04 91 25 05 37

RESTAURANT CALYPSO
3, rue Catalans
13007 Marseille
04 91 52 64 00

RESTAURANT CAMORS
82, plage Estaque
13016 Marseille
04 91 46 58 21

RESTAURANT MICHEL
6, rue Catalans
13007 Marseille
04 91 52 30 63

LA MIRAMAR
12, quai du Port
13002 Marseille
04 91 91 19 40

L'OLIVERAIE
10, place des Huiles
13001 Marseille
04 91 33 34 41

RESTAURANT PASSÉDAT
Anse de Maldormé
13007 Marseille
04 91 59 25 92

LE SUD EN HAUT
80, cours Julien
13006 Marseille
04 91 92 66 64

UNE TABLE AU SUD
2, quai du Port
13002 Marseille
04 91 90 63 53

LE TIBOULEN DE MAÏRE
La Calanque Blanche
chemin Les Goudes
13008 Marseille
04 91 25 26 30

TOINOU
3, cours Saint-Louis
13001 Marseille
04 91 33 14 94

LES TROIS FORTS
36, boulevard Charles Livon
13007 Marseille
04 91 15 59 00

Index

Africa:
North, 19, 159, 185, 215, 229,
242
sub-Saharan, 17, 19–20
aïoli, 62
Aix-en-Provence, 26
Aix-Marseille, Université, 21, 37
Algeria, 13, 16, 17, 108, 115, 177,
185, 193, 196, 249
Algerian:
honey fritters, 249–50
Ramadan soup, 115–16
almond(s):
in black olive clafoutis,
234–35
custard ice cream, 251–52
lamb stew with prunes and,
185
in Moroccan chicken rolls,
181–82
alouettes sans tête, 198–99
Alsop, William, 9
Amouyal, Jäelle, 193–94, 196
anchoïade, 57
anchovies:
eggplant stew with, 214
in escarole tart, 105
and garlic paste, 57
in tapenade, 55
anise Corsican cookies, 247–48
appetizers, 71–93
anise fish terrine, 90

Armenian-style cheese
turnovers, 77
basil fish terrine, 90
Chez Etienne's pan-fried
calamari with parsley and
garlic, 88–89
chicken liver terrine, 93
chickpea cakes, 73–74
curry fish terrine, 90
fish blinis, 83–84
fish terrine, 90
Moroccan savory turnovers,
81–82
octopus terrine, 91–92
Parmesan and black olive
biscuits, 75
Provençal-style eggs in
cocotte, 76
ricotta sesame rolls, 80
salmon crumble, 85–86
tuna tartare with fresh herbs
and panisses, 87
warm baklava of herbed goat
cheese, 78
apples:
baked, with a caramel of nuts
and spices and brioche
French toast, 224–25
caramelized, in ravioli, 223
flambé of pan-fried, with
gingerbread crumbs,
221–22

Arax, 19, 21
Arendt, Hannah, 16
Armenia, 14, 16, 19, 21, 38, 49,
77, 96, 97, 101, 210
Armenian:
pizza, 101–2
-style cheese turnovers, 77
Arsenaulx, Les, 28
Art et Les Thés, L', 159
Ashkenazi Jews, 16
Asia, Southeast, 242
Aubagne, rue d', 17, 19, 20–21
Aubert, Bernard, 4
Aubin, Alain, 117
Au Royaume de la Chantilly, 19

bacon:
Canadian, in open-faced
Marseille-style BLT,
188–89
slab, in Provençal beef rolls,
198–99
bacon laitue tomate Marseillais,
188–89
Baghtchejian, Berthe, 77, 101,
210
baklava of herbed goat cheese,
warm, 78–79
banana basil cake, 228
Bandikian, David, 19, 20–21
Bandikian, Vartan, 19
Bandol, 162, 244

Bandol wine jus, 163

Banjo (McKay), 186

Bar de la Marine, 26

Barras, Paul-Nicolas-François, 148

basil:

 banana cake, 228

 and garlic sauce, 61

 ice cream, 253

 panisses, 73–74

 potato chips, 209

 in Provence-style sardine spread, 60

 vegetable soup with garlic and, 109–10

bass:

 sea, Napoleon of, and tapenade with tomato confit and peas, 155–56

 striped, nut-encrusted, fillet, with Asian spices and soy mushroom consommé, 157–58

Beau Rivage, 26

beef, 190–203

 braised, in cannelloni, 192

 ground, in croquettes for *dafina*, 196

 ground lean, in Armenian pizza, 101–2

 rib steak with garlic fries, 202–3

 rolls, Provençal, 198–99

 Sephardic Sabbath stew, 193–95

 steak au poivre with caramelized shallots, 200–201

 stew, Provençal, 190–91

beignet de truffes au chocolat Gianduja, 238–39

beignets:

 chocolate hazelnut truffle, 238–39

 see also fritters

beignets de courgettes, 210

Belle de Mai, 11, 115

Bergero, Aimé, 30, 46, 48

Besson, Luc, 5

beurre blanc, saffron, 149

biscuits, Parmesan and black olive, 75

biscuits au Parmesan et olives noires, 75

bisque, seafood, prawn and scallop brochette with, 172

Biton, Gilbert, 10

black olives, *see* olives, black

Blancarde, La, 247

blinis, fish, 83–84

blinis de poisson, 83–84

Bluzet, Dominique, 3

Bogart, Humphrey, 10

bohémienne, la, 213

Boiron, Eric, 202, 236

Bompard, 30

Bonnadier, Jacques, 60, 109

Bonne Mère, La, 23

boreg au fromage, 77

bouillabaisse, 121–43

 about, 28, 29, 30, 36, 46, 47, 122–26

 chef's vs. fisherman's, 125–26

 chicken, 141

 fisherman's, 132–33

 fish stock for Marseille-style, 127–28

 green pea, 139–40

 Marseille-style, 129–31

 mussel broth for Marseille-style, 128

 one-eyed, 138

 origins of, 122–24

 salt cod, 142–43

 spinach, 139–40

 stock for, 125

 terrine, 134–35

 vegetable stock for, 136–37

Bouillabaisse, La, 126

bouillabaisse borgne, 138

bouillabaisse de morue, 142–43

bouillabaisse d'épinards, 139–40

bouillabaisse de poulet, 141

bouillabaisse du pêcheur, 132–33

bouillabaisse Marseillaise, 129–31

Boulanger, Patrick, 15

Boule Bleue, La, 33

boulettes de poisson à la sauce tomate, 159

Boulud, Daniel, 73

bourride, 117–19

Bovis, Marcel, 16

braised beef cannelloni, 192

Braque, Georges, 7

bread:

 dough, 97–98

 Provençal round sweet, 231–32

breadsticks, 103–4

Breton, André, 16

brioche French toast, for baked apples with a caramel of nuts and spices, 224 brochette, prawn and scallop, with seafood bisque, 172–73

brochette de langoustines aux Saint Jacques, bisque de crustacés, 172–73

brousse de Rove, 38

brownie "Dakatine," 237

Brunet, Renée, 105, 136, 138, 139, 164, 190, 213

Burkina Faso, 20

butter, clarifying of, 155

butter sauce:
  Caribbean curry, 153–54
  saffron beurre blanc, 149

Cadiou, Yvon, 75, 111, 215, 228, 237, 253, 254

Café Parisien, 10

Caillat, Apollon, 124, 125, 126

cake à la banane et basilic, 228

calamari, Chez Etienne's pan-fried, with parsley and garlic, 88–89

Calanques, 6, 32

Calvados, in flambé of pan-fried apples with gingerbread crumbs, 221

Calypso, 7

Canadian bacon, in open-faced Marseille-style BLT, 188–89

Canebière, La, 7, 17, 23

Canistrelli, 247–48

cannelloni, braised beef, 192

cannelloni de daube, 192

Cap Orient, 17–18

Cappai-Silvestri, Martine, 30

caramelized apple ravioli, 223

caramelized shallots, steak au poivre with, 200–201

caramel of nuts and spices, baked apples and brioche French toast with, 224

Carbone, 28

Caribbean curry butter sauce, fish fillets with, 153–54

Carrese, Philippe, 13, 147

carrots, glazed, with black olives and cumin, 207

Casablanca, 10

Casanis, 42

Cassaro, Etienne, 48, 88, 99

casserole, Yvon's vegetable, 215

Cassis, 6, 41

caviar de sardine à la Provençale, 60

Cendrars, Blaise, 2

Centre d'Océanologie de Marseille, 32

César, 5

Cézanne, Paul, 7

Chagall, Marc, 16

Chandler, Raymond, 12, 13

chapon, 129

Charles Livon, Le, 28, 155, 166, 209, 224

Charte de la Bouillabaisse Marseillaise, 129

Château d'If, 6

cheese:
  Armenian-style turnovers, 77
  in basil and garlic sauce, 61
  see also specific cheese

Chez Aldo, 160

Chez Etienne, 88, 97, 99, 103

Chez Etienne's pan-fried calamari with parsley and garlic, 88–89

Chez Fonfon, 132, 171, 223

Chez Madie, 28

Chez Magali, 73, 240

Chez Salem, 17–18

chichi-fregi, 7, 240–41

chicken, 177–82
  bouillabaisse, 141
  breasts, gingerbread-crusted, with licorice sauce, 179–80
  couscous with chickpeas, onions, and raisins, 177–78
  -liver terrine, 93
  rolls, Moroccan, 181–82

chickpea(s):
  in Algerian Ramadan soup, 115–16
  basil panisses, 73–74
  cakes, 7, 73–74
  in chicken couscous with onions and raisins, 177–78
  flour, in panisses, 74
  panisse fries, 73–74
  in Sephardic Sabbath stew, 193–95

chocolate:
  brownie "Dakatine," 237
  -chip Corsican cookies, 247–48
  and hazelnut truffle beignets, 238–39
  "soup," 236

chorba, 115–16

cigares de pastilla, 181–82

Ciotat, La, 50

clafoutis aux olives noires confites, 234–35

cocotte de legumes, 215

cod, salt, bouillabaisse of, 142–43

Comoros, 17, 19, 20, 22, 48, 88

compote:

    honey mango, 230

    tomato-pepper, 189

compote de mangue au miel, 230

compressé de bouillabaisse Port de l'Orient, 134–35

Condroyer, Guy, 238

confit:

    black olive, for clafoutis, 234

    lemon and onion, mashed potatoes with, 208

confiture d'échalotes au vin rouge, 65

confiture de tomates et gingembre, 66

confiture d'oignons, 64

Considerable Town, A (Fisher), 36

consommé, soy mushroom, nut-encrusted striped bass fillet with Asian spices and, 157

cookies, Corsican, 247–48

    anise, 247–48

    chocolate chip, 247–48

    orange Corsican, 247–48

    raisin Corsican, 247–48

cookies, Marseille Candlemas, 245–46

Coq d'Or, 19

Coquillages Toinou, 7

coquilles Saint-Jacques au sel d'orange, endive caramelisée, 168–69

Corniche Kennedy, 31–33

Corsica, 14, 15, 49, 210, 233, 247

Corsican cookies, *see* cookies, Corsican

côte de boeuf et frites à l'ail, 202–3

Coudoux, 47

coulis de tomates Provençal, 68

Count of Monte Cristo, The (Dumas), 6

Cours d'Estienne d'Orves, 29

Cours Julien, 26, 213

couscous, chicken, with chickpeas, onions, and raisins, 177–78

couscous fassi, 177–78

crème anglaise, see custard

"crêpes" Marocaines, 81–82

croquettes, ground beef, for *dafina,* 196

crumble de saumon, 85–86

crumble topping for salmon, 85–86

cumin, glazed carrots with black olives and, 207

curry ice cream, 254–55

custard, almond, ice cream, 251–52

dafina, 193–95

Danjard, Georges-Jean, 148

daube Provençale, 190–91

Derain, André, 7

desserts, 219–55

    Algerian honey fritters, 249–50

    almond custard ice cream, 251–52

    baked apples with a caramel of nuts and spices and

    brioche French toast, 224–25

    banana basil cake, 228

    basil ice cream, 253

    brownie "Dakatine," 237

    caramelized apple ravioli, 223

    chocolate hazelnut truffle beignets, 238–39

    chocolate "soup," 236

    Corsican cookies, 247–48

    curry ice cream, 254–55

    flambé of pan-fried apples with gingerbread crumbs, 221–22

    gingerbread, 229

    honey mango compote, 230

    L'Estaque-style funnel cakes, 240–41

    Marseille Candlemas cookies, 245–46

    poached pears in red wine, 244

    Provençal round sweet bread, 231–32

    roasted fig dumplings with a red wine caramel sauce, 242–43

    semolina pudding, 233

    tomatoes stuffed with caramelized fruits and nuts, 226–27

dips:

    anchovy and garlic paste, 57

    Provençal garlic mayonnaise, 62

    tapenade, 55

    see also spreads

Docks, 11

dough:
  bread, 97–98
  chichi-fregi, 97–98
  pizza crust, 97–98
Doullay, Lolita, 109
Ducasse, Alain, 28, 48, 73, 188
Duchamp, Marcel, 16
Dufy, Raoul, 7
Dumas, Alexandre, 6, 7, 124
dumplings, roasted fig with a red
  wine caramel sauce,
  242–43
Dupuy, Jacques, 46, 47, 63, 129,
  130
Durand, Charles, 124, 125

Echevins, Les, 28, 38, 40, 76, 114,
  139
eggplant:
  caviar, 212
  stew with anchovies, 214
  and tomato stew, 213
eggs:
  in cocotte, Provençal-style, 76
  endive, caramelized, in
    sautéed sea scallops with
    orange salt, 168–69
  poached, in one-eyed
    bouillabaisse, 138
  poached, in salt cod
    bouillabaisse, 142–43
  poached, in spinach
    bouillabaisse, 139–40
Egypt, 16
Emmental cheese:
  in *pistou*, 61
  in pizza "Chez Etienne,"
    99–100

Epuisette, L', 48, 238
Ernst, Christian, 155, 166, 172,
  209, 224
Ernst, Max, 16
Escale, L', 41
escarole tart, 105
Escoffier, Auguste, 124, 233
Espig, Frédéric, 17, 18
Estaque, L', 5, 7, 130, 240

Fanny, 5
Fassone, Enzo, 103, 231, 240
Fausse-Monnaie, 31
Femmes D'Ici et D'Ailleurs, 81,
  181
fennel-stuffed salmon fillet with
  onion jam, 151
Fernandel, 1, 126
fielas (conger eel), 129
Fiesta Des Suds, La, 4, 81
fig, roasted, dumplings with a
  red wine caramel sauce,
  242–43
*figues rôties en papillotes, caramel
  au vin rouge*, 242–43
*filet de boeuf poêlé au poivre
  concassé sur échalotes
  confites*, 200–201
*filet de poisson au beurre de
  Colombo*, 153–54
*filet de poissons aux aromates dans
  son fumet de champignon*,
  157–58
*filet de saumon farci de fenouil,
  gratiné à la confiture
  d'oignon*, 151
*filet de sole farci aux épinards,
  beurre blanc safranée*, 149

*filet de volaille au pain d'épice et
  crème de réglisse*, 179–80
fish, 145–73
  about, 146–48
  and anise terrine, 90
  balls in tomato sauce, 159
  and basil terrine, 90
  blinis, 83–84
  Chez Etienne's pan-fried
    calamari with parsley and
    garlic, 88–89
  and curry terrine, 90
  fillets with Caribbean curry
    butter sauce, 153–54
  fisherman's stew,
    164–65
  grilling of, 160–61
  monkfish and prawn stew
    with Bandol wine jus,
    162–63
  Napoleon of sea bass and
    tapenade with tomato
    confit and peas, 155–56
  nut-encrusted striped bass
    fillet with Asian spices and
    soy mushroom consommé,
    157–58
  octopus terrine, 91–92
  salmon crumble, 85–86
  salmon fillet, fennel-stuffed
    with onion jam, 151
  salmon fillets, zucchini-
    wrapped with goat cheese
    and tomato sauce, 150
  salt cod bouillabaisse,
    142–43
  sardine and Swiss chard
    gratin, 216–17

fish *(cont.)*
  sole fillet stuffed with spinach
    in a saffron beurre blanc,
    149
  soup with aïoli, Provençal,
    117–19
  stock, for Marseille-style
    bouillabaisse, 127–28
  stock for bouillabaisse, about,
    125
  terrine, 90
  trout, fillet of, with tomato,
    152
  tuna tartare with fresh herbs
    and panisses, 87
  types of and use in
    bouillabaisse, 129
  whole, grilled in the
    style of L'Escale,
    160–61
  see also bouillabaisse;
    shellfish; *specific fish*
Fisher, M. F. K., 22, 36
fisherman's bouillabaisse,
  132–33
fisherman's stew, 164–65
504 (restaurant), 28, 177
flambé of pan-fried apples with
  gingerbread crumbs,
  221–22
Flaubert, Gustave, 21, 124
fond de légumes pour
  bouillabaisse, 136–37
fond de poisson pour bouillabaisse
  Marseillaise, 127–28
Fonky Family, 5
Fort St. Jean, 23
Fort St. Nicolas, 23

fougasse:
  olive, 103–4
  rosemary, 103–4
fougasse au romarin, 103–4
Four de Navettes, 245
404 (restaurant), 177
French Connection, The, 5
French Revolution, 21–22
French toast, brioche, for baked
  apples with a caramel of
  nuts and spices, 224
French West Indies, 17, 19
Frérard, Dominique, 83, 87, 242,
  251
Friche Belle de Mai, La, 11
fritters:
  Algerian honey, 249–50
  zucchini, 210
fromage de chèvre rôti aux herbes
  en croute de baklava, 78–79
Fromion, André and Eric, 30
Fry, Varian, 16
funnel cakes, L'Estaque-style, 7,
  240–41

Galia Viande, 19
galinette (gurnard), 129
Gallois, Louis, 3
gambas rôtis au miel et gingembre,
  171
garlic:
  and anchovy paste, 57
  Chez Etienne's pan-fried
    calamari with parsley and,
    88–89
  fries, 202–3
  mayonnaise, Provençal, 62
  and parsley, 76

sauce, spicy
  vegetable soup with basil and,
    109–10
Garnier, Gilles and Karine, 153
Garrigues, Gérard, 49
gigot d'agneau aux parfums de
  garrigue, 184
ginger:
  honey shrimp, 141
  -tomato jam, 66
gingerbread:
  basic, 229
  crumbs, flambé of pan-fried
    apples with, 221–22
  crumbs, preparation of,
    179–80, 221
  -crusted chicken breasts with
    licorice sauce, 179–80
Giraffe, La, 28, 149, 212, 237
glace au basilic, 253
glace aux amandes, 251–52
glace aux capucins, 254–55
glazed carrots with black olives
  and cumin, 207
goat cheese:
  herbed, warm baklava of,
    78–79
  zucchini-wrapped salmon
    fillets with tomato sauce
    and, 150
Gollin, Claude, 12
Goudes, Les, 30, 31, 41, 160
Grand culinaire, Le (Escoffier),
  124
Grand Dictionaire de Cuisine,
  124
Grand Hôtel du Louvre et de la
  Paix, 124

gratin de blettes à la Provençale, 216

Greece, 14, 15, 16, 17, 19, 21, 38, 160

green beans, *see* haricots verts

green pea bouillabaisse, 138–40

gressins, 103–4

griouch, 249–50

ground beef croquettes for *dafina*, 196

Gruyère cheese:
    in Armenian-style cheese turnovers, 77
    in eggplant and tomato stew, 213
    in eggplant stew with anchovies, 213–14
    in one-eyed bouillabaisse, 138
    in *pistou*, 61
    in pizza "Chez Etienne," 99–100
    in Provençal "short" soup, 114
    in Provence-style Swiss chard gratin, 216

Guedigian, Robert, 5

Guigou, 7

Guinea, 20

Habaieb, Salem, 17

Halle Delacroix, 18, 19

haricots verts:
    soup "Roucas Blanc," 112–13
    in vegetable soup with basil and garlic, 109–10

Harmelin, Jean-Georges, 32

Haussmann, Baron, 8

hazelnut, chocolate truffle beignets, 238–39

Henri Bardouin, 43

herbes de Provence, 56

herbs:
    dried, Provence-style, 56
    fresh, tuna tartare with panisses and, 87

honey:
    fritters, Algerian, 249–50
    in gingerbread, 229
    ginger shrimp, 171
    -lemon salad dressing, 235
    and mango compote, 230

Hôtel de Ville, 16, 26, 28

Hôtel du Département, 9

Hotel Mercure, 28

huile d'olive glacée, 69

Iala, Karim, 177

IAM, 5, 134

ice cream:
    almond custard, 251–52
    basil, 253
    curry, 254–55

If, 32

immigration, 15–17

Indochina, 17

Italy, 14, 15, 16, 17, 21, 38, 49, 96, 192

Ivory Coast, 17, 20

Izzo, Jean-Claude, 12, 13

jams:
    onion, 64
    oven-roasted tomatoes, 67
    shallot and red wine, 65
    tomato-ginger, 66

Jews, 159
    Ashkenazi, 16
    Sephardic, 16, 49, 193, 196

Julius Caesar, 3

kouclas, 196

Krull, Germaine, 16

lahmajoun, 101–2

lamb, 184–85
    boneless shoulder or neck, in Algerian Ramadan soup, 115–16
    chops, in Provençal "short" soup, 114
    ground lean, in Armenian pizza, 101–2
    roast leg of, with thyme and rosemary, 184
    stew with prunes and almonds, 185

Langevin, Germaine, 112

Larousse Gastronomique, 233

Lebanon, 14, 17, 21

Le Corbusier, 9–10

lemon:
    caramel, in semolina pudding, 233
    -honey salad dressing, 235
    and onion confit for mashed potatoes, 208

Lemon Grass, 28, 48, 80, 157

Lévy, Lionel, 28, 48–49, 85, 168, 188, 207, 226, 234

Lhu, Van, 88–89

Lisle, Claude-Joseph Roget de, 21–22

Longchamp, boulevard, 8

Longue-des-Capucins, rue, 17, 19
Loubat, Bernard, 198
Lunch, Le, 41

McKay, Claude, 186
Madagascar, 17, 19
Madrague, 31
Maghreb, 16
Maison Dorée, La, 55
Maison du Fada, 9
Maisons d'Estaque, 7
Mali, 20
Malmousque, 31
mango honey compote, 230
marc de Provence, in Provençal
    beef stew, 190–91
Marcelinho, Adriano, 33
Marché d'Afrique, 20
Marchetti, François, 231
marinade, for Provençal beef
    stew, 190
Marius and Jeannette, 5
marmite du pêcheur, 164–65
Marquet, Albert, 7
marrowbones, for rib steak with
    garlic fries, 203
"Marseillaise, La," 21–22
Marseille:
    Candlemas cookies, 245–46
    culinary traditions of,
        36–49
    cultural life of, 3–8
    history and description of,
        1–34
    savon de, 14–15
    -style BLT, open-faced,
        188–89
    -style bouillabaisse, 129–31

Marsiho, 7
mashed potatoes with lemon and
    onion confit, 208
Massalia, 6
mayonnaise, Provençal garlic, 62
Mazargues, 30, 47
meats:
    braised beef cannelloni,
        192
    ground beef croquettes, for
        dafina, 196
    lamb stew with prunes and
        almonds, 185
    medallion of veal with an
        eight-spice semolina pilaf,
        183
    Provençal beef rolls, 198–99
    rib steak with garlic fries,
        202–3
    roast leg of lamb with thyme
        and rosemary, 184
    Sephardic Sabbath stew,
        193–95
    steak au poivre with
        caramelized shallots,
        200–201
    stuffed mutton tripe with
        sheep's trotters, 186–87
    see also beef; chicken; lamb;
        veal
*médaillon de veau et sa semoule
    aux huit saveurs*, 183
medallion of veal with an eight-
    spice semolina pilaf, 183
merlan (hake), 30
Méry, Joseph, 6
Meynier, Monsieur, 55
Middle East, 19, 21

*millefeuille de loup en croustillant
    de tapenade, tomates confit
    et poêlée de differents pois*,
    155
Minguella, Pierre and Jean-
    Michel, 29, 30
Miramar, Le, 28, 29
Moholy-Nagy, Laszlo, 16
monkfish, 129
monkfish and prawn stew with
    Bandol wine jus, 162–63
Montand, Yves, 1
Morard, Clément Marius, 124
Moréni-Garron, Jacques, 40
Moréni-Garron, Jeanne, 38, 76,
    114, 139
Morgiou, Calanque de, 6
Moroccan:
    chicken rolls, 181–82
    lamb stew with prunes and
        almonds, 185
    savory turnovers, 81–82
Morocco, 14, 16, 17, 49, 97, 159,
    177, 181, 185, 196, 207
mozzarella cheese, in pizza
    "Chez Etienne," 99–100
mussel broth, for Marseille-style
    bouillabaisse, 128
mutton tripe, stuffed with
    sheep's trotters, 186–87

Napoleon of sea bass and
    tapenade with tomato
    confit and peas, 155–56
navettes Marseillaises, 245–46
Nazet, Marion, 164
N'Diaye, Fallou, 4
Noailles quarter, 18–21

noix de Saint Jacques poêlées aux légumes, panisses au basilic et tapenade avec tomates confites, 166–67

North Africa, 19, 159, 185, 215, 229, 242

Notre-Dame-de-la-Garde, 22–23

nut-encrusted striped bass fillet with Asian spices and soy mushroom consommé, 157–58

octopus terrine, 91–92

oeufs en cocotte Provençale, 76

Old Port (Vieux Port), 1, 7, 9, 12, 14, 16, 17, 22, 23, 26, 28, 31, 73, 186

olive oil:
    in Marseille cookery, 39
    Provençal, 12
    spread, cold, 69

Oliveraie, L', 28, 153

olives, black:
    confit, in clafoutis, 234
    in fougasse, 103–4
    glazed carrots with cumin and, 207
    in Parmesan biscuits, 75
    purée, 56
    tapenade, 55

Olympique de Marseille (OM), 21–22, 33

Omori, Ali, 88

one-eyed bouillabaisse, 138

onions:
    in chicken couscous with chickpeas and raisins, 177–78

confit of lemon and, mashed potatoes with, 208

jam, 64

open-faced Marseille-style BLT, 188–89

orange Corsican cookies, 247–48

orange salt, for sautéed sea scallops with caramelized endive, 168

Orsoni, José, 247

O' Stop, 198

oven-roasted tomatoes, 67

Pagnol, Marcel, 5

pain d'épice, 229

Palais du Pharo, 29

Palazzolo, Janine, 141, 233

pancetta, in open-faced Marseille-style BLT, 188–89

Panier, 10–11

Panier des Arts, Le, 202, 236

panisse fries, 73–74

panisses, 7, 73–74

Papa, Kassem, 20, 22

Parmesan cheese:
    and black olive biscuits, 75
    in eggplant and tomato stew, 213
    in one-eyed bouillabaisse, 138
    in *pistou,* 61
    in Provençal "short" soup, 114

Passage to Marseille, 10

Passédat, Gérald, 48, 69, 91, 134

Pastis, 42, 51

pastis de Marseille, 40–45
    Ange Scaramelli, 43–44
    Frédéric Poitou, 44

history and description of, 42–43

pâte à pain, 97–98

pears in red wine, poached, 244

peas:
    green, in bouillabaisse, 138–40
    green, in Napoleon of sea bass with tomato confit and, 155–56
    split, in soup, 111

Perez, Neige, 30, 152, 164

Pernod, 42

persillade, 76

pétanque, 50–51

Pet de Mouche et la Princesse du Désert (Carrese), 13

Petit Pavillon, Le, 33

petits légumes farcis au caviar aubergine, 212

Philippi, Giselle, 56, 64, 78, 90, 93, 151, 200, 211

Phocaea, 6

phyllo:
    dough, use of, 78–79
    in Napoleon of sea bass and tapenade with tomato confit and peas, 155–56
    in warm baklava of herbed goat cheese, 78–79

pieds et paquets Marseillais, 186–87

pieds-noirs, 16

Pinna, Alexandre, 223

Pires, Gérard, 5

pissaladière, see escarole tart

pistou, 61

pizzas and tarts, 95–105
    Armenian, 101–2
    "Chez Etienne," 99–100
    dough for, 97–98
    escarole, 105
    gressins, 103–4
    olive fougasse, 103–4
    rosemary fougasse,
        103–4
Place Jean-Jaurès, 26
Plaine, 26
plantains, in fish fillets with
    Caribbean curry butter
    sauce, 153–54
poached pears in red wine, 244
poêlé de Royal Gala au pain
    d'épice, 221–22
poires pochées au vin rouge, 244
poisson grillé à L'Escale, 160–61
Poitou, Frédéric, 44, 49
Pomègues, 32
pommes au four et son caramel aux
    fruits secs et aux épices,
    brioche perdue, 224–25
pommes de terre fourées au basilic,
    209
pompe à l'huile, la, 231–32
Pompey, 3
Portugal, 14
potatoes:
    chips, basil, 209
    garlic fries, 202–3
    mashed, with lemon and
        onion confit, 208
    powder, instant mashed, 212,
        237
pouding à la semoule, 233
Pouillon, Fernand, 9, 26

prawns, *see* shrimp
Provençal:
    beef rolls, 198–99
    beef stew, 190–91
    eggs in cocotte, 76
    fish soup with aïoli, 117–19
    garlic mayonnaise, 62
    round sweet bread, 231–32
    sardine spread, 60
    "short" soup, 114
    Swiss chard gratin, 216
    tomato sauce, 68
Provençal olive oil, 12
Provence, 14, 18, 49, 103, 190,
    207, 210, 213, 216, 229, 231,
    242, 245
prunes, in lamb stew with
    almonds and, 185
pudding, semolina, 233
Puget, Pierre, 10
purée de pommes de terre au fondant
    de citron et oignon, 208

Quai de Rive Neuve, 23, 26, 28,
    29, 31
Quai des Belges, 23, 26, 29, 30
Quai du Port, 23, 26, 28

ragoût d'aubergines à l'anchois,
    214
ragoût de carottes et olives de
    Nyons, 207
ragoût de lotte et gambas au jus de
    Bandol, 162–63
raisins:
    chicken couscous with
        chickpeas, onions and,
        177–78

    in Corsican cookies, 247–48
Ramadan soup, Algerian, 115–16
rascasse (scorpion fish), 129
ratatouille, *see* eggplant, and
    tomato stew
Ratonneau, 32
ravioli, caramelized apple, 223
raviolis comme les auraient aimés
    les soeurs Tatin, 223
Renoir, Pierre Auguste, 7
République, rue de la, 8
Réserve, La, 124
Restaurant Camors, 130
Restaurant L'Escale, 160
Restaurant Michel, 7
Restaurant Passédat, 30, 41, 69,
    91
Rhazi, Fatima, 81, 181
rib steak with garlic fries, 202–3
Ricard, 42
Ricard, Paul, 42, 43
rice:
    Basmati, for monkfish and
        prawn stew with Bandol
        wine jus, 163
    cooked, in chicken
        bouillabaisse, 141
ricotta sesame rolls, 80
Rieusset, André, 130
roasted fig dumplings with a red
    wine caramel sauce,
    242–43
Rofritsch, Hervé and Maurice, 33
rolls, ricotta sesame, 80
Roman de la Sardine, Le
    (Bonnadier), 60
rosemary:
    fougasse, 103–4

fresh, in roast leg of lamb with thyme and, 184
Roucas Blanc, Le, 112
rouget (red mullet), 30, 46
rouille, 63
rouleaux de fromage au sésame, 80
Rozzonelli, Aldo-Christian and Renée, 73, 240

saffron, 17
  history of, 18
Sahnoune, Zohra, 115, 185, 249
St. Just, 9
Saint Pierre (John Dory), 129, 146–47
Saint Victor Abbey, 231, 245
salad, for black olive clafoutis, 234–35
salad dressings:
  black olive purée, 56
  honey-lemon, 235
salmon:
  crumble, 85–86
  fennel-stuffed fillet, with onion jam, 151
  in fish terrine, 90
  mousse loaf, *see* fish terrine
  tartare, 85–86
  zucchini-wrapped, fillets with goat cheese and tomato sauce, 150
Samaritaine, 10, 28
sardine(s):
  fresh, preparation of, 217
  Provence-style, spread, 60
  and Swiss chard gratin, 216
sauces:
  basil and garlic, 61

Caribbean curry butter, fish fillets with, 153–54
  chunky fresh tomato, for Provençal beef rolls, 199
  lemon caramel, for semolina pudding, 233
  licorice, for gingerbread-crusted chicken breasts, 179
  Provençal garlic mayonnaise, 62
  Provençal tomato, 68
  red wine caramel, for roasted fig dumplings, 243
  saffron beurre blanc, fillet of sole stuffed with spinach in a, 149
  spicy garlic, 63
Saugeron, Florent, 48, 80, 157, 179, 183, 221
saumon en peau de courgette et chèvre frais, et coulis de tomates, 150
sausage, sweet country, in haricot vert soup "Roucas Blanc," 112–13
sautéed sea scallops with caramelized endive and orange salt, 168–69
Savon de Marseille, 14–15, 39
Savon de Marseille, Le (Boulanger), 15
scallops:
  and prawn brochette with seafood bisque, 172–73
  sautéed sea, with caramelized endive and orange salt, 168–69
  sea, with sautéed vegetables,

basil panisses, tapenade, and tomato confit, 166–67
Scaramelli, Ange, 43
semolina:
  grains, in ginger honey shrimp, 171
  pilaf, eight-spice, with medallion of veal, 183
  pudding, 233
Senegal, 17, 20
Sephardic Jews, 16, 49, 193, 196
Sephardic Sabbath stew, 193–95
sesame ricotta rolls, 80
shallots:
  caramelized, 200–201
  and red wine jam, 65
shellfish:
  ginger honey shrimp, 171
  monkfish and prawn stew with Bandol wine jus, 162–63
  prawn and scallop brochette with seafood bisque, 172–73
  sautéed sea scallops with caramelized endive and orange salt, 168–69
  sea scallops with sautéed vegetables, basil panisses, tapenade, and tomato confit, 166–67
  see also scallops; shrimp
shrimp:
  ginger honey, 171
  and monkfish stew with Bandol wine jus, 162–63
  in Provençal fish soup with aïoli, 117–18

shrimp *(cont.)*
   and scallop brochette with
      seafood bisque, 172–73
Sicily, 73
Silvestri, Roger, 47
soap, 14–15
sole, 30
sole fillet stuffed with spinach in
      a saffron beurre blanc, 149
Soleil d'Egypte, Le, 19
Somalia, 20
Sormiou, Calanque de, 6, 41
soupe au chocolat, 236
soupe au pistou, 109–10
soupe courte, 114
*soupe de haricots verts comme au
      "Roucas Blanc,"*
      112–13
soupe de pois cassés, 111
soups, 107–19
   Algerian Ramadan, 115–16
   fish soup with aïoli,
      Provençal, 117–19
   haricot vert, "Roucas Blanc,"
      112–13
   Provençal "short," 114
   seafood bisque, prawn and
      scallop brochette with, 172
   soy mushroom consommé,
      for nut-encrusted striped
      bass fillet with Asian spices
      and, 157–58
   split pea, 111
   vegetable with basil and
      garlic, 109–10
   see also bouillabaisse
Sourrieu, Guillaume, 48
Southeast Asia, 242

soy mushroom consommé, for
   nut-encrusted striped bass
   fillet with Asian spices,
   157–58
Spain, 14, 15, 16, 17, 18, 49
Spigol, 17–18
spinach:
   bouillabaisse, 139–40
   stuffing for fillet of sole in a
      saffron beurre blanc, 149
   wilted, in sea scallops with
      sautéed vegetables, basil
      panisses, tapenade, and
      tomato confit, 166–67
split pea soup, 111
spreads:
   anchovy and garlic paste, 57
   basil and garlic sauce, 61
   black olive purée, 56
   cold olive oil, 69
   Provence-style sardine, 60
   tapenade, 55
   see also dips
squid:
   Chez Etienne's pan-fried
      calamari with parsley and
      garlic, 88–89
   in fisherman's stew, 164–65
   see also calamari
Stade Vélodrome, 22
steak au poivre with caramelized
      shallots, 200–201
stew:
   eggplant, with anchovies, 214
   eggplant and tomato, 213
   fisherman's, 164–65
   lamb, with prunes and
      almonds, 185

monkfish and prawn, with
      Bandol wine jus, 162–63
   Provençal beef, 190–91
   Sephardic Sabbath, 193–95
   see also bouillabaisse
stock:
   fish, for bouillabaisse, 125
   fish, for Marseilles-style
      bouillabaisse, 127–28
   vegetable, for bouillabaisse,
      136–37
striped bass fillet, nut-encrusted,
      with Asian spices and soy
      mushroom consommé,
      157–58
stuffed mutton tripe with sheep's
      trotters, 186–87
stuffed vegetables with eggplant
      caviar, 212
stuffing:
   bacon, garlic, and parsley, for
      Provençal beef rolls, 198
   for braised beef cannelloni,
      192
   caramelized fruits and nuts,
      for tomatoes, 226–27
   eggplant caviar, for
      vegetables, 212
   spinach, for fillet of sole in
      a saffron beurre blanc,
      149
Suarès, André, 7
sub-Saharan Africa, 17, 19–20
Sud en Haut, Le, 78, 90, 151,
      200
Supervielle, Jules, 26
*supions frits en persillade "Chez
      Etienne,"* 88–89

Swiss chard:
    in braised beef cannelloni,
        192
    gratin, sardine and, 216
    Provence-style gratin of, 216
syrup, red wine, for poached
        pears, 244

Table au Sud, Une, 28, 49, 85,
        168, 226
tagine d'agneau aux pruneaux et
        amandes, 185
Taha, Rachid, 4
Tam Ky, 19
tapenade, 55
tartare de thon mariné aux herbes
        frâiches et panisso, 87
tarte à la scarole, 105
Tassara, Adrienne, 125, 132
Tatin, Stephanie and Caroline,
        223
Taxi, 5
Temime, Emile, 21, 32, 37
terrine de courgette, 211
terrine de foie de volaille, 93
terrine de poisson, 90
terrine de poulpe, 91–92
terrines:
    anise fish, 90
    basil fish, 90
    bouillabaisse, 134–35
    chicken liver, 93
    curry fish, 90
    fish, 90
    octopus, 91–92
    Provençal beef stew, molded
        and chilled, 190–91
    zucchini, 211

TGV Mediterranée, 3
Théâtre du Gymnase, 3
Tiboulin de Maïre, Le, 30, 41, 46,
        160
Togo, 17
tomates de pays farcies
        caramelisées, 226–27
tomato:
    chunky fresh, in sauce for
        Provençal beef rolls,
        199
    condiment for salmon
        crumble, 85–86
    confit, 67
    and eggplant stew, 213
    fillet of trout with, 152
    -ginger jam, 66
    oven-roasted, 67
    -pepper compote, for open-
        faced Marseille-style BLT,
        189
    sauce, Provençal, 68
    stuffed with caramelized
        fruits and nuts, 226–27
tomettes, 8
Total Khéops (Izzo), 13
Transbordeur, 26
Trilogie Marseillaise, 5
tripe, stuffed mutton, with
        sheep's trotters, 186–87
Trois Forts, Les, 28, 29, 83, 87,
        251
trout fillet with tomato, 152
truffle, chocolate hazelnut
        beignets, 238–39
truite à la tomate, 152
tuna tartare with fresh herbs and
        panisses, 87

Tunisia, 14, 16, 17, 73, 159, 177,
        196, 242
Turkey, 14, 16, 17
turnovers:
    Armenian-style cheese, 77
    Moroccan savory, 81–82
Twain, Mark, 7–8, 14

Univers Alimentaire, L', 20

Vacon, rue, 17
Vallon des Auffes, 31, 125, 132,
        171
veal medallion with an eight-
        spice semolina pilaf, 183
vegetable(s), 205–17
    casserole, Yvon's, 215
    Provence-style Swiss chard
        gratin, 216
    sardine and Swiss chard
        gratin, 216–17
    soup, with basil and garlic,
        109–10
    stock for bouillabaisse,
        135–37
    stuffed with eggplant caviar,
        212
Vettorel, Olivier, 66, 150, 210,
        212, 237
Vielle Charité, 10–11, 159
Vietnam, 19, 88
Vieux Port, *see* Old Port
View of the Gulf of Marseille, 7
vinaigrette fouettée aux olives
        hoires, 56
Vong, 179
Vongerichten, Jean-Georges,
        179

walnuts, in brownie "Dakatine,"
    237
Werfel, Franz, 16
whitefish fillets with Caribbean
    curry butter sauce,
    153–54
whole fish grilled in the style of
    L'Escale, 160–61
wine:
    Bandol red, syrup for
        poached pears, 244
    Bandol reds, 162
    jus, Bandol, 163

red, and caramel sauce for
    roasted fig dumplings,
    243
red, and shallot jam, 65
red, pears poached in,
    244
wonton skins, for caramelized
    apple ravioli, 223
World Cup of 1998, 3
World War I, 18
World War II, 9, 16–17

Yvon's vegetable casserole, 215

Zarokian, Serge, 41, 46, 101, 102,
    117, 160, 162, 208
Zidane, Zinedine, 32
Zola, Emile, 124
zucchini:
    fritters, 210
    sliced, for salmon wrap,
        150
    terrine, 211
    -wrapped salmon fillets with
        goat cheese and tomato
        sauce, 150
Zuili, Benjamin, 159

MARS

La Belle de Mai

Palais Longchamp

La Canebière

Cours Ju

Gare St. Charles

Bd d'Athenes   Cours Lieutard

Cours Belzunce   Rue de Rome

Porte d'Aix   la République   Quai des Belges

Rue de   LE PANIER

La Vieille   Hotel   VIEUX
Charité   de Ville   PORT

Quai du Port   Quai de Rive Neuve

Cathédrale de la Major

Les Docks

Fort   St.
St. Jean

L'ESTAQUE

BASSIN DE LA GRANDE JOLIETTE

Palais du Phare

N

Marseille

Mediterranean Sea

Iles Frioul

L'huile

M